Gender and punishment in Ireland

Manchester University Press

Gender and punishment in Ireland

Women, murder and the death penalty, 1922–64

Lynsey Black

MANCHESTER UNIVERSITY PRESS

Published by Manchester University Press
Oxford Road, Manchester M13 9PL

www.manchesteruniversitypress.co.uk

British Library Cataloguing-in-Publication Data
A catalogue record for this book is available from the British Library

ISBN 978 1 5261 4528 4 hardback
ISBN 978 1 5261 8234 0 paperback

First published 2022

The publisher has no responsibility for the persistence or accuracy of URLs for any external or third-party internet websites referred to in this book, and does not guarantee that any content on such websites is, or will remain, accurate or appropriate.

Typeset
by Cheshire Typesetting Ltd, Cuddington, Cheshire

For my parents, Caroline and Don, for Emmett,
and for Catherine

Contents

Tables

Acknowledgements

The idea of this book has consumed me for over a decade. I read Anette Ballinger's *Dead Woman Walking* in 2010, and wondered what a similar project in Ireland would reveal. Now, I suppose, I have an answer. Except, of course, it's not the definitive answer. The work of understanding and interpreting is never done, and there is so much more to do in unpicking the past and present of gender and punishment in Ireland.

For now, though, this is what I have to offer, and for that I would like to express my huge gratitude to Lizzie Seal and Ivana Bacik. They have been inspirational mentors throughout.

Many thanks to my colleagues in the Department of Law at Maynooth University, and to David Doyle, Ian O'Donnell, Donal Coffey and Louise Brangan, who read chapters and sections of the book in draft form and offered invaluable feedback.

A big thank you to Emma Brennan and all at Manchester University Press for guiding me through this process.

The staff of the National Archives of Ireland made the book possible. Particular thanks to Ken, Paddy and Christy. I'm also very grateful to Noelle Dowling in the Dublin Diocesan Archives. The Department of Justice facilitated access to key Department of Justice files, as did the Department of An Taoiseach. These materials hugely enriched the discussion throughout. For very generous access to documentaries, media clips and other publications, I'm grateful to TG4, the RTÉ Archives and the Garda Review. I would also like to thank Sean Reynolds for taking hours out of his day to walk me through the museum at Mountjoy Prison. A big thank you to Ray Kavanagh, Elaine Farrell, Tom Reddy and Bill Vaughan, who offered advice and support when the research was in its early stages.

I am so happy to be able to put this book into the world with such a beautiful cover, featuring *Garden Green* by Norah McGuinness. I am very grateful to the Hugh Lane Gallery and the estate of Norah McGuinness for this privilege.

To my truly exceptional friends.

Finally, to my parents and to Emmett – thank you for everything.

Introduction

At 7.45 a.m. on 25 October 1924, 31-year-old Annie Walsh entered Fedamore Garda (police) Station, County Limerick. She told the officer present that her 60-year-old husband Edward had been killed the previous night, shot dead by his nephew, 23-year-old Michael Talbot. When asked why she had not reported the killing sooner, Walsh said she had feared for her life, terrified of what Talbot might do next. When Gardaí arrived at Walsh's home, they found the victim lying in a pool of blood, fully clothed with his cap and boots on. Walsh recounted that at around midnight, she had been in bed with her husband, when they were awakened by Talbot banging on the door of the cottage. Walsh told Gardaí that after the initial commotion, her husband and Talbot had spoken quietly in the kitchen when suddenly the younger man had struck Edward on the head, produced a revolver and shot him.

Talbot was discovered hiding in his mother's house. When questioned, his version of events was somewhat different: 'You may arrest Mrs Walsh as well as me. I did not kill him. She killed him with a hatchet. I held his hands while she killed him.' When Edward's body was examined, there was no trace of a bullet wound; rather, he had been killed by heavy blows to the head with a hatchet-like instrument. The medical evidence clearly suggested that Walsh was lying.

The prosecution case against Annie Walsh was damning. It was alleged that she and Talbot were engaged in a sexual relationship, and that she had recruited her paramour in the killing with hopes of receiving compensation for her husband's murder. Annie Walsh was convicted and sentenced to death on 10 July 1925;

Michael Talbot had been similarly sentenced in a separate trial the day before. Although Walsh received a strong recommendation to mercy from the jury, she was not reprieved. On the morning of 5 August 1925, she was executed, hanged in Dublin's Mountjoy Prison by the English executioner Thomas Pierrepoint at 8.45 a.m., just 45 minutes after Talbot. She left behind a key, a purse, a Post Office savings book containing a small sum of money and her rosary beads.[1]

As the only woman to die by the hangman's noose after independence in 1922, her case is assured a certain status in the annals of Irish criminal justice history. However, while she may have been alone in facing execution, many of the aspects of her story are far from unique. Between independence in 1922 and the enactment of the Criminal Justice Act in 1964, 292 women and girls were prosecuted for murder in Ireland.[2] Their cases are inevitably those which came under suspicion; although the 'dark figure' of undetected killings of adults would have been relatively insignificant, not all women who killed infants came under suspicion. While this cannot then be claimed as a 'true' figure of such cases, the sample *does* reflect the picture of women and murder as glimpsed through the machinery of criminal justice. At this remove, such a perspective offers one of the few windows into the lethal violence of the past.

Inevitably, not all women experienced the entirety of a criminal trial for murder; some had their case dismissed entirely, others pleaded guilty to lesser offences and others again were found unfit to plead. Of those who did experience a trial, some were found guilty but insane, while many were acquitted by juries and discharged. Ultimately, 22 women found themselves convicted of murder and condemned to die. Through close analysis of all 292 cases, however, this book explores the contours of women and lethal violence in Ireland from 1922 to 1964. Through the following chapters, the themes that came up time and again are examined: themes of domestic desperation, the deep criminogenic shame of illegitimacy, sexual intrigue, constructions of madness and familial conflicts over inheritance and status. The cases are interpreted against the backdrop of post-colonial Ireland and the processes of historical change that occurred in the four decades from 1922.

The book makes no apology for its focus on women. Traditionally, Irish historiography had spilled its ink almost entirely on men, although a rich seam of Irish women's history has worked to counter this bias. In the present context, the justifications for a gendered analysis of homicide lie with the particular insights that the research on Ireland can offer; in decades of closely prescribed gender and sexual relations, notions of the 'double deviance' of women and girls suspected of lethal violence can illuminate fault lines in Irish society related to the position of women while also contributing to the literature on gender and punishment.[3]

Women who kill: bringing in the case of Ireland

Male violence is understood to occur on a continuum: when men commit acts of violence, it is not outwith the meanings of masculinity. The criminalisation of working-class men in particular, and the resulting association between 'public violence, public man',[4] ensures some normalisation in cases where men perpetrate lethal violence. This is not the case with women's violence, where gender instantly assumes greater salience. Victorian ideals of women as moral guardians are,[5] to an extent, embedded throughout historical *and* contemporary attempts to 'get to grips with' female violence.

Women's lethal violence is also qualitatively 'different' from men's; women are less likely to kill, and when they do, they tend to kill within their own families. Both the 'typical', such as the killing of infants, as well as the atypical cases, such as those few cases where women were charged with killing strangers, form the subject of this book. The literature has identified the need to engage with this latter category: of women who kill in uncommon circumstances. Seal has outlined the necessary work undertaken on women who kill infants and women who kill abusive partners, noting that they offer 'ideologically sound' categories of women's lethal violence.[6] Feminist scholarship has yet to engage as fully with the more unusual cases of women who kill. Consideration of the spectrum of women's lethal violence allows for a fuller investigation of the connections between gender and justice in this period in Ireland. Discourses in the cases in which women killed children and husbands illuminate responses when archetypal standards are threatened. Examination of killings which are far beyond the contextually acceptable gender roles of the time can shed light on what happens when the standards are smashed.

The book therefore contributes to the emerging body of work on women who kill. In recent years there has been an explosion of scholarship on this subject, a development which has enriched criminological understandings of gender, crime and punishment. The literature spans both historic work and contemporary sociological criminology. Scholarship on punishment has generally identified differential responses to male and female offending behaviour. Much of this is typified in the mindset, identified by O'Brien, of women as 'not dangerous' and as more malleable than men to moralising reform.[7] Institutional responses rose to meet this conception of women. In Ireland, the intensification of 'coercive confinement' post-independence has been documented with regard to institutions such as Magdalen laundries and mother and baby homes.[8] The broader literature on the institutional responses to female 'deviance' demonstrates continuities with the Irish case; for example, Ruggles's examination of Philadelphia's Magdalen Asylum from 1836 to 1908 demonstrated the use of terminology which was substantially similar to mid-twentieth-century Ireland, including the differentiation of women based on classed notions of 'incorrigibility'. An 1856 quote from the meeting of the Board of Managers cited their wish to attract 'a better class (who have not yet been so deeply steeped in crime)'.[9] In 1941, an Irish probation officer noted similarly that Our Lady's Home on Dublin's Henrietta Street was for the 'better types'.[10] Closer to home, McCormick's exploration of female sexuality in twentieth-century Northern Ireland likewise records the use of a range of denominational institutions for non-conforming women and girls.[11] The book explores the extent to which religious institutions formed a key component of Ireland's gendered punishment regime well into the twentieth century.

Conceptions of women's malleability to reform have suggested contrasting regimes to those considered suitable for men; these ideologies have also been noted in contemporary criminological scholarship on women in prison. In her ethnography of a US women's prison in the 1990s, McCorkel observed astonishingly cruel practices within the drug rehabilitation programmes available to women.[12] These programmes expected cannibalism of the self and an enforced internalisation of the perceived 'shame' that criminal women should experience. Contemporary accounts of women and punishment continue to remind us that for women caught in the criminal justice system, appropriate responses are often seen as capturing bodies and minds. A further commonality identified across time periods has been the resort to pathology in cases of women who commit acts of violence. Zedner concluded that 'psychiatric diagnoses were found to be particularly plausible in explaining female deviance' in nineteenth-century England.[13] A century later, Allen suggested that women who appeared before the courts for serious offences were often 'rendered harmless' by pathology.[14]

On women and capital punishment, the international literature has explored the gender differential in the operation of the death penalty. Across centuries, and across jurisdictions, the fact that a condemned person was female could inform execution methods.[15] Similarly, the roster of capital crimes was different for women, and included the offence of *petit treason* – the act of killing one's husband.[16] Gender also figured in considerations of 'decency'. The use of the electric chair in New York prompted an 1888 report which fretted that hanging was an indecent mode of death for women.[17] Considerations of 'protection' also impacted rates of reprieve. Discussing the US, Streib has remarked on the 'male' character of capital punishment.[18] This is evident across many jurisdictions, and is particularly stark in New Zealand where only one woman was ever executed.[19] While the research has tended to show that women experienced commutation more frequently than men, Ballinger noted of England and Wales that when the cases of women who had killed children were removed, women who had murdered men were *less* likely than men to be commuted.[20] Some categories of women's lethal violence are clearly considered more threatening than others.

Throughout the literature, one constant has been the public and media interest in women's lethal violence. For Heidensohn, this interest stems from the rarity of women's crime.[21] Others have interpreted it against the prevailing expectations of women's 'inherent' nature. Wiener, for example, commented on the stereotype of idealised Victorian womanhood, which ensured fascination with cases of condemned women, their dress and their demeanour.[22] Much of the literature on women who kill has closely examined the reactions of the media and the public. This work has theorised societal, cultural and official responses, demonstrating how these are informed by normative gender expectations. This is hardly surprising: Lloyd memorably stated that offending women are perceived as 'doubly deviant', labelled as such because they have betrayed their gender and contravened the criminal law.[23] This double deviance is compounded when women kill. The social context in which women's lethal violence plays out is shaped in part by the gender role expectations such women must navigate. Seal's study of cases of women who kill from mid-twentieth-century England, for example, has shown how the creation of acceptable narratives was heavily dependent on the particular moment in time in which they were formed.[24]

Both historical and more contemporary research emphasises the centrality of place and time. Zedner writes of her own research in Victorian England that 'A principal theme of this study is the relationship between responses to female criminality and prevailing social values and concerns. It is not possible to understand the history of crime, or its control, in isolation.'[25] Post-colonial Ireland offers an intriguing background against which to examine women's lethal violence. Post-independence, Ireland experienced a rising atmosphere in which women's public presence was marginalised, and in which women were relegated to the domestic sphere as part of a conservative and Catholic nation-building project.[26] The intensely patriarchal aspirations of the new state created a very particular moment in time in which the influence of the Catholic Church, both in terms of its moral teachings and as a social 'superstructure',[27] is significant. Mahon noted that 'One has to examine women's lives to appreciate the significance of Catholicism.'[28] In this context, an analysis of women who kill is an opportunity to examine the clash between the ideals of Irish womanhood and the aberrant actions of those women charged with murder.

Gender discourses

Morrissey has argued that when women kill, the rupture between expectation and behaviour creates tension which must be resolved.[29] Women who kill demand explanation, absolution and reconciliation, or neutralisation. To achieve these ends, a narrow range of habitable roles for women who kill has evolved. The literature has identified these stereotypes; 'typologies' in the language of Seal, or 'stock stories' in the words of Morrissey. These gender discourses were formed through inductive processes of interpretation from the official, public and press responses to violent women. Worrall suggested that criminal justice professionals use ideologies of domesticity, pathology and sexuality when attempting to comprehend offending women.[30] Drawing on this, in her study of executed women in twentieth-century England and Wales, Ballinger used the concepts of sexuality, respectability, domesticity and motherhood through which to analyse the discourses.[31] Seal too devised typologies by which women who killed were understood: the masculine woman, the muse/mastermind dichotomy, the damaged personality, the respectable woman and the witch.[32] Fox articulated a further framework of woman as more evil than man, of woman as the dupe of man and of woman as mad.[33] Within these approaches, the suggested categories are understood as constructs of a patriarchal society. Typologies such as these were typically generated from cases in England and Wales, Australia or the United States. The book examines the feasibility of these categories in the context of Ireland, drawing on the social, economic and cultural space of post-independence to assess whether there is some universality in the representation of women who kill. In the challenge of casting Irish cases within the existing mould, the book examines the convergences and divergences which render Ireland a new case study of women's lethal violence.

While these gender discourses are useful, for example in the utility of pinpointing particular societal gender roles in play at a particular time and place, there are inevitably limits to their analytic capacities. Zedner, for one, notes that gender discourses are reified 'types' only.[34] The chapters that follow therefore explore the *limits* of normative gender discourses. To take one example, let us consider the case of Annie Walsh, which served as an opening to this chapter. The 1925 case of Annie Walsh can be compared to a later 1929 case with a protagonist also named Annie Walsh. These two cases were strikingly similar, involving a woman enlisting her lover to murder an unwanted husband. Nevertheless, the ultimate outcomes were very different. In 1925, Walsh and her co-convicted lover were executed. In the 1929 case, Walsh, along with her co-convicted lover, were reprieved.[35] While there was little to differentiate between the gender dynamics at work, specific legal factors were instrumental in ensuring reprieve in 1929, particularly the fact that the convictions rested on the evidence of children. It is clear that gender norms were not always the most relevant influence shaping criminal justice and public responses. Individual cases invariably reveal the contingency of gender and the salience of many other factors, including those inextricably linked to the national context.

In Ireland, political associations collided with perceptions of the death penalty to render its status somewhat ambivalent. As Doyle and O'Donnell argued, the Irish collective memory linked capital punishment to English tyranny. The resulting reluctance to execute condemned persons sprang from a deep well of Irish 'antipathy and unease (perhaps even revulsion) towards the practice'.[36] Accordingly, a form of penal parsimony in the use of judicial death contributed to decision-making on commutation in some cases that would otherwise have seemed to warrant death. In Ireland, the twin influences of class and rurality also heavily influenced the treatment of women in the sample. The majority of women charged with murder were women of the labouring classes working in an agricultural milieu. As Conley found, in a late nineteenth-century context, these circumstances could serve to make gender a less relevant marker of identity for women before the courts.[37]

Gender norms are therefore not static, but are dynamic and contingent, reliant on the interplay of factors such as class, rurality, place and legal factors. The stock stories, typologies or stereotypes identified above do not map absolutely onto women's experiences of criminal justice. Instead, they offer a useful shorthand. There are other scripts and other circumstances that are instrumental in how vaguely articulated gender discourses are interpreted in specific cases. The chapters to come trace the nuances of such discourses, exploring the complexity of storytelling in the responses to women who kill. Additionally, beyond the stories spun *about* the women, the book also presents glimpses of the lived experience of these women, drawn from the archival material on their cases, and informed by the words of the women themselves. Inevitably, the presentation of these biographies represents another form of story-telling, but one that attempts to make space for the women's voices.

Irish historiography

The book has been informed by a substantial body of work from Ireland which blends scholarship from criminology and history. In particular, there is a substantial Irish literature on infanticide.[38] Within the context of a prescriptively Catholic nation with high levels of community conformity, such studies reveal much about Irish responses to female deviance. The existing studies on infanticide have unearthed trends and offered detailed insights into infant murder prosecutions and their social meanings. Infanticide was a frequent occurrence through the nineteenth and into the twentieth century.[39] It was an offence which came with suitably specialised and gendered explanatory discourses. In her exploration of the relationship between homicide and insanity in the nineteenth century, for example, Prior showed that women were most likely to be found insane in cases of infant murder.[40]

Perhaps unsurprisingly considering this pathologised lens, the literature on infanticide has identified a tendency towards leniency. Only a very small percentage of women suspected of the murder of an infant were ultimately convicted of this offence.[41] Of those who *were* convicted of infant murder, no one in the decades from 1850 was executed.[42] In all these cases, sentences of death were followed by commutation. The case of Edward O'Connor, though, suggests that leniency was not a function of gender alone. O'Connor, the only man in the research period convicted of the murder of his illegitimate infant, spent just three years in prison following commutation.[43]

Illegitimacy was the context for the overwhelming majority of women who killed infants, representing 84.7 per cent of Farrell's

nineteenth-century sample.[44] Such women were faced with considerable shame and stigma. At the creation of the new Irish state,
institutional networks catering for the confinement of the unmarried mother were established in response to a perceived crisis of
immorality.[45] Many of these institutions, which recur throughout
the chapters to come, were run by religious organisations, particularly by Catholic Church orders and congregations. The impact of
Catholic Church moral philosophies was evident also in the legislative curtailments to women's reproductive choices. From the late
1920s, McAvoy documents prohibitions on birth control and the
failure to provide welfare support for unmarried mothers as key
features of a society hostile to women's sexual autonomy.[46]

Beyond significant work on infanticide, others have approached
the subject of women who kill from different perspectives. Conley,
exploring homicides from 1866 to 1892, noted that women committed considerably fewer homicides and were more likely to be
victims than perpetrators.[47] Conley argued that considerations
of gender were often subordinate; as the majority of homicides
occurred in rural areas and were committed by members of the
'labouring classes', Conley contended that women's recreational
violence was afforded considerable tolerance. Even with this inter-
sectional reading, women were still more likely to receive a lighter
sentence than men who were convicted of manslaughter.[48]

There is little in the literature on women who killed adults in
twentieth-century Ireland. Brennan investigated family homicides
committed by both men and women from 1930 to 1944, identifying eight cases of women.[49] Only one of these eight was ultimately
convicted of murder, while another pleaded guilty to manslaughter.
Brennan argues that these acquittals were in part grounded by evidential hurdles but further suggests that there were men convicted
in equally challenging circumstances, suggesting that gender may
have offered a protective factor.

Beyond the lens of gender, other work which has tackled the
question of lethal violence in Ireland includes Vaughan's substantial
work on murder trials from 1866 to 1914,[50] McMahon's examination of violence in pre-Famine Ireland,[51] and work by McCullagh
on the motivations for homicide in the late nineteenth century.[52]
This research has all tended to concentrate on the nineteenth

century, although Brewer et al. offered insights on homicide in their general overview of crime in Ireland from 1945 to 1995.[53]

Regarding study of the death penalty, Irish historiography in this area was notably absent for many years. However, the past decade has seen a new enthusiasm for studies of this nature. This work has proceeded from a number of perspectives. O'Donnell investigates the cases of men and women sentenced to death in Ireland from 1922, creating a framework through which to understand clemency, as representing either justice, mercy or caprice.[54] Doyle and O'Callaghan meanwhile offer a history of the death penalty in the decades post-1922 which details its trajectory and meanings within the legal, political and social context.[55] Doyle and O'Donnell have presented a numerical overview of the death penalty post-1922, arguing that the differential in commutation by gender is the most striking feature of its operation.[56] O'Brien meanwhile has explicated the arguments for and against abolition advanced over the decades post-independence.[57] Elsewhere, I have written on the operation of paternalism in the treatment of women sentenced to death post-1922.[58]

A persistent thread in the literature has been a focus on capital punishment as a tool by the British to rout Irish Republican violence. O'Donnell notes for example that for the Irish public, capital punishment was 'a practice long tainted by association with the colonial power'.[59] As a result of this political lens, discussion on violence in Ireland often implicitly understood violence according to its maleness. This book offers a remedial exercise, providing the first comprehensive account of women, murder and the death penalty in Ireland, which considers the full spectrum of women's lethal violence in the years from 1922 until 1964.

Irish legal framework

On independence in 1922, Ireland inherited the English legal framework that made death the mandatory sentence for murder.[60] Regardless of the views of the judge or jury on whether the convicted person *should* hang, or indeed even in cases where it was highly unlikely that the convicted person *would* hang, the judge had no choice but to impose a sentence of death once a jury had found an accused guilty of murder. Death-eligible killings were first restricted in 1949 with the passing of the Infanticide Act. This ensured that a woman who had killed her own infant aged up to 12 months could be prosecuted for infanticide, an offence akin to manslaughter, instead of murder, thereby avoiding the necessity of passing a death sentence. Under the Criminal Justice Act 1964, the death penalty regime was further significantly reformed through the creation of a two-tier framework of capital and non-capital murder. Henceforth, the great majority of murders committed in Ireland would receive a mandatory sentence of life imprisonment. Capital murders, which included killings such as the murder of a member of An Garda Síochána while on duty, would continue to attract a death sentence. Although some persons were sentenced to death under this framework, no one was executed, and the death penalty was abolished in the Criminal Justice Act 1990. In a 2001 referendum, all reference to the death penalty was removed from the Irish Constitution and its future reintroduction was prohibited. This study focuses on the years from independence in 1922 to the enactment of the Criminal Justice Act 1964 in March 1964, which so substantially reformed the law on murder and the death penalty in Ireland.

Sources

The book draws on sources held by the National Archives of Ireland. Much of this material consisted of officially generated documents of governing, including files from the Department of Justice and Department of An Taoiseach. Some earlier cases were heard at the Dublin Commission and those records are also stored within this archive. Trials Record Books, the State Books for the Central Criminal Court, provided data on the numbers of women prosecuted with murder from 1922 to 1964, and State Files by County offer further documents on many of these cases. 'Death Books', one of which was stored on-site at Mountjoy Prison in Dublin, recorded those women who were convicted of murder and sentenced to death. For these women also, their individual prison files provided a rich source of information on their cases and post-reprieve experiences. In some cases, where there was an appeal against conviction and sentence, entire transcripts of the trial exist in the Court of Criminal Appeal files which illuminate the narratives at play. The tables which appear in the chapters to follow were compiled using the information from these archival sources.

The voices of the women in the sample are occasionally heard: through the petitions written by condemned and imprisoned women, and through their statements and evidence. Although these voices are mediated by their instrumental purposes, and are influenced by other actors such as prison chaplains and investigating Gardaí, they nonetheless offer insights into the experiences and thoughts of some of these most abject women. Letters retained on the women's individual files in the Department of Justice and Department of An Taoiseach archives also provided a glimpse of public reactions to their cases. Although these extant letters are a partial glimpse only, they inform our knowledge of wider public narratives. Many of these narratives are mirrored in contemporary press reporting, which was consulted extensively through digital newspaper databases. For the historical researcher the inability to observe trials means that much nuance is lost. Kaufman, referring to contemporary death penalty research and the reliance on trial transcripts, underlines just how much is missed without trial observation.[61] At this remove, newspaper reporting, in addition to providing factual information that may not be present in the state archive, offers some of the few glimpses of behaviour and emotion in trials, thus facilitating a greater understanding of the process. In press coverage we can glimpse the contumacious defendant, the truculent witness or the rowdy courtroom audience. The rarity of women who kill means that many of their cases caught the interest of the press. This facet of discourse provides compelling insights into the media narratives on individual cases. Across the entirety of the sample, the press reporting also allows for broader themes of representation to be ascertained. One notable absence among the sources consulted herein is the lack of access to any files held by the religious orders and organisations which operated the institutions in which many women found themselves detained. This silence compounds the legacy of harm such sites have left in their wake. In the case of women convicted by the courts and sent to institutions by state actors, it represents a particular failing.

The examination of women's lethal violence in the chapters that follow relies on the fragments left behind in officially produced documentation, in surviving letters and in the press reports of the time. The informal judgements made on the women herein are all situated judgements, and the specific contexts of official, press and public discourses are considered in light of the existing literature. To illustrate, Irish press reporting on cases of women and murder was notably muted and skirted away from sensationalism. While commentators such as Carter Wood and Miller have scrutinised the media fascination with high-profile cases of women who kill in Britain and the US,[62] the Irish media context threw up considerable barriers to similar reporting styles, not the least of which was the censorship introduced from the dawn of the new Irish state.[63] In a similar vein, the judgements of Gardaí reflected the views of members of an organisation formed in the mould of an idealised Irish nationalism, and linked to a traditional view of Irish life.[64] Throughout the analysis here, the contexts in which representations are formed and decisions made are considered.

Structure

The book focuses on the processes of criminal justice and punishment, and the meanings attached to women who kill in Ireland in this period. The following chapters therefore explore key steps on the women's journeys, such as the trial and (for some) their conviction, including arguments for insanity, the extension of clemency and the commutation of sentence, as well as the prison and confinement experiences of reprieved women.

Chapter 1 provides an overview of the 292 cases of women tried for murder in Ireland from 1922 to 1964, including an examination of the legal outcomes and profile of the prosecutions. The chapter also spotlights the 22 cases of women convicted of murder and sentenced to death. Chapter 2 explores the operation of clemency for these condemned women. Of these 22, only Annie Walsh was ultimately executed, while 21 benefited from various overtures of mercy from official quarters and the public. Chapter 3 investigates questions of insanity through the trial, exploring the broad themes which motivated discourses of insanity in the Irish context, particularly the idea of heredity and 'weak-mindedness', as well as an examination of those women found unfit to plead or guilty but insane, or those certified insane post-conviction. Chapter 4 focuses on the sentencing and punishment of women prosecuted for murder and convicted of lesser offences. This analysis explores the detention of such women, exploring the meanings of both imprisonment and religious institutionalisation in these years. Chapter 5 investigates the women who had their sentence of death commuted to penal servitude for life. Examining the post-reprieve journey of these women, the chapter presents an overview of the imprisonment experiences of reprieved women and the confinement of women in religious institutions, as well as their post-release experiences, analysing the involvement of actors such as probation officers and prison chaplains. Chapter 6 turns to the question of motherhood and child-killing. Motherhood was a central organising concept around which women's identities were constructed, not least because a significant proportion of the women tried for murder were tried for the killing of an infant. The chapter also looks beyond the cases of infant murder to the ideologies and practices of motherhood which run through so many of the cases. Chapter 7 continues the examination of the central themes through which women were made explicable, exploring marriage and sexuality. The chapter looks at notions of idealised womanhood and considers these in the Irish context, particularly ideas of domesticity and figures such as the poisoner and the abortionist. Chapter 8 situates the prosecuted women within their class and community, exploring how such positionalities went towards how they were understood within the criminal justice apparatus. The Conclusion seeks to explore and explain the experiences of women prosecuted for murder in these decades, making sense of the Irish case within the broader literature.

The chapters draw on the existing secondary literature to contextualise the archival and press sources used. Throughout, the archival sources themselves are drawn on heavily to bring to life the cases of prosecuted women. Although the cases within the sample represent a statistical anomaly and are in some ways entirely unrepresentative of the experiences of Irish women in these years, in many ways they tell a story that would have been recognisable to women at the time. Paradoxically, the cases offer a compelling and all too familiar glimpse of the lives of women in Ireland post-independence. The women's crimes were the triggers which ensured the details of their lives would be recorded for posterity.

Notes

1 National Archives of Ireland (hereafter NAI) State Files Central Criminal Court (hereafter SFCCC) Limerick 1925; Department of Justice, H1004/275.

2 The figure is drawn from the number of women prosecuted for murder as listed in the State Books for the Central Criminal Court. The figures presented are all those cases for which evidence was found that a woman had been prosecuted for murder. In some cases, this evidence was fragmentary, and inevitably, earlier cases have left fewer traces in the records. After the Infanticide Act 1949, women charged with the murder of their own infant aged under 12 months were eligible to be charged with this lesser offence. These post-1949 cases are excluded from this tally unless the women were sent to the Central Criminal Court on a murder charge.

3 Work remains to be done in the area of masculinity, although see Katie Barclay, 'Performing emotion and reading the male body in the Irish court, c.1800–1845', *Journal of Social History*, 51:2 (2017) 293–312.

4 Elizabeth A. Stanko, 'Challenging the problem of men's individual violence', in Tim Newburn and Elizabeth A. Stanko (eds), *Just Boys Doing Business? Men, Masculinities and Crime* (London: Routledge, 1995).

5 Lucia Zedner, *Women, Crime and Custody in Victorian England* (Oxford: Clarendon, 1991).

6 Lizzie Seal, *Women, Murder and Femininity: Gender Representations of Women Who Kill* (Basingstoke: Palgrave Macmillan, 2010), p. 3.

7 Patricia O'Brien, 'Crime and punishment as historical problem', *Journal of Social History*, 11:4 (1978) 508–20.

8 Eoin O'Sullivan and Ian O'Donnell, 'Coercive confinement in the Republic of Ireland', *Punishment and Society*, 9:1 (2007) 27–48. See also James M. Smith, *Ireland's Magdalen Laundries and the Nation's Architecture of Containment* (Manchester: Manchester University

Press, 2008); Frances Finnegan, *Do Penance or Perish: A Study of Magdalen Asylums in Ireland* (Oxford: Oxford University Press, 2004).

9 Steven Ruggles, 'Fallen women: the inmates of the Magdalen asylum of Philadelphia, 1836–1908', *Journal of Social History*, 16:4 (1983) 65–82, cited at p. 71.

10 Dublin Diocesan Archives, Archbishop John Charles McQuaid. AB8/b/ XXVIII/983. Memorandum prepared by E. M. Carroll, probation officer at Dublin Metropolitan Courthouse, forwarded in a letter of 9 July 1941; NAI, Department of Justice 234/1744. Letter from Kathleen Sullivan, 21 June 1930.

11 Leanne McCormick, *Regulating Sexuality: Women in Twentieth-Century Northern Ireland* (Manchester: Manchester University Press, 2011).

12 Jill McCorkel, *Breaking Women: Gender, Race and the New Politics of Imprisonment* (New York: New York University Press, 2013).

13 Zedner, *Women, Crime and Custody in Victorian England*, p. 264.

14 Hilary Allen, 'Rendering them harmless: the professional portrayal of women charged with serious violent crimes', in Kathleen Daly and Lisa Maher (eds), *Criminology at the Crossroads: Feminist Readings in Crime and Criminology* (Oxford: Oxford University Press, 1987/1998).

15 Camille Naish, *Death Comes to the Maiden: Sex and Execution, 1431–1933* (London: Routledge, 1991).

16 Shelley A. M. Gavigan, 'Petit treason in eighteenth century England: women's inequality before the law', *Canadian Journal of Women and the Law*, 3:2 (1989/1990) 335–74.

17 David Garland, *Peculiar Institution: America's Death Penalty in an Age of Abolition* (Oxford: Oxford University Press, 2010), cited at p. 118.

18 Victor L. Streib, 'America's aversion to executing women', *Women's Law Journal*, 1 (1997) 1–8.

19 Lynley Hood, *Minnie Dean: Her Life and Crimes* (London: Penguin, 1995).

20 Anette Ballinger, *Dead Woman Walking: Executed Women in England and Wales, 1900–1955* (Dartmouth: Ashgate, 2000).

21 Frances Heidensohn, *Women and Crime*, 2nd edition (Basingstoke: Palgrave Macmillan, 1996).

22 Martin Wiener, *Men of Blood: Violence, Manliness and Criminal Justice in Victorian England* (Cambridge: Cambridge University Press, 2004).

23 Ann Lloyd, *Doubly Deviant, Doubly Damned: Society's Treatment of Violent Women* (London: Penguin, 1995).

24 Seal, *Women, Murder and Femininity*; Lizzie Seal, 'Issues of gender and class in the Mirror Newspapers' campaign for the release of Edith Chubb', *Crime Media Culture*, 5 (2009) 57–78.
25 Zedner, *Women, Crime and Custody in Victorian England*, p. 7.
26 Maryann Gialanella Valiulis, 'Power, gender and identity in the Irish Free State', *Journal of Women's History*, 6:4/7:1 (1995) 117–36.
27 Evelyn Mahon, 'Ireland: a private patriarchy?', *Environment and Planning A*, 26:8 (1994) 1277–96.
28 Mahon, 'Ireland: a private patriarchy?', p. 1978.
29 Belinda Morrissey, *When Women Kill: Questions of Agency and Subjectivity* (New York: Routledge, 2003).
30 Anne Worrall, *Offending Women: Female Lawbreakers and the Criminal Justice System* (London: Routledge, 1990).
31 Ballinger, *Dead Woman Walking*.
32 Seal, *Women, Murder and Femininity*.
33 Marie Fox, 'Crime and punishment: representations of female killers in law and literature', in John Morison and Christine Bell (eds), *Tall Stories? Reading Law and Literature* (Dartmouth: Ashgate, 1996).
34 Zedner, *Women, Crime and Custody in Victorian England*.
35 NAI, SFCCC Galway 1929–1931; Court of Criminal Appeal (hereafter CCA) 16/1929; Department of An Taoiseach S.5904; Department of Justice 234/2599.
36 David M. Doyle and Ian O'Donnell, 'The death penalty in post-independence Ireland', *Journal of Legal History*, 33:1 (2012) 65–91, p. 69.
37 Carolyn A. Conley, *Melancholy Accidents: The Meaning of Violence in post-Famine Ireland* (Lanham, MD: Lexington, 1999).
38 Although the term infanticide had no specific legal meaning until the Infanticide Act of 1949, it had been generally used throughout the nineteenth and twentieth centuries to refer to the killing of an infant. Ian O'Donnell, 'Lethal violence in Ireland, 1841 to 2003: famine, celibacy and parental pacification', *British Journal of Criminology*, 45:5 (2005) 671–95. Farrell has noted that prior to its enshrinement as a separate offence in 1949, it was often used in a much wider sense, and could refer to the killing of older children. Elaine Farrell, *'A Most Diabolical Deed': Infanticide and Irish Society, 1850–1900* (Manchester: Manchester University Press, 2013). For other work on infanticide in Ireland, see Karen M. Brennan, '"A fine mixture of pity and justice": the criminal justice response to infanticide in Ireland 1922–1949', *Law and History Review*, 31:4 (2013) 793–841; Karen M. Brennan, 'Punishing infanticide in the Irish Free State', *Irish Journal*

of Legal Studies, 3:1 (2013) 1–35; Elaine Farrell, '"Infanticide of the ordinary character": an overview of the crime in Ireland, 1850–1900', *Irish Economic and Social History*, 39 (2012) 56–72; Clíona Rattigan, *'What Else Could I Do?': Single Mothers and Infanticide, Ireland 1900–1950* (Dublin: Irish Academic Press, 2012); Louise Ryan, 'The press, the police and prosecution perspectives on infanticide in the 1920s', in Diane Urquhart and Alan Hayes (eds), *Irish Women's History* (Dublin: Irish Academic Press, 2004).

39 Although Farrell and O'Donnell both demonstrate that figures declined considerably from the mid-nineteenth century. O'Donnell, 'Lethal violence in Ireland'; Farrell, *'A Most Diabolical Deed'*.

40 Pauline M. Prior, *Murder and Madness: Gender, Crime and Mental Disorder in Nineteenth-Century Ireland* (Dublin: Irish Academic Press, 2008).

41 Brennan found that of 160 cases, 124 women were convicted of lesser charges, 26 were acquitted and 8 were convicted of murder. Brennan, 'A fine mixture of pity and justice'. Similarly, Rattigan found that of 71 cases of suspected infanticide from 1900 to 1921, 38 women were convicted of concealment of birth, 8 of manslaughter, 10 were acquitted and only 3 were found guilty of murder. From 1922 to 1950, of 195 women tried, 64 were convicted of concealment of birth, 67 were found guilty of manslaughter, 27 were found not guilty and 9 were convicted of murder. Rattigan, *'What Else Could I Do?'*.

42 Farrell, *'A Most Diabolical Deed'*, p. 211.

43 Ian O'Donnell, *Justice, Mercy, and Caprice: Clemency and the Death Penalty in Ireland* (Oxford: Oxford University Press, 2017).

44 Farrell, 'Infanticide of the ordinary character'.

45 Maria Luddy, 'Moral rescue and unmarried mothers in Ireland in the 1920s', *Women's Studies*, 30:6 (2001) 797–817.

46 Sandra McAvoy, 'The regulation of sexuality in the Irish Free State, 1929–1935', in Greta Jones and Elizabeth Malcolm (eds), *Medicine, Disease and the State in Ireland, 1650–1940* (Cork: Cork University Press, 1999).

47 Conley, *Melancholy Accidents*.

48 Ian O'Donnell, 'Killing in Ireland at the turn of the centuries: contexts, consequences and civilising processes', *Irish Economic and Social History*, 37 (2010) 53–74.

49 Karen Brennan, 'Murder in the Irish family, 1930–1945', in Niamh Howlin and Kevin Costello (eds), *Law and the Family in Ireland: 1850–1950* (London: Palgrave, 2017). Brennan excluded killings of an infant aged under one year.

50 W. E. Vaughan, *Murder Trials in Ireland, 1836–1914* (Dublin: Four Courts Press, 2009).

51 Richard McMahon, *Homicide in pre-Famine and Famine Ireland* (Liverpool: Liverpool University Press, 2013).

52 Ciaran McCullagh, 'A tie that blinds: family and ideology in Ireland', *Irish Economic and Social Review*, 22:3 (1991) 199–211.

53 John D. Brewer, Bill Lockhart and Paula Rogers, *Crime in Ireland, 1945–95: 'Here Be Dragons'* (Oxford: Clarendon, 1997).

54 O'Donnell, *Justice, Mercy, and Caprice*.

55 David M. Doyle and Liam O'Callaghan, *Capital Punishment in Independent Ireland: A Social, Legal and Political and History* (Liverpool: Liverpool University Press, 2019).

56 Doyle and O'Donnell, 'The death penalty in post-independence Ireland'.

57 Gerard O'Brien, 'Capital punishment in Ireland, 1922–1964', in N. M. Dawson (ed.), *Reflections on Law and History* (Dublin: Four Courts Press, 2006).

58 Lynsey Black, '"On the other hand the accused is a woman …": women and the death penalty in post-independence Ireland', *Law and History Review*, 36:1 (2018) 139–72, p. 139.

59 O'Donnell, *Justice, Mercy, and Caprice*, p. 13.

60 Ireland gained independence from the United Kingdom in 1922. Following the War of Independence (1919–21), the Anglo-Irish Treaty was signed in London in 1921. This provided for the partition of the island of Ireland. Six counties in the north, remaining within the United Kingdom, became Northern Ireland, while the other 26 counties became the Irish Free State. Ireland became a republic in 1949, following passage of the Republic of Ireland Act 1948. Throughout the book, the term 'Ireland' refers to the 26 counties that comprised, first, the Free State, and then the Republic of Ireland.

61 Sarah Beth Kaufman, *American Roulette: The Social Logic of Death Penalty Sentencing Trials* (Oakland: University of California Press, 2020).

62 John Carter Wood, *The Most Remarkable Woman in England: Poison, Celebrity and the Trials of Beatrice Pace* (Manchester: Manchester University Press, 2012); April Miller, 'Bloody blondes and bobbed-haired bandits: the execution of justice and the construction of the celebrity criminal in the 1920s popular press', in Su Holmes and Diane Negra (eds), *In the Limelight and under the Microscope: Forms and Functions of Female Celebrity* (London: Continuum, 2011).

63 Sandra McAvoy, 'Before Cadden: abortion in mid-twentieth-century Ireland', in Dermot Keogh, Finbarr O'Shea and Carmel Quinlan (eds),

Ireland in the 1950s: The Lost Decade (Cork: Mercier Press, 2004). Finola Kennedy has noted that 'Abortion was a term rarely mentioned in public in Ireland until the 1980s', see Finola Kennedy, *Cottage to Crèche: Family Change in Ireland* (Dublin: IPA, 2001), p. 38.
64 Vicky Conway, *Policing Twentieth Century Ireland: A History of An Garda Síochána* (Manchester: Manchester University Press, 2013).

1

Women prosecuted for murder

From 1922 until 1964, 292 women were prosecuted for murder. Of these, only 22 were convicted on this charge, and of these 22, only one was executed. Of the total number prosecuted, the case involved an infant victim in 253 cases, a child in 5 cases and in 34 cases an adult. Table 1.1 gives an overview of prosecutions by year and victim status. Through the 1920s, the 1930s and the 1940s, the most remarkable trend was the stability of the numbers of women before the courts on a murder charge. The Infanticide Act 1949 ushered in a new era of female murder prosecutions by largely removing infant murders from the ranks of those prosecuted. This change coincided with a decade in which very few women were prosecuted for child or adult murder. Ireland in the 1950s, dubbed by Brady as 'a policeman's paradise', remained isolated from the post-war crime increases experienced elsewhere.[1] As O'Donnell noted, homicide levels plummeted to just 1.7 per 1,000,000 in 1954.[2]

Most of the women charged with murder did not seek to put the state on proof, avoiding the unpredictability of a jury trial. As Table 1.2 shows, while 86 women were tried by jury, 158 pleaded guilty to a lesser, non-capital offence. From this remove, it is a fraught endeavour to speculate on the extent to which such decisions were directed by legal counsel or by the women themselves. The experiences of some, such as the few who pleaded guilty to the capital charge, suggest little guidance from the appointed barristers. Although the legal fiction is that defendants instruct counsel, and that plea decisions remain within the defendant's domain, it is perhaps more accurate to describe the defendant as a passive actor

Table 1.1 Women prosecuted by year and victim status

Year	Infant	Child	Adult	Total
1922	0	0	0	0
1923	1	0	0	1
1924	9	0	2	11
1925	5	0	3	8
1926	18	0	6	24
1927	15	0	0	15
1928	13	1	2	16
1929	21	0	1	22
1930	11	0	0	11
1931	10	0	1	11
1932	4	0	1	5
1933	14	0	2	16
1934	9	0	3	12
1935	11	0	0	11
1936	5	0	0	5
1937	7	1	0	8
1938	9	0	0	9
1939	3	0	1	4
1940	8	0	1	9
1941	11	0	0	11
1942	9	0	2	11
1943	11	0	0	11
1944	9	0	0	9
1945	7	1	1	9
1946	5	1	1	7
1947	6	0	0	6
1948	7	0	0	7
1949	4	0	2	6
1950	3	1	0	4
1951	0	0	0	0
1952	0	0	0	0
1953	4	0	0	4
1954	1	0	0	1
1955	1	0	0	1
1956	0	0	1	1
1957	1	0	0	1
1958	0	0	0	0
1959	1	0	0	1
1960	0	0	1	1
1961	0	0	0	0

Table 1.1 (continued)

Year	Infant	Child	Adult	Total
1962	0	0	2	2
1963	0	0	1	1
1964	0	0	0	0
Total	253	5	34	292

Table 1.2 Jury trials and pleas, 1922–64

Decade	Jury trial	Nolle prosequi and discharged	Pleaded guilty to a lesser offence	Partial (trial and plea)	Unknown	N/A (e.g. unfit to plead, put back, etc.)	Total
1920s	31	4	38	6	14	4	97
1930s	36	0	42	10	0	4	92
1940s	12	2	70	0	1	1	86
1950s	4	1	8	0	0	0	13
1960s	3	0	0	0	0	1	4
Total	86	7	158	16	15	10	292

amid legal professionals.[3] Carlen went so far as to term defendants 'dummy players' in their own cases.[4]

Of those who did not have a jury trial (and had not pleaded guilty to a lesser offence) some were found unfit to plead,[5] for others a *nolle prosequi* was entered and they were discharged from court.[6] Significantly, the numbers of women opting for jury trials collapsed through the 1940s, as it became increasingly likely that women would plead guilty to a non-capital offence.

The pattern in those pleading guilty was skewed by offence type, with clear differences between those charged with murdering an adult and those charged with murdering an infant or child. Of 34 women prosecuted for the murder of an adult, 23 pleaded not guilty at trial. Of the 23 who put their case to a jury, ten were convicted of murder and death-sentenced, ten were found not guilty and discharged from court and three were found guilty of manslaughter. Only four women pleaded guilty to lesser offences, three of whom pleaded guilty to manslaughter while another pleaded guilty as an accessory to murder. A further four were found unfit to plead, one woman's case was put back and in two cases the state entered a *nolle prosequi* and the women were discharged from court.

Meanwhile, Table 1.3[7] sets out the 154 cases of women charged with infant/child murder (predominantly infant murder[8]) who pleaded guilty to lesser offences (of cases for which information is available). The overwhelming majority pleaded guilty to either concealment of birth or manslaughter.[9] The pattern tells a story of the gradual replacement of concealment of birth by manslaughter. While concealment of birth was considerably more numerous as a plea in the 1920s, it had collapsed in frequency by the 1940s. In the decade in which more women than ever pleaded guilty to a lesser offence, that offence was generally manslaughter. Why did this happen? Manslaughter carried a potentially much harsher sentence, with a maximum penalty of penal servitude for life. In contrast, under section 60 of the Offences Against the Person Act 1861, concealment of birth carried a maximum punishment of two years' imprisonment with or without hard labour. Despite significant differences in the maximum penalty, there was little difference in the sentences handed down for manslaughter or concealment in cases of infant death (with the caveat that all women sentenced to penal servitude had necessarily been convicted of manslaughter). As the years wore on, it became increasingly likely that women would plead guilty to manslaughter (and then infanticide after 1949).

In many ways, verdicts in infant murder could often appear arbitrary. Judicial discussion of sentencing on this could be insightful;

Table 1.3 Women pleading guilty to lesser offences, infant/child murder, 1922–64

Decade	Concealment	Manslaughter	Infanticide (post-1949)	Other	Total
1920s	25	8	N/A	3	36
1930s	19	19	N/A	3	41
1940s	14	55	0	0	69
1950s	0	1	7	0	8
1960–64	0	0	0	0	0
Total	58	83	7	6	154

Justice Johnston made two remarks four years apart that high-lighted this capriciousness. Although Elizabeth Hannon was con-victed of murder and death-sentenced in 1927, Johnston confided to the Department of Justice that had she been convicted of conceal-ment he would have sentenced her to six months' imprisonment.[10] Four years later, Johnston, in sentencing Mary Kiely to two years' imprisonment with hard labour following her guilty plea to man-slaughter, noted that 'He had power to impose penal servitude for life, but would not do that, although the sentence must be severe.'[11] In many cases, there was little on the facts to distinguish cases as more fitting for a murder conviction, a lesser conviction or an acquittal.

Some women, when called upon to plead, pleaded guilty to murder. These few cases seem to demonstrate the intense vulner-ability of many women before the courts. In 1924, 18-year-old Isabella Snow, who eventually pleaded guilty to the manslaughter of her infant, had first pleaded guilty to murder:

> That plea took the prosecution by surprise, if not by bewilderment. The judge at the last sessions, fearing he would have to accept the plea, put the accused back, for, had he accepted it, there was no other course open to him but to go through the horrible formality of putting on the black cap and imposing the death sentence – a sentence which would not be carried out.[12]

The recent Infanticide Act 1922 (England and Wales) was cited as a reason why a guilty plea should not be accepted. When Snow instead entered a plea to manslaughter, it was accepted by state counsel, who again cited the new legislation across the Irish Sea. While this suggested that Irish courts would henceforth shy away from capital convictions for infant murder, there were to be 12 death sentences for this offence before reform in 1949. It remained the case that if a woman put the state on proof, the jury could find the defendant guilty on the most serious charge.

In cases of infant murder, despite the risk of pleading not guilty and facing the unknown of a jury verdict, a considerable number of women did just that. Arguably, it was not a high-stakes game. The expectation was that women convicted of infant murder would be swiftly reprieved.[13] However, the strain of the capital verdict for some was extreme.[14] Shown in Table 1.4, for some who opted for a jury trial, it ended more fortuitously. In the 1920s, for women who put the state on proof in adult murder cases, a death sentence was the most likely outcome. However, for infant murder cases, acquittal and discharge from court was most likely. In the 1930s, of 30 women who underwent a jury trial when charged with infant or child murder, 17 were found not guilty and discharged from court, while five were convicted of murder. Adult murder cases were more likely to end in the women's discharge after acquittal in this decade too in five of six cases (with one woman being convicted of murder). By the 1940s, the number of women pleading not guilty had collapsed.

To a great extent, jury trial is a 'black box'. Sarat quoted United States Supreme Court Justice John Paul Stevens that, 'If the state wishes to execute a citizen, it must persuade a jury of his peers that death is an appropriate punishment for his offence.'[15] Yet, how juries interpret the information presented to them is far from clear. More than strictly legal considerations assailed jurors as they weighed up guilt or innocence, and many verdicts appeared perverse given the evidence. However, once the matter was in the hands of the jury, it became the sole arbiter of fact. In some cases, juries seemed to engage in 'jury nullification', returning a not guilty verdict despite overwhelming evidence to the contrary. Howlin has documented the gradual silencing of the Irish jury by the late nineteenth century,[16] including diminishing tolerance for 'perverse' verdicts, but even this now-muzzled jury could occasionally return verdicts at odds with the facts and with judicial expectation. This was clear in infant murder trials, as juries were occasionally exhorted to 'find verdicts of wilful murder' despite sympathy for the defendant.[17] In the 1926 case of Nora Kearney, Justice Johnston, in response to the jury's verdict of manslaughter, stated pointedly that 'he would accept the verdict, which was rather unfortunate as there was no evidence of manslaughter'.[18] As Justice Conor Maguire noted in summing up the evidence for the jury in Alice Jones's trial for infant murder in 1938, 'It was difficult to avoid an air of unreality about trials of infanticide.'[19] Despite the seemingly high-stakes legal peril, infant murder trials were strange affairs: a case of the law hybridised by long practice to a form in which it was

Table 1.4 Jury trials and outcomes, 1922–64

Decade and offence type	Death sentence	Convicted of murder but underage	Guilty of manslaughter	Guilty of concealment	Guilty but insane	Not guilty and discharged
1920s – adult	5	0	2	N/A	0	1
1920s – infant/child	6	1	3	4	1	8
1930s – adult	1	0	0	N/A	0	5
1930s – infant/child	5	0	3	3	2	17
1940s – adult	3	0	0	N/A	0	2
1940s – infant/child	1	0	0	0	1	5
1950s – adult	1	0	3	N/A	0	0
1950s – infant/child	0	0	0	0	0	0
1960–64 – adult	0	0	1	N/A	0	2
1960–64 – infant/child	0	0	0	0	0	0

tolerable to contemporary norms. Juror indecision was occasionally a cause of annoyance too, as in Annie Cox's first trial at which she faced a charge of murdering her newborn infant. The jury returned after 90 minutes to declare that they could not agree a verdict. Justice Johnston, exasperated, stated, 'All I can say, gentlemen, is if a jury cannot agree on a simple case like this the sooner they are discharged the better. I discharge you, gentlemen – gladly discharge you for the rest of the Commission.'[20] In contrast, in a number of cases, jury acquittals were met with approval by the judge,[21] while in others, the judge directed acquittal.

Other cases saw the jury struggle with returning a verdict which amounted to a death sentence, as in the 1929 case of Mary Kiernan in which the jury initially brought in a verdict of guilty 'but not responsible for her actions'.[22] In the 1944 case of Ellen Keogh, in which she was initially found guilty of murder, the jury rider went so far as to suggest that she not been the blameworthy party in the killing; this rider ultimately led to the quashing of her conviction in the Court of Criminal Appeal.[23] In the case of Mary Moynihan, capitally convicted for the murder of her employer in December 1924, a juror later wrote to the Department of Justice experiencing 'qualms of conscience'.[24] One juror in the 1963 case of Kathleen Clogher took action to ensure he would not find himself in such a position, and was permitted to stand down after declaring his opposition to capital punishment:

> I could not conscientiously act as a juror in this case as I am against the death penalty and have addressed public meetings in favour of its abolition. I have been agitating for the abolition of the death penalty for a number of years.[25]

It was possible, then, for juries to bring in verdicts that seemed at odds with the facts, and there were moments throughout in which jurors raised their heads above the parapet and become visible to the historical researcher. Further, returning to Justice Stevens's aphorism, which presupposed that in bringing a capital prosecution the state 'wishes to execute a citizen', this statement was far from being an accurate reflection of Ireland in these years. For one, as infant murder charges comprised the significant bulk of murder prosecutions, there were a great many cases in which the state brought

capital proceedings but had no notion of executing the defendant if
she was to be found guilty. More broadly, as explored in Chapter 2,
there was little zeal to execute even those women convicted of the
murder of an adult.

Women convicted of murder

Twenty-two women were convicted of murder and sentenced
to death, as outlined in Table 1.5. The first was Hannah Flynn,
condemned to death on 27 February 1924.[26] Mamie Cadden was
the last woman sentenced to death, on 1 November 1956.[27] A
further two women successfully appealed their murder convictions,[28] while others also attempted to have their case heard in the
Court of Criminal Appeal.[29] Unlike the case of Annie Walsh (1929),
however, whose appeal failed,[30] not all appeals were heard in full.
In the case of Mary Daly, her appeal was refused but the case was
referred to the Supreme Court on a point of law of exceptional

Table 1.5 Women convicted of murder and sentenced to death, 1922–64

Name	Convicted	Age	Location	Victim
Hannah Flynn	27 February 1924	28	Co. Kerry	Margaret O'Sullivan (former employer)
Mary Moynihan	12 December 1924	22	Co. Cork	Nora Horgan (employer)
Hannah O'Leary	30 June 1925	37	Co. Cork	Patrick O'Leary (brother)
Annie Walsh	10 July 1025	31	Co. Limerick	Edward Walsh (husband)
Elizabeth Doran	3 June 1926	40	Co. Wicklow	Own Infant
Mary Kiernan	28 October 1926	22	Co. Westmeath	Own Infant
Elizabeth Hannon	12 December 1927	30	Co. Westmeath	Own Infant
Mary Anne Keane	10 June 1929	23	Co. Roscommon	Own Infant

Table 1.5 (continued)

Name	Convicted	Age	Location	Victim
Deborah Sullivan	13 June 1929	21	Co. Kerry	Own Infant
Annie Walsh	21 June 1929	42	Co. Galway	Sonny Dan Walsh (husband)
Catherine Ahearne	25 June 1929	26	Co. Wexford	Own Infant
Christina Russell	27 November 1930	28	Co. Dublin	Own Infant
Margaret Finn	3 March 1931	25	Co. Clare	Own Infant
Jane O'Brien	8 June 1932	52	Co. Wexford	John Cousins (nephew)
Elizabeth and Rose Edwards	28 March 1935	20 and 28	Co. Roscommon	Infant of Elizabeth
Mary Somerville	15 Nov 1938	50	Co. Monaghan	Infant grandchild
Kate Owens	22 November 1943	36	Co. Westmeath	Own Infant
Agnes McAdam	15 February 1946	53	Co. Monaghan	James Finnegan
Mary Daly	29 April 1949	27	Dublin City	Mary Gibbons
Frances Cox	21 November 1949	30	Co. Laois	Richard Cox
Mamie Cadden	1 November 1956	64	Dublin City	Helen O'Reilly

public importance; that Court quashed her conviction, but she was again capitally convicted of murder at the retrial.[31]

As outlined in Table 1.6, more death sentences were handed down to women from the period 1922 to 1929 than in any other decade post-1922. The number of death sentences in each decade dropped considerably following this peak. As Doyle and O'Donnell found, the rate of all death sentences peaked in the period 1923

Table 1.6 Women sentenced to death by decade

Women sentenced to death	Decade
11	1922–29
6	1930–39
4	1940–49
1	1950–59
0	1960–64

to 1929 but declined in the decades thereafter.[32] The exception to this decline occurred during the Second World War, a period known in Ireland as the 'Emergency'. During this period, what Doyle and O'Donnell termed the 'mercy ratio' shifted, as security fears fomented punitivism within the Department of Justice, and more persons were executed than reprieved. These trends applied to men only. The occurrence of female death sentences had an almost unbroken downward trend from the peak of 11 from 1922 to 1929; this figure halved in the following decade and experienced no late spikes or reversals, unlike the trend for male death sentences.

All women prosecuted for murder: profile of the cases

Within the cases, there were 281 victims: 242 infants (aged under 12 months), 6 children and 33 adults. The disparity between the numbers of women prosecuted and the number of victims is a feature of those cases in which multiple family members were prosecuted for murder. Other women were prosecuted for multiple murders, such as Kate Owens, who was initially prosecuted with three counts of infant murder,[33] or Mary Agnes Staunton, prosecuted on six counts of murder and who pleaded guilty to six counts of infanticide.[34]

The character of female-perpetrated homicides is different to those perpetrated by men. Women commit homicides at lower rates than men, and when women do kill, their victims are more likely to be drawn from their immediate family, typically children or partners.[35] The identity of the victim in homicides is intertwined with how the killing is understood. Most of the cases within the scope of this work are legible as 'typically' female killings, such as the killing of infants or intimate partners. Seal has argued that women who kill are understood within narrow heteronormative standards, bound by marriage and motherhood, but that focusing solely on these cases marginalises and renders unknowable the cases which fall beyond this.[36] While more 'typical' cases form the bulk of the cases herein, there are also those that fall beyond it, presenting glimpses of the 'unknowable' female-perpetrated killing.

For instance, O'Donnell's analysis of homicides in the 1890s showed that 15.2 per cent of homicides occurred as a result of disputes between employers and employees, none of which had been committed by women.[37] The cases of Hannah Flynn and Mary Moynihan herein fit this profile. The killing of an employer signalled a reversal of the natural order. Kennedy observed that the structure of the Irish household for the first decades of the twentieth century imposed strict binary hierarchies of husband/wife, parent/child and master/servant. In this matrix of duty, the killing of employers was particularly insidious, and aggravated when perpetrated by live-in domestic servants.[38] It is perhaps no surprise that both Flynn and Moynihan were convicted of murder.

Killings which occurred during the commission of another offence accounted for 5.6 per cent of the homicides in the 1890s but, again, none had been committed by women.[39] The cases of Mary Daly and Mamie Cadden arguably match this description.[40] Cadden was performing an abortion procedure prohibited under the Offences Against the Person Act 1861 (and it was only this fact which allowed her to be prosecuted for murder), while Daly had been attempting to rob Mary Gibbons in a Dublin church when the killing occurred. Both women were convicted of murder. Of all the women prosecuted for murder, only Mary Daly and Mary Flynn had killed persons entirely unknown to them, which is exceptionally rare for female-perpetrated killings. At Flynn's trial in February 1962, for the murder of Maurice Ryan, she was found guilty of manslaughter.[41] Flynn had killed Ryan during a brawl after Flynn and her family, who were Travellers, had been driven from the nearby town by locals.[42] This disposal, a manslaughter conviction, and Flynn's sentence of 18 months' imprisonment, corresponded with prevailing patterns a century before, when deaths resulting from drunken brawls and fights were more likely to result in relatively short terms of imprisonment.[43] This suggests a scale of culpability for homicides which was intimately connected to the means of killing.

Throughout the cases, there were implications related to the means of killing, which is evident in how each case was understood. Certain cases were considered particularly heinous because of how the victim died. The case of Frances Cox, who murdered her brother by strychnine poisoning, provoked particular comment.[44] The association of poison with murders committed by women, and the framing of such killings as cruelly deliberate, was evident through the discourse on the killing. However, a slew of cases in which women were prosecuted and acquitted for the murder of their husbands by poisoning suggest greater nuance is needed, and that there was far from blanket condemnation of suspected poisoners.[45] Alternatively, the categorisation of gun violence as 'male' was evident in the masculinisation of women who killed by shooting, as in the case of Jane O'Brien.[46] The only other women prosecuted for a death by shooting, Kate Duffy[47] and Bridget Daly,[48] had both killed their husbands and were both found unfit to plead.

The question of motivation throughout the prosecutions often turned on the societal censure directed towards illegitimacy, as most women were prosecuted for infant murder. The shame experienced by these women was intensely criminogenic. For those who killed adults, motivations fell under the headings of financial gain, inheritance and land, family disputes and extramarital relationships, although many cases demonstrated multiple sources of conflict.[49]

As shown in Table 1.7, most women prosecuted were aged in their twenties.[50] The mean age of women in the sample was 28 (of 226 cases where age was known) and the median was 25. There was a disparity in age between those women prosecuted for adult murder and women prosecuted for infant murder;[51] women before the courts for infant murder were younger (with mean/median ages of 24/27) compared to those prosecuted for adult murder (with mean/median ages of 39/40).

The youngest was 15-year-old Mary Cole, while the eldest was Margaret O'Brien, who was prosecuted for the murder of her infant grandchild in 1953 (and who walked free after the state entered a

Table 1.7 Age ranges of prosecuted women

Number of women	Age range
32	15–19
115	20–29
47	30–39
14	40–49
10	50–59
8	60–69
0	70+

nolle prosequi on the charge). Fifteen-year-old Mary Cole was convicted, on 23 March 1928, for the murders of two children in her care; due to her age she was not sentenced to death and was instead detained 'at the pleasure of the Governor General'.[52]

Of the 268 cases in which marital status could be ascertained, 59 women were married, 186 were unmarried, nine were married but separated and a further nine were widowed.[53] As explored in subsequent chapters, marital status was key to how women were understood by the courts and legal professionals, and constituted a significant means of reading cases and informing sentence and punishment. Marital status tended to shape both the killings women stood accused of and the criminal justice responses they faced.

The women before the courts on charges of murder were almost entirely drawn from the labouring classes. Few women had means, something which threw them into crises when, as had happened in many of the cases, they became pregnant. In 1928, 30-year-old farm servant Margaret Slattery was discharged from court and a *nolle prosequi* entered. Slattery had been charged with the murder of her newborn infant, and had been living rough prior to the birth: 'For some days before her confinement the woman had lived in the open fields, sleeping at night in a ditch, "like a cow or other animal".'[54] Such intense precariousness was evident in the 1929 case of Mary Anne Keane who was convicted of the murder of her infant. Keane gave birth in a county home but 'had no real home to go to' on discharge as her husband had turned her out months before.[55] Keane wandered from place to place on foot; a neighbour she met on the road later reported that she 'appeared to be distressed, and was

almost crying'.[56] These cases represent the acute edge of precariousness, but the circumstances of women across the decades more often
than not spoke to lives of meagre means.

The profile of killings was predominantly rural or semi-rural.
Comparing the secular profile of homicide in 1890 and 1990,
O'Donnell noted that homicide in Ireland became a more urban
phenomenon.[57] Although crime was increasingly occurring in
urban areas from the turn of the century, Brewer et al. found that
homicide remained a typically rural offence until later in the twentieth century, with the particulars of the offence governed by its rural
location so that victims and perpetrators would typically have been
known to each other.[58]

Reflecting the relative monoculture of Ireland in these years,
the overwhelming majority of prosecuted women were Catholic.
For the women for whom religion could be ascertained, only a
handful identified as non-Catholics. Of the women condemned to
death, Mary Somerville and Frances Cox were Church of Ireland.
Mamie Cadden, while initially identifying as Catholic, later con-
troversially declared as 'No Religion'. Cadden's resistance to being
identified as Catholic was evident in her outburst from the dock
following her death-sentencing: 'Well, I am not a Catholic. Take
that now.'[59]

Religious affiliation offered many women support in the form
of petitions from local priests and religious figures, and the intervention of the prison chaplain and religious visitors to women
in prison. Prison visiting often provided women with their only
outside contact. In particular, chaplains frequently involved themselves in cases of women reprieved from sentences of death and took
efforts to petition for their release to religious institutions. For those
women who were not Catholics, they engaged with different sup-
ports, reflecting the highly religiously segregated voluntary sector of
these decades. Mary Somerville, as the only Protestant woman who
was reprieved and transferred from prison to a religious institution,
went to the Protestant Bethany Home.[60] Similarly, Frances Cox was
supported by the Salvation Army.[61]

Of the 22 condemned women, six had been previously convicted.
Table 1.8 presents the range of offences, from minor infractions
related to the distillation of home-made alcohol to manslaughter.

Table 1.8 Previous convictions for condemned women

Name	Number	Details
Annie Walsh (1929)	1	26 June 1928, 'keeping spirits unlawfully made and distilled'
Elizabeth Edwards	1	19 Dec 1933, 'larceny of turkeys'
Rose Edwards	1	19 Dec 1933, 'larceny of turkeys'
Kate Owens	1	25 April 1934, 'concealment of birth'
Frances Cox	1	22 July 1949, 'manslaughter of her infant'
Mamie Cadden	3	5 May 1939, 'conspiracy to abandon a child' and 'child abandonment'
		27 April 1945, 'intent to procure a miscarriage'

The sentences imposed ranged from fines, in the case of Annie Walsh (1929) and Elizabeth and Rose Edwards, to being bound over to keep the peace in the case of Kate Owens. Mamie Cadden was sentenced to 12 months and five years' imprisonment for her 1939 and 1945 convictions respectively. Frances Cox was discharged on her recognisance to keep the peace for two years following her conviction for the manslaughter of her infant, but immediately after her trial she was arrested for the murder of her brother, for which she would ultimately be convicted and sentenced to death. The fact of a woman's prior conviction could render her a more likely target for suspicion and surveillance. The Garda report on Elizabeth and Rose Edwards noted that:

> At the time, it was generally expected that the larceny episode was merely the forerunner of other inevitable incursions into crime, and, unfortunately, the popular opinion of the day proved to be only too well founded.[62]

In the case of Mamie Cadden,[63] her previous convictions relating to child abandonment and intent to procure a miscarriage meant that suspicions were immediately brought to her door when the body of Helen O'Reilly was found on Hume Street, following her death as a result of an abortion procedure. Cadden's notoriety and association with other crimes of a similar hue were instrumental when piecing together the circumstantial evidence during her trial. As McAvoy suggested, it was her devalued reputation, 'as much as her proximity to the spot where the body was found, [which] made her the chief suspect'.[64]

At least seven women beyond those condemned also had previous convictions. Many of these related to previous 'infanticide-related' offences.[65] As Garrett noted, the terminology of crime pervaded discussion of illegitimacy, and for women who became pregnant outside of marriage, their 'fall' was often referred to in language interchangeable from criminality.[66] Mary Brady pleaded guilty to concealment in 1927:

> Mr Carrigan, prosecuting, pointed out that this was the girl's second offence, and it was arranged that she should go to the High Park Convent, Mr Justice Johnston imposing a suspended sentence of six months' imprisonment.[67]

Annie McNamara was found guilty of concealment in 1929. Her sentence of 12 months' imprisonment was to run concurrently with an earlier sentence of four months' imprisonment imposed at Limerick Circuit Court on 11 February 1928, which had been suspended upon her entering into recognisance to keep the peace for two years, and which was now triggered by her second conviction.[68] Delia Murphy pleaded guilty to the manslaughter of her infant in 1935 and was sentenced to nine months' imprisonment; it was noted that she had a previous conviction for concealment from 20 October 1929 following which conviction she had been released on probation.[69] Mary Clarke was found guilty of concealment in 1943. She had previously been convicted at Dublin District Court on 25 October 1940 for soliciting, for which she had been subject to a probation order for two years. On her second conviction, she was sent to High Park laundry for three years in lieu of a two-year suspended sentence.[70]

The 'state of the country'

The background of political violence was evident through some cases, although none could be defined as political killings. In 1932, Jane O'Brien shot her nephew John Cousins and attempted to make the crime seem politically motivated.[71] Cousins's killing happened just two weeks after Fianna Fáil won their first election victory against Cumann na nGaedheal, the party for which Cousins worked as an election agent. The murder, occurring at Easter, the night before commemorations of the 1916 Easter Rising, suggested a political element, and his shooting was initially considered within this context. The case of Mary Moynihan also speaks to wider themes of political violence. Moynihan was convicted for the murder of her employer, Nora Horgan, which had taken place on 9 September 1922 at which time much of the country was affected by violence related to the Civil War.[72] Due to the instability in rural Cork, where the killing took place, the crime was not fully investigated until late 1923. Some newspapers reported that Republican forces in the area held their own inquest following the murder.[73] Moynihan also named as the perpetrator a local man who was a known Republican, suggesting she was exploiting the tumult for her own ends.[74] Beyond these cases, there was a tendency for letter writers appealing on behalf of the condemned women to urge clemency by referencing the patriotic pasts of particular women's families. Letter writers also invoked the Republican pasts of various ministers for justice in an appeal to leniency.[75]

The fact of the border also appeared across some cases, representing the new post-partition reality on the island. Mary Somerville, convicted of the murder of her infant grandchild in 1938, was swiftly brought to a Garda station because of fears she would evade capture by crossing the border from her home in Monaghan: 'In the ordinary course this would not have been done, but owing to the close proximity of the Border and the likelihood of her absconding, it was deemed necessary.'[76] In 1947, Maggie McGrory gave birth and killed her infant in Donegal before fleeing across the border to Northern Ireland where the Irish authorities required the assistance of the Royal Ulster Constabulary to apprehend her.[77]

Maleness

The criminal justice apparatus remained explicitly predicated on the male offender. While the very delayed reform of the law on infant murder, for instance, ensured that hundreds of women faced a capital trial, they did so within a system which was capable of accounting for them only by modification. Its presumed 'maleness' was evident even in certain official documentation on which 'he/his' was crossed out in pen and replaced with a handwritten 'she/her'.[78] As demonstrated throughout, the death penalty, and even imprisonment, were considered unfitting for women in these decades.

The gendering of capital punishment as 'male' in Ireland springs in part from an association of the death penalty with the execution of men for subversive offences; the death penalty was therefore often understood as a political weapon of suppression.[79] Beyond this, as Chapter 2 demonstrates, the judicial killing of women was an obscene prospect for many in government. Prison too was often viewed as an inappropriate response to women's offending. The falling numbers of women who were committed to prison post-1922 led to the closure of a number of prisons for women and the emergence of female prisoners as a negligible and forgotten population.[80] As explored in later chapters, although the numbers of women imprisoned was falling for much of the post-1922 period, women *were* being confined in semi-penal sites, often in religious institutions, creating a shadow and deeply gendered punishment regime.

Conclusion

The profile of women prosecuted for murder in the decades after independence speaks to the strange phenomenon whereby hundreds of women were capitally prosecuted in circumstances in which there was no notion of eventual execution. The legal frameworks which persisted until the reform of the law on infanticide ensured that a punitive regime prevailed for women suspected of killing their illegitimate infant. Throughout, the profile of these women was signally different from the cases of women prosecuted for the murder of an adult, reflected in the individual circumstances of the women before the courts and the criminal justice responses.

Despite the intensely gendered nature of crime and punishment in these decades, in which separate gendered regimes of punishment were devised for women, the criminal justice apparatus was always predicated on the male offender. This presumed 'maleness' obscures the female experience of these processes and regimes. An analysis of murder and punishment in Ireland from this perspective creates an alternative map of significance.[81]

Notes

1 Conor Brady, *Guardians of the Peace* (Dublin: Gill and Macmillan, 1974), p. 240.
2 Ian O'Donnell, 'Lethal violence in Ireland, 1841 to 2003: famine, celibacy and parental pacification', *British Journal of Criminology*, 45:5 (2005) 671–95.
3 Cyrus Tata, *Sentencing: A Social Process – Re-thinking Research and Policy* (London: Palgrave Macmillan, 2020).
4 Pat Carlen, *Magistrates' Justice* (London: Martin Robertson, 1976), p. 81.
5 See Chapter 3.
6 Ellen Sullivan was put back, and her case does not seem to have come before the court again. The principal state witness in this case had been found insane. NAI, State Books Central Criminal Court (hereafter SBCCC) 'Change of venue cases for all counties', June 1925 to December 1926; SFCCC Limerick 1925–28.
7 Not included are those cases which began as jury trials but later incorporated pleas (there were three concealment pleas in the 1920s; three concealment pleas, two manslaughter pleas and one other plea in the 1930s).
8 Five women were charged with the murder of a child over 12 months, three of whom pleaded guilty to manslaughter.
9 Women also pleaded guilty to a number of other offences. In 1923, Maggie Redmond pleaded guilty to child neglect, see 'Alleged Infanticide', *Leinster Express* (14 July 1923), p. 4. In 1924, Margaret Hillis pleaded guilty to incitement, see NAI, Dublin Commission Monaghan 1924. In 1926, Johanna O'Donnell pleaded guilty to attempted suicide, see NAI, SFCCC Limerick 1925–28. In 1930, Mary Goss pleaded guilty to intent to prevent a coroner's inquest, see NAI, SBCCC November 1927 to June 1935; SFCCC Kildare 1929–30. In 1930, Margaret Browne pleaded guilty to wilfully abandoning a child (contrary to section 12 of the Children Act 1908), see 'Charge against

Mother', *Irish Times* (16 October 1930), p. 4; NAI, SBCCC Dublin City 1930. In 1933, Kathleen McKenna pleaded guilty to abandon-ment, see NAI, SBCCC November 1927 to June 1935. In 1934, Mary Reilly pleaded guilty to abandonment and cruelty (abandoning a child contrary to section 27 of the Offences Against the Person Act 1861 and cruelty contrary to section 12(1) of the Children Act 1908), see NAI, SBCCC Dublin City 1934.

10 NAI, Department of Justice 234/2016. Letter from Justice Johnston, 12 December 1927.
11 'Infanticide Charge', *Evening Herald* (27 March 1931), p. 1.
12 'Virginia Girl's Trial', *Anglo-Celt* (15 November 1924), p. 1.
13 See Chapter 5 for the 'working rule' which stipulated that such women should spend two years in prison before release to a home.
14 See Chapter 5.
15 *Spaziano v Florida*, 468 US 447, 490 (1984) cited in Austin Sarat, *When the State Kills: Capital Punishment and the American Condition* (Princeton, NJ: Princeton University Press, 2018), p. 127.
16 Niamh Howlin, 'Passive observers or active participants? Jurors in civil and criminal trials', *Journal of Legal History*, 35:2 (2014) 143–71.
17 'Murder Charge against Domestic Servant', *Cork Examiner* (7 December 1927), p. 8.
18 'Body in River', *Evening Herald* (11 March 1926), p. 1.
19 'Woman on Trial for Murder', *Evening Herald* (5 May 1938), p. 10.
20 'Infant's Body in Bucket', *Evening Herald* (15 June 1935), p. 1. Annie Cox pleaded guilty to manslaughter, on 12 November 1935, at her second trial.
21 When Kate Shanley was acquitted, there was applause in the court-room, 'Failure of Meath Murder Case', *Irish Press* (23 March 1933), p. 7. Likewise, when Susan Doyle was acquitted in 1935, the verdict was welcomed by the judge, 'Howth Infanticide Charge', *Irish Independent* (16 July 1935), p. 7.
22 'Baby in Canal', *Cork Examiner* (29 October 1926), p. 2.
23 NAI, CCA 56/1944.
24 NAI, Department of Justice 234/1744. Handwritten note, 18 December 1924.
25 'Woman Said to Have Put Strychnine on Fish Tea', *Irish Press* (7 May 1963), p. 4.
26 NAI, SFCCC Kerry 1923; Department of Justice 18/2769A Hannah Flynn.
27 NAI, CCA 36/1956; Department of An Taoiseach S.16116; Department of Justice 18/3562. Only one woman was sentenced to death after

1964: Marie Murray was convicted of capital murder in the Special Criminal Court on 9 June 1976. Murray subsequently had her capital murder conviction quashed and was convicted at the retrial of non-capital murder. See, *DPP v Noel Murray and Marie Murray* [1977] 111 ILTR 65. See also David M. Doyle and Liam O'Callaghan, *Capital Punishment in Independent Ireland: A Social, Legal and Political History* (Liverpool: Liverpool University Press, 2019), ch. 6.

28 Mary Lenihan was ultimately acquitted, see *Attorney General v Mary Lenihan* [1929] 63 ILTR 100. Ellen Keogh pleaded guilty to man-slaughter, see NAI, Department of Justice, 18/7448A.

29 Mary Moynihan, Hannah O'Leary, Annie Walsh (1929), Christina Russell, Jane O'Brien, Elizabeth and Rose Edwards, Mary Somerville, Agnes McAdam, Frances Cox and Mamie Cadden.

30 NAI, SFCCC Galway 1929–31; CCA 16/1929; Department of An Taoiseach S.5904; Department of Justice 234/2599.

31 NAI, SFCCC Unknown Counties 1949; CCA 68/1948; Department of an Taoiseach S.14430; Department of Justice 170/7622.

32 David M. Doyle and Ian O'Donnell, 'The death penalty in post-independence Ireland', *Journal of Legal History*, 33:1 (2012) 65–91. Doyle and O'Donnell excluded the 81 executions which occurred during the Civil War.

33 NAI, SFCCC Westmeath 1943. Statement of Kate Owens, 8 May 1943.

34 NAI, SBCCC January 1953 to December 1956; SFCCC Kildare 1953–54.

35 In an Irish context: Enda Dooley, *Homicide in Ireland: 1972–1991* (Dublin: Stationery Office, 1995); Enda Dooley, *Homicide in Ireland: 1992–1996* (Dublin: Stationery Office, 2001); Carolyn A. Conley, *Melancholy Accidents: The Meaning of Violence in post-Famine Ireland* (Lanham, MD: Lexington Books, 1999).

36 Lizzie Seal, *Women, Murder and Femininity: Gender Representations of Women Who Kill* (Basingstoke: Palgrave Macmillan, 2010).

37 Ian O'Donnell, 'Killing in Ireland at the turn of the centuries: contexts, consequences and civilising processes', *Irish Economic and Social History* 37 (2010) 53–74.

38 Finola Kennedy, *Cottage to Crèche: Family Change in Ireland* (Dublin: IPA, 2001).

39 O'Donnell, 'Killing in Ireland at the turn of the centuries'.

40 In the case of Mamie Cadden, it was the fact of death occurring during the commission of an illegal abortion that rendered the death a murder, *Attorney General v Mary Anne Cadden* [1957] 91 ILTR 97.

41 NAI, SBCCC 1962 to July 1964.

42 This case is more fully explored in Chapter 8.

43 O'Donnell, 'Killing in Ireland at the turn of the centuries'; Conley, *Melancholy Accidents*.

44 NAI, Department of An Taoiseach S.14689; Department of Justice 18/11757.

45 See Chapter 7.

46 NAI, Department of An Taoiseach S.8653; Department of Justice 18/2737.

47 NAI, SBCCC November 1933 to 22 April 1941.

48 NAI, SBCCC (Counties) 1957 to 1961.

49 McCullagh identified three sources of conflict: land, exploitation of labour by parents and the selection of one son to inherit. Ciaran McCullagh, 'A tie that blinds: family and ideology in Ireland', *Economic and Social Review*, 22:3 (1991) 199–211. O'Donnell adds spousal disharmony to this trio, O'Donnell, 'Killing in Ireland at the turn of the centuries'.

50 Table 1.7 presents age at trial of 226 women for whom ages are known. Some women were unsure of their exact year of birth. In other cases, conflicting ages were given and the most reliable age was selected.

51 The median/mean ages of those prosecuted for child murder was skewed by the very small number of women in this category and the ages of 15-year-old Mary Cole and 17-year-old Kathleen Harmon who were prosecuted for such killings.

52 'Double Murder Trial Ends', *Irish Times* (24 March 1928), p. 5. In 1922, all persons aged 16 and over could be capitally convicted. Section 29 of the Children Act 1941 raised the age limit to 17.

53 For a handful of women it was unclear whether they were widowed or separated. Likewise, some women came to court unmarried but pledged to marry the father of their infant victim in the immediate future.

54 'Infanticide Charge', *Irish Times* (18 July 1928), p. 11.

55 NAI, Department of Justice 18/3540. Memorandum.

56 NAI, SFCCC Roscommon 1929–31. Deposition of Patrick McGowan.

57 O'Donnell, 'Killing in Ireland at the turn of the centuries'.

58 John D. Brewer, Bill Lockhart and Paula Rodgers, *Crime in Ireland, 1945–1995: 'Here Be Dragons'* (Oxford: Clarendon, 1997).

59 NAI, Department of An Taoiseach S.16116. Trial judge's charge to the jury.

60 NAI, Department of An Taoiseach S.11040; Department of Justice 18/3110A.

61 NAI, Department of An Taoiseach S.14689B.

62 NAI, Department of Justice 18/885A. Garda report, 2 April 1935.

63 NAI, CCA 36/1956; Department of An Taoiseach S.16116; Department of Justice 18/3562.
64 Sandra McAvoy, 'Before Cadden: abortion in mid-twentieth-century Ireland', in Dermot Keogh, Finbarr O'Shea and Carmel Quinlan (eds), *Ireland in the 1950s: The Lost Decade* (Cork: Mercier Press, 2004), p. 147.
65 See discussion of Margaret Walsh in Chapter 4.
66 Paul Michael Garrett, '"Unmarried mothers" in the Republic of Ireland', *Journal of Social Work*, 16:6 (2000) 708–25.
67 'Central Criminal Court', *Irish Independent* (17 December 1927), p. 11.
68 NAI, SBCCC November 1927 to June 1935.
69 'Manslaughter Charge', *Irish Times* (3 April 1935), p. 2.
70 NAI, SFCCC Dublin 1943.
71 NAI, CCA 9/1932; Department of An Taoiseach S.8653; Department of Justice 18/2737.
72 NAI, SFCCC Cork 1923–October 1924; CCA 17/1924; Department of Justice 234/1744.
73 For example, 'County Cork Murder Mystery', *Irish Times* (18 January 1924), p. 5.
74 NAI, Department of Justice 234/1744. Statement of Jeremiah Horgan, 19 October 1923.
75 For example, in the case of Elizabeth and Rose Edwards, NAI, Department of Justice 18/885A, or Mary Daly, Department of Justice 170/7622.
76 NAI, Department of An Taoiseach S.11040. Garda report, 17 November 1938.
77 NAI, SBCCC February 1946 to 1952; SFCCC Clare, Donegal and others 1955; 'Murdered Baby Charge', *Irish Press* (18 August 1947), p. 1.
78 This was evident throughout a number of the archival records on the 22 death-sentenced women, for example in the licences issues to women who were released from prison while serving sentences of penal servitude for life.
79 Gerard O'Brien, 'Capital punishment in Ireland, 1922–1964', in N. M. Dawson (ed.), *Reflections on Law and History* (Dublin: Four Courts Press, 2006).
80 Christina Quinlan, *Inside: Ireland's Women's Prisons Past and Present* (Dublin: Irish Academic Press, 2011); Mary Rogan, *Prison Policy in Ireland: Politics, Penal Welfarism and Political Imprisonment* (London: Routledge, 2011).

81 O'Donnell's inclusion of gender in his analysis of rates of lethal violence highlights the need to incorporate gendered understandings in this
way. Ian O'Donnell, 'Lethal violence in Ireland, 1841 to 2003: famine,
celibacy and parental pacification', *British Journal of Criminology*,
45:5 (2005) 671–95.

2

Clemency for the condemned

Inevitably, a book which explores women and the death penalty in Ireland must deal in large part with reprieve. In discussing death, we find mostly clemency. As only Annie Walsh (1925) was executed, this chapter explores how it came to be that the other 21 women were *not* executed. The chapter maps the formal and informal processes of clemency, and considers the rationales for mercy which were expressed from many quarters, including by juries, judges, the Department of Justice and the public.

The application of mercy as a function of gender is also explored: how mercy operated for women *qua* women. The chapter considers whether there was a de facto system of 'mercy by gender'. The specific Irish example complicates the concept of 'double deviance', which theorises that offending women are punished more severely because they have contravened both the law and their gender.[1] A significant amount of research has challenged the concept of 'double deviance', demonstrating that women generally receive more lenient criminal justice outcomes than men.[2] Writing on colonial Kenya and Nyasaland (now Malawi), Hynd found that gendered and racialised ideologies ensured that women were viewed as insufficiently developed to face execution.[3] The contention is not straightforward though. Ballinger argued that certain classes of British female murderer received less favourable outcomes than men.[4] She found that from 1900 to 1949, 90.8 per cent of women and 40.3 per cent of men had their death sentences commuted, but women who had killed an adult were *less* likely than men to have sentence commuted.

In Ireland, the outcomes for women convicted of murder would also seem to contradict the notion of 'double deviance'. Removing the 12 cases of infant murder convictions (where execution was unthinkable), only 10 per cent of condemned women were executed from 1922 to 1964. Rather than 'double deviance', the Irish cases show a penal landscape rooted in the prevailing social milieu – the inferior position of women and an attendant paternalism which facilitated 'chivalry'.[5] While certain women were vilified by criminal justice actors, they nevertheless escaped the ultimate punishment. In Chapters 4 and 5, the double-edged sword of paternalism is explored in greater depth by consideration of the post-conviction experiences of women in religious institutions.

Formal and informal processes of mercy

Mercy could be extended at various stages following a murder conviction. Between 1922 and 1964, death was the mandatory sentence for murder. However, as Doyle and O'Callaghan stress, death itself remained discretionary due to the prerogative of mercy.[6] For the first decade and more after independence, decisions on commutation of sentence were made by the Executive Council,[7] and were communicated to the Governor General.[8] Thereafter, decisions were made by the government and communicated to the President.

Judge and jury

Post-conviction, there were a number of stages at which recommendations for mercy could be given or mitigation argued. A jury recommendation was the initial means of articulating a desire for leniency. Following the verdict, a jury could choose to add recommendations, or riders, to verdicts, in some cases expressing a recommendation, or a strong recommendation, to mercy.[9] Most women condemned to death received such recommendations. O'Donnell notes that 49 of 78 persons convicted of murder and sentenced to death as a result of a jury trial received a recommendation to mercy, 19 of 22 women compared to 30 of 56 men.[10]

In the days following conviction, the judge wrote to the Department of Justice, passing on any jury riders and confiding his own views. In his correspondence, the judge could choose to endorse the jury's recommendation and discuss any relevant aggravating or mitigating circumstances.[11] In 19 of the 22 cases, the jury gave a recommendation to mercy. The judge endorsed all but three, withholding endorsement for Annie Walsh (1925), Kate Owens and Jane O'Brien. In the case of Hannah O'Leary, the jury recommendation to mercy was partial only, expressed by 7 of the 12 jurors, and was not endorsed by the judge.[12] Only three women received no jury recommendation: Annie Walsh (1929), Frances Cox and Mamie Cadden. In these cases, the judge's communication to the Minister reflected evidential and legal issues in the cases. In the absence of jury riders in the case of Annie Walsh (1929), the judge recommended that her sentence be commuted because she had been convicted on the evidence of children.[13] In the case of Frances Cox, the judge was circumspect in his parsing of the arguments:

> in my opinion, the verdict was fully justified by the evidence. There was no defence of insanity or any suggestion of mental instability and I formed the impression the accused was normally intelligent. I do not recall any extenuating circumstances in the evidence. I cannot speak as to her background and upbringing as the evidence did not deal sufficiently with these matters.[14]

In the case of Mamie Cadden, the judge was equally non-committal:

> The only special feature in this case viz. that the malice involved in the charge of murder was 'constructive' and not 'actual' malice, is presumably known to the Minister ... and I have therefore no observations to make which would be of any assistance.[15]

In the later capital cases of Cox and Cadden (occurring in 1949 and 1956), judges likely felt less urgency to enumerate rationales for mercy as there was little expectation these women would hang. In the 1943 case of Kate Owens the judge wrote that he had 'no comments to make on the Jury's recommendation to mercy, as I deem this to be the sole prerogative of the Minister and the Government'.[16] As an infant murder case, there was no reasonable expectation that the sentence would be carried out.

Garda reports

In every case, the views of the judge and jury were compiled in
a memorandum by the Department and disseminated to government. The Department also included Garda reports on condemned
persons, offering information which could not be presented at trial,
relating to the background character of women and their families.
These often consisted of little more than rumours and tended to
present an unfavourable picture. As a result, Garda reports typically expressed more punitive attitudes to condemned women, more
likely to caution against reprieve.

These reports served to situate a woman within her local and
familial context. Seal noted the importance of appeals to respectability in letters sent regarding condemned persons in mid-century
Britain.[17] In this vein, the mechanisms by which certain persons were
identified as worthy of reprieve differed little from earlier conceptions of respectability identified by Hay.[18] Lacey found that despite
a growing acceptance of culpability as an interior phenomenon, the
notion of character and respectability remained evident throughout
the nineteenth century.[19] In Ireland, Doyle and O'Callaghan found
that community and respectability continued as key themes used to
make sense of condemned persons.[20] This is evident throughout the
cases of condemned women, such as in the report on Mary Kiernan:

> Nothing was ever known against her parents or any other member of
> the family. Her relatives from father's and mother's side are all very
> respectable people. Some of them are shop-keepers … while others
> are respectable, well-to-do farmers in that district.[21]

Garda reports presented arguments counter to mercy. In the case of
Jane O'Brien, they were determinedly opposed to her reprieve:

> The murder was fully premeditated, carefully planned and carried
> out with great callousness. To add to the horror of the crime, the
> murdered man was the assassin's nephew. I have gone through the
> reports fully and I can find no reason why the law should not be per-
> mitted to take its course in this case.[22]

In a separate report, it was noted that 'The local people appear
to have no sympathy for the accused and are indifferent as to the

punishment which may be awarded.'[23] In the case of Elizabeth and Rose Edwards too, the Garda report noted that 'anything in the nature of a too-generous commutation of sentence will undoubtedly negative the work that has been put into this case'.[24] The body of the infant in this case had not been recovered despite weeks of searching; the need to justify such efforts is evident in Garda correspondence. The views expressed within Garda reports were clearly representative of their situatedness; their investigative work was vindicated by punishment which granted them a stake in the outcome.

The reports also offered local insight. The case of Annie Walsh (1929) saw a groundswell of support from the local community, much of which was premised on the belief that the victim, Sonny Dan Walsh, had met his death accidentally.[25] Sonny Dan had been found face down in a stream near his home and his death was only investigated following the persistence of his family which sought to implicate his widow Annie and a man named Martin Joyce. The seemingly grassroots support enjoyed by Walsh and Joyce was given some context by Gardaí,[26] who claimed that the momentum was provoked by animosity towards the victim's family. Occasionally, the Minister sought or accepted other opinions too. Cecil Lavery, the senior counsel who had acted for the prosecution, was asked to provide his opinion on the Walsh (1929) case, responding that 'The evidence falls short of actual demonstration of guilt as is only natural but I am personally satisfied that both accused are equally guilty.'[27]

Public petitioning

The public sometimes made their voices heard on behalf of condemned women (although Doyle and O'Callaghan suggest that correspondence from the public mattered little in the final decision[28]). Members of the public could put their name to the petitions commonly prepared by condemned women's solicitors while others sent individual letters. Almost universally, correspondence from the public sought reprieve. The petitions sent on behalf of Annie Walsh (1929)[29] and Jane O'Brien[30] had been signed by significant numbers of local persons and respected figures from politics and the church.

The greater volume of letters within their files seemed to reflect the perception that these women were particularly 'at risk' of execution.[31] As noted, Walsh (1929) had received no recommendation to mercy from the jury,[32] and O'Brien, although she had received a recommendation to mercy based on her age and sex, remained an unsympathetic character. Both had murdered adult men, a victim status which was viewed as more 'serious' and more subversive. Annie Walsh had murdered her husband, while Jane O'Brien murdered her nephew. The 1929 case of Annie Walsh, in particular, closely echoed the facts of the earlier 1925 case of Annie Walsh. Occurring only four years after the execution of Annie Walsh and Michael Talbot, this would have resonated with the public. Additionally, the Garda reports on both women implicated them in previous undetected murders. The date of the murders in 1929 and 1932, respectively, occurring earlier within the period under review, also made commutation a more contested decision. That there was no presumption of reprieve seems evident from a note on O'Brien's file from before her commutation which reads: 'Telephone enquiry received from the "Irish Press" asking whether the death sentence on Mrs O'Brien fixed for the 28th instant by the Court of Criminal Appeal had been reprieved.'[33]

Clergy

Religion also played a role in petitions for commutation, albeit not in a straightforward way. In 1932, the Eucharistic Congress was held in Ireland. This was also the year in which Jane O'Brien was sentenced to death and, in a case with few mitigating features, the fact of the Congress featured heavily. The Catholic Archbishop of Dublin petitioned:

> I understand that there is a woman at present in Mountjoy jail under sentence of death for murder. I hope I will not seem to presume too much if I ask you to consider the question of granting a reprieve in her sentence. I feel that an execution would cast a sinister shadow over the glorious celebrations of the Congress and I think that an act of clemency would come most appropriately at this time. I am not familiar with the facts of the case and base my appeal solely on the grounds of mercy and consideration for the sacred festivities of the Congress.[34]

A letter in the *Irish Press* likewise argued that 'it would not be in keeping with the spirit of the Congress that any unfortunate prisoner should, during its progress, lie under sentence of death'.[35] The Bishop of Galway wrote on behalf of Annie Walsh (1929) and Martin Joyce, quoting the belief of local people that the death had been accidental: 'I believe that there is a possibility, one might even say a probability, of mistake.'[36] However, even this takes as its premise the innocence of the condemned persons rather than principled objection. Perhaps surprisingly, there was little intervention by clergy in matters of capital punishment.[37] While individuals occasionally benefited from a letter written by a local priest, the extent to which there was general silence from the Catholic Church was unexpected, especially considering the extent to which various religious organisations were involved in the administration of criminal justice in these decades.

Family

Not every condemned woman had a family that would (or could) put pen to paper in her defence. One condemned woman who did benefit from such support was Elizabeth Doran, whose son wrote: 'We all beg your mercy to spare my mother from hanging.'[38] The sister of Annie Walsh (1929) also petitioned on her behalf.[39] In the case of Agnes McAdam, a letter sent on her behalf by a senator was apparently motivated by overtures made by her family.[40] However, the failure of family support was referenced explicitly by Hannah Flynn's defence counsel as a fact in mitigation of her actions; her counsel was critical of her family's failure to travel to Dublin for the trial and complained that 'Not one of these moved to help her.'[41] This was despite his acknowledgement of their poverty and the difficulties of travelling from Kerry. The case of Mary Daly is an unusual instance in which the family of the victim petitioned for clemency; the grown children of the victim, Mary Gibbons, wrote that if the sentence of death was commuted, Daly should swiftly be allowed to rejoin her husband and child. This letter also presented the words of their mother, providing an appeal to commutation from the victim herself: 'I bear her no illwill [*sic*] – the poor creature, she did not know what she was doing.'[42]

Rationales for mercy

Motivations for mercy fell along formulaic lines. Seal identified themes of doubt, mitigation, arbitrariness, inequity and retributive objections to reprieve in the public's responses to condemned persons.[43] Within the current sample, mitigation was most frequently invoked, with the personal circumstances of the condemned woman cited as justification. More abstract humanitarian reasons were explicitly invoked in a minority of cases only.[44] As O'Brien writes, in most cases there was only 'loud public indifference'.[45]

Personal mitigation

The age of women, too old or too young, was often invoked. Such mitigation was begged for women in their twenties, and for women aged over 50. In practice, there were few life stages which could not attract such a plea. Recommendations to mercy could also be justified by reference to the 'low mentality' of women which worked to diminish their culpability. Doyle and O'Callaghan record this as the most common rationale for men and women in this period.[46] 'Low mentality' was explicitly referenced by the jury in the case of Hannah Flynn, in which the recommendation was 'grounded on the fact that [her] mentality was stated to be defective'.[47] These judgements were often reinforced by the views of prison medical officers. The reporting of 'low mentality' arguments in newspapers could prompt members of the public to pick up the thread in their correspondence. One letter writer appealed on behalf of Elizabeth Doran on the basis that 'I understand she is weak minded'.[48] Some women considered 'weak-minded' were also judged to be at risk from the mental strain of a death sentence. The judge in Elizabeth Hannon's case urged commutation '<u>at the earliest moment</u>' due to the strain.[49] This was also evident in the case of Mary Daly, in which the judge expressed the view that she was 'a very highly strung young woman', who could not endure the shadow of death for long.[50]

The maternal role of various women also grounded calls for mercy. In a petition written by Annie Walsh (1929), she appealed on behalf of her children, arguing that 'The shame that their mother was hanged will follow my unfortunate children forever and I do wish to spare them this disgrace and live for their sake.'[51] In the case of Mary Somerville, one letter writer argued that 'Any <u>mother must</u> understand the woman's impulse to shield her <u>own</u> young daughter of 18 years.'[52] Somerville, who had been convicted of the murder of her illegitimate grandchild, was judged by some petitioners to have acted in the best interests of her daughter, evident in one appeal from the Society for the Abolition of the Death Penalty that 'the grandmother's motive – to save her daughter from disgrace – was not wholly selfish'.[53] Another letter prioritised Somerville's gender and her motherhood as motivations which could not be fairly judged by men:

> It would be impossible for any *man* to put himself in a woman's place, but oh I wish you would just ask your wife if she was an old forlorn widow, friendless & alone, with one little daughter aged seventeen, & no friends to help, or husband to advise her, & no means of hiding her child's disgrace, doesn't she think any woman might become temporarily quite insane? I wish you would ask Mr. Justice O'Byrne & the Chief Justice to ask their wives the same question? All laws, of every country, Your Excellency, are made by men <u>for</u> men, & are as a rule, well made, but there is something wrong in the law that allows a seducer to get scot free, & a poor demented mother to be hanged.[54]

In the case of Mary Daly, who was convicted of the murder of Mary Gibbons in a Dublin church, motherhood was again a strong feature in favour of mitigation. One writer stated, 'She could not desert her Baby, whose duty was it to feed her & her Baby & pay rent & keep her a home.'[55] Some letter writers referenced their own motherhood in their appeals,[56] such as the letter on the Daly case: 'I am too busy to write much more & feel compelled, after bathing my little family tonight, to sit down and write this little letter to you.'[57]

In some cases, men were blamed.[58] Somewhat tangentially, Mary Daly's husband was criticised for his failure to provide: 'where is the man who brought her to this state in life to commit such a deed'?[59] The shifting of blame to men was most explicit in cases of women convicted of infant murder. Many petitioners expressed the view that it was unconscionable that a woman should be held culpable when the father of the infant received no censure. One letter from Canada on the case of Elizabeth and Rose Edwards queried, 'what of the father of the child'?[60] Another on the same case asked 'How many unfortunate <u>innocent</u> girls has [*sic*] been and is every day "let down" by cowardly skunks of men who run away and hide when the harm is done?'[61] A letter from England on the case of Margaret Finn made more explicit the paternalism of this viewpoint, stating: 'I need not remind you how important it is for the state to protect its weaker members against callous, and wicked men, who bring ruination on them.'[62]

In the case of Ellen Keogh, the jury rider explicitly made reference to the influence of another.[63] Keogh was capitally convicted on 29 April 1944 for the murder of her infant, but the jury rider stated that she had 'in the circumstances, no option but to aid and abet'. This was a reference to John Mitchell, the father of the infant. On appeal, the jury rider constituted 'reasonable doubt', and Ellen's murder conviction was quashed.[64] At her retrial, she pleaded guilty to manslaughter. Ellen was viewed by the jury as a submissive partner in the commission of the crime, a view which was complicated by the acquittal of John Mitchell at his own trial.[65] This created a somewhat anomalous position; sympathy was extended by the jury to the female participant in view of the larger part played by the male participant, who had nevertheless escaped legal censure. Keogh herself expressed it bitterly while in prison: 'it is terrible to think Mitchell is out and I here for his crime'.[66] A Department of Justice document went further, claiming that the 'ultimate result of the case was that Mitchell who was really the principal got off scot-free while the accomplice Mrs Keogh is serving a term of three years' penal servitude'.[67]

Legal reasons and doubt

Pleas for mitigation could also be grounded in legal reasoning. Hannah Flynn's solicitor argued that they had been given insufficient time to prepare the case.[68] Mamie Cadden's counsel sought to rely on the manner in which the *mens rea* requirement for murder was met.[69] There were a number of cases, such as those of Mary Moynihan and Annie Walsh (1929), in which commutation was partially motivated by uncertainty as to guilt. In the case of Mary Moynihan, the judge himself expressed doubt: 'The evidence against her was entirely circumstantial and it is possible that the fatal blows were not inflicted by her.'[70] He suggested that even if Moynihan had inflicted the injuries, she could have been acting under the influence of Jeremiah Horgan, the victim's husband, and the man she had implicated in the dock following the verdict.[71] In this case, a departmental review of the evidence ultimately favoured the guilty verdict.[72] However, the suspected influence of Horgan weighed heavily in the establishment of sympathy for Moynihan. As noted already, the only mitigating feature available to the judge in the Annie Walsh (1929) case was that the prosecution case rested on the evidence of children.[73]

Public sentiment

While few petitioners questioned the death penalty per se, in some cases Ireland's revolutionary past was cited as sufficient cause for mitigation, suggesting that some petitioners drew on the notion of capital punishment as un-Irish. In the case of Elizabeth and Rose Edwards, one letter writer appealed to the experience of the Governor General who had himself been imprisoned for his part in the 1916 Easter Rising.[74] A person writing on behalf of Mary Daly wrote to the Minister for Justice that: 'I am sure that as one who once received a death sentence yourself you will not treat this appeal lightly.'[75] The persuasive function of petitioning is crucial to understanding the use of such entreaties. Seal has written that letter writers could 'deploy shared meanings … draw on personal experiences, and make direct appeal'.[76] Such tactics are evident in rationales based on the personal experiences of government figures. The conceptual association of the infliction of capital punishment with the British was evident in these exhortations. Appeals for mercy based on patriotism drew on the idea of the death penalty in Ireland as a British invention.[77] Appealing to the revolutionary pasts of various government figures represented an example of Seal's claim of petitioning as 'constitutive acts of citizenship' in which, in this specific case, a common Irish identity was evoked.[78] As Sutton

writes, public engagement in clemency campaigns suggested participation in national conversations on crime and punishment.[79]

The volume of letters received on behalf of each woman was
reflective of the newspaper coverage each received. Cases which
provided novel circumstances garnered more column inches and
were more likely to entice members of the public to put pen to
paper. Wood observed that newspaper accounts necessarily framed
the information received by the public.[80] Seal has argued that rather
than the press leading public discourse, reporting was 'painted
from a shared cultural palette' which relied on cultural touch-
stones held by readers and writers alike.[81] However, the concept of
'public responses' remains 'elusive',[82] and care must be taken when
attempting to glean public sentiment from letters received on capital
cases, which only ever comprised a minority of the public.

That said, there is no obvious abolitionist thread through
either the newspaper reporting or the letters. There was little sustained momentum in Ireland for reform or abolition of capital
punishment. An eclectic array of organisations corresponded with
government on the issue: groups such as the Religious Society of
Friends, the Society for the Abolition of the Death Penalty,[83] the
Irish Association for Civil Liberty, the Irish Women Workers'
Union, the People's Rights Association, the Gaelic League and Old
Cumann na mBan. High-profile individuals also made their voices
heard, such as Senator Owen Sheehy-Skeffington who appealed for
Mamie Cadden, on more humanitarian grounds than was typical:

> I am morally certain that you and the Cabinet will decide to commute
> the sentence of death on Miss Cadden. I am writing this letter merely
> to say that I am convinced that in so doing you will be acting with the
> approval of a very wide section of public opinion. My own feeling is
> that our society would lose a measure of self-esteem and degrade itself
> if by its actions this wretched creature were to be hanged.[84]

The publicity achieved by each case also shaped the public response
from international letter writers.[85] A telegram from an Irishman
living in England purported to express the feelings of other Irish in
his local area that the death penalty was inappropriate in the case
of Agnes McAdam.[86] Similarly, a letter from an Irishman who was
a member of a religious order in England, wrote, with reference to

Margaret Finn, that 'It is the opinion of several Irishmen here that the penalty is most drastic.'[87] Two letters from Canada on behalf of Elizabeth and Rose Edwards following the report of their sentence in a Canadian newspaper demonstrated that public interest was inextricably bound up with publicity; this letter also warned that the execution would be 'a blot on Ireland's fair name that will last for fifty years'.[88] These letters represent both the cultural significance of newspaper reporting on Irish issues for the Irish abroad, and the view of Ireland from abroad, both of which featured in appeals for mercy.

Seal noted that, post-1945, letters sent to the Home Office in British capital cases moved from a profile in which the sender was frequently known to the condemned to a profile of persons unknown to the condemned; these later cases drew instead on 'imagined communities' to appeal for justice.[89] Appeals to a shared history of revolution spoke to a sense of Irishness, which was especially pronounced in the early years after independence. Despite these traces of an imagined community, though, the volume of letters is more accurately characterised by its meagreness.

There was no sustained anti-death penalty movement in Ireland. Irish feelings on capital punishment were marked by apathy and ambivalence. O'Brien has suggested that the small number of death sentences hampered momentum as campaigning vigour dwindled between executions: 'The gathering of people at the prison gates on the morning of an execution may have betokened interest or curiosity but not necessarily concern.'[90] The relatively low numbers of letters sent on behalf of the condemned women (a notable volume of correspondence numbered from five to ten letters) is stark when compared with the volume of letters on cases identified in England and Wales.[91] However, the volume of correspondence from the public may have reflected the relative poverty of Ireland in these decades, rather than apathy.

One thing which is clear is that a woman's sex was relevant. If some commentators, as discussed below, felt that the exemption of women from hanging was unjust, this was not a view shared by letter writers. If, as Seal writes, these letters can be read as acts of citizenship,[92] then the public response to condemned women highlights that sex was sufficient cause for reprieve much of the time.

The limits of mercy

Any discussion of mercy must grapple with the 1925 execution of Annie Walsh.[93] Walsh was convicted on 10 July 1925 for the murder of her husband Edward at their County Limerick home. Michael Talbot was convicted separately for the same offence and both were executed in Mountjoy Prison on 5 August. Walsh could have expected a reprieve; a woman had not been hanged in Ireland since Mary Daly in 1903.[94] During Annie Walsh's confinement in prison, a fellow inmate, Hannah O'Leary, *was* reprieved, while her brother Con O'Leary was executed.[95] The O'Leary case provided an example in which a man and a woman were convicted of the same murder and in which the woman received mercy above the man. While Annie Walsh received a strong recommendation to mercy from the jury, Hannah O'Leary received only a partial recommendation. Similarly, in the case of Annie Walsh (1929), who was *also* convicted of the murder of her husband with the aid of a man with whom she was in a relationship, although she received no jury recommendation, her sentence was commuted (as noted above, largely because the conviction rested on the evidence of children[96]). This renders the earlier Annie Walsh case worthy of closer examination.

The great majority of executions carried out in the early 1920s were linked to political violence; for O'Brien it was therefore incongruous that a woman would hang for a 'crime of passion', and he speculated that the revolutionary years fomented more punitive attitudes while Victorian-era judges may have taken a more conservative stance through the decade.[97] The facts of the 1903 Mary Daly case also bore some resemblance to Walsh's, possibly creating a precedent for execution. The failure of the judge to endorse the jury recommendation can also be contrasted with the later 1929 Annie Walsh case.[98] Without this endorsement, 'the Executive Council felt unable to give effect to [the jury] recommendation'.[99] Irish public opinion did not appear to be clamouring for a reprieve either:

> Little, if any, public interest was aroused in the execution which took place this morning. Beyond the presence of a few policemen

and newspaper reporters outside the entrance to the prison, there was nothing else to indicate the grim scene which was about to be enacted within its walls. Shortly before eight o'clock a few women collected outside the avenue leading to the main entrance. The hour had scarcely struck when a warder emerged from the prison, and placed the usual notice on the gate.[100]

There were no letters appealing for clemency within the extant archives on Annie Walsh. The execution of Annie Walsh was therefore signally different from high-profile cases of women executed in Britain in the twentieth century; unlike the cases of Edith Thompson or Ruth Ellis, Annie Walsh's execution aroused no feelings of outrage or disgust.[101] Her execution passed unremarked and without fanfare.

The lack of interest may have stemmed from the genuine expectation that Annie Walsh would be reprieved.[102] It is likely that the newspapers expected a late-hour reprieve: 'For the first time in 20 years in Ireland a woman is to be hanged this morning. Up to midnight last night there was no variation of the death sentence.'[103] It was only on 6 August that reporting could give voice to these expectations by reference to Walsh's own hopes of reprieve: 'The female prisoner was hoping to the last that her sentence would be commuted. She was very nervous and walked with faltering steps to the scaffold, praying all the while.'[104]

It seems that Annie Walsh was denied reprieve due to a confluence of factors, including the judge's failure to endorse the jury recommendation, the nature of the crime she had committed, her sexual relationship with the co-convicted and, crucially, her dominant role in the killing relative to Talbot. The killing of a husband by his wife and her lover is an offence of cultural significance. Husband-murder was historically considered a disruption of a natural hierarchy, once considered a form of *petit treason*. Ballinger noted that 'Women who kill their husbands/partners have always been punished more harshly than men who kill their spouses.'[105]

The government could not have spared Walsh and hanged Talbot, because the burden of culpability did not neatly divide along gender lines. A comparison of the cases of Walsh and Talbot to Hannah and Con O'Leary elucidates this difficulty of reprieving only Walsh.

Both Annie Walsh and Hannah O'Leary were in the condemned cells during the summer of 1925. Their cases offer a comparison of reverse symmetry; in one the dominant partner was the woman and in the other the dominant partner was the man. The less culpable woman, Hannah O'Leary, had her sentence commuted, while the less culpable man, Michael Talbot, was executed along with his female co-accused. Annie Walsh *could not* be reprieved because there was a male partner who was complicit; commutation of Walsh's sentence would have led to the reprieve of the less culpable Talbot. While Annie Walsh was not executed because of her gender, it could be argued that she was denied commutation due to the gender of her co-convicted. To reprieve both parties was a bridge too far.

Later attempts to rationalise Walsh's execution underlined the singularity of her death. This was pronounced in the case of Jane O'Brien, who had shot dead her nephew. The crime was considered particularly callous and presented the very real prospect that O'Brien would be executed. In light of this, petitioners worked hard to distinguish her case from the only other woman executed in recent memory. The arguments relied heavily on the notion that Walsh was executed because she was the dominant party:

> In the case of Mrs Walsh, it was a murder committed under brutal circumstances in which the woman took the leading part, and in which her paramour over whom she had control was also sentenced to death, and her reprieve would have meant the reprieve of the man in the case.[106]

A letter from Jane O'Brien's solicitor reinforced this:

> We understand that the last woman hanged was Mrs Walsh. We enquired from Mr Brereton-Barry (who defended her) as to the circumstances of that case and it appears to us that she was convicted of a particularly brutal murder – one of savage brutality. We think it would have been very difficult to have reprieved her and hanged her lover, so we presume that the Executive Council at that time felt they could not let one off and hang the other. They were both hanged. Mrs Walsh was the only woman to be hanged since the establishment of the Irish Free State.[107]

The decision not to commute the sentence of Annie Walsh could be considered a 'hard decision', made within a set of very particular factors. However, it should be noted that there is little within the archives which could shed light on this decision. This dearth of documentation may be because a decision of this nature, *not* to reprieve, was essentially a 'non-decision' and required little formal documentation. There is also an argument that Walsh's execution was almost an oversight, and that the government stumbled into her hanging, thereafter quietly determining that no further women would be executed.

Considering clemency and gender

Doyle and O'Donnell highlight the differential application of mercy between men and women as one of the defining characteristics of capital punishment in Ireland; half of all condemned men were executed but only one in ten women condemned for the murder of an adult was executed (one in 22 when infant murder convictions are included).[108]

O'Donnell has considered the exercise of clemency under a tripartite framework of justice, mercy and caprice.[109] Clemency is, as he notes, always lenient treatment, whatever form it takes, but these forms vary. Decisions which reflect 'justice' incorporate mitigating factors which cannot be accounted for when a sentence is mandatory. In the case of mothers convicted of infant murder, clemency was justice, because 'the state had a legal but not a moral right to take their lives'.[110] Mercy, meanwhile, was grounded in sympathy, and occurred 'when deserved punishment was softened out of compassion for the offender's plight'.[111] Caprice, finally, 'involved a sudden and unpredictable change of direction'.[112] By necessity, when categorising the commutation of women in Ireland, none could be classified as caprice. As there was little expectation women would hang, any decisions made which confirmed this could hardly be unpredictable. (If anything, the decision *not* to commute in the Annie Walsh (1925) case was an example of capricious decision-making.) Reviewing the cases in which clemency was exercised for women, O'Donnell identified 17 examples of 'justice' and four of 'mercy' (Jane O'Brien, Kate Owens, Frances Cox and Mamie Cadden).

O'Donnell considers the case of Kate Owens as the lone exception among those women convicted of infant murder whose
reprieve could not be characterised as justice. O'Donnell instead
regards this as mercy, arguing that the judge's failure to endorse the
jury recommendation was evidence that he was not averse to her
execution. Although the evidence suggested that Owens had committed multiple similar offences, to my mind this does not betoken a
willingness to let the law take its course. The judge's actions instead
seem to represent a mark of symbolic condemnation which he
neither expected nor wished to see fulfilled. By the 1940s, it would
have been unthinkable to hang a woman in such circumstances.
I would also recategorise the commutation of Mamie Cadden as
'justice' rather than 'mercy'. Adequate *mens rea* for Cadden's crime
(an accidental killing of a client during an abortion procedure) was
only found through the doctrine of 'constructive malice'. Although
he did not recommend Cadden to mercy, the judge noted the use
of this doctrine in his remarks to the Minister. The doctrine was
abolished eight years later in the Criminal Justice Act 1964. As
with the necessity to temper the law in the case of infant murder,
Cadden's case necessitated remedial action post-conviction. Beyond
individual quibbles of classification, O'Donnell's framework offers
a tool to engage in questions of capital punishment and gender.

O'Donnell identifies five women who were spared solely because
of their gender.[113] Certainly, in the cases of Frances Cox or Jane
O'Brien, there was little to recommend the women to mercy
beyond this (although in Cox's case, the considerations extended
to women who had recently given birth were likewise extended
to her as she had killed her newborn infant just days before she
killed her brother). However, beyond gender, there were other
facts which suggested clemency in some of these cases. In Hannah
O'Leary's case, it was repeatedly noted that she seemed to be possessed of defective reasoning. Similarly, in the case of Mary Daly,
her frenzied attack against an elderly woman in a Dublin church
raised questions about her mental state. However, to highlight such
arguments in mitigation ignores the fact that there were many men
hanged for whom similar mitigating circumstances *could* have been
found but were not. In reality, sex mattered, and the Secretary at
the Department of Justice explicitly listed 'sex' alongside 'youth,

deficient mentality or provocation' as an acceptable extenuating circumstance.[114]

Some women were simply reprieved because they were women. This is evident across many of the cases, such as in the rationale for commutation proposed by the Department of Justice for Elizabeth Hannon that 'The fact that the condemned person is a woman is a very relevant consideration. Women are executed in very exceptional circumstances only.'[115] In the case of Mary Somerville, the judge outlined her heinous crime, before concluding, 'On the other hand, the accused is a woman and, however illogical it may be, this is a matter which cannot be overlooked.'[116] The extension of clemency to women was established practice and was generally reinforced by the letter-writing public. One petitioner in the case of Elizabeth and Rose Edwards wrote that, while logically it was no worse to hang a woman than a man, 'most people will agree that there is something peculiarly revolting in the idea of men deliberately and officially killing a woman'.[117] In cases which were less obviously sympathetic, such as that of Annie Walsh (1929), such inclinations were also evident; as one petitioner argued:

> It would be, in my deliberate & earnest opinion, a shocking thing to hang a woman. Things have been bad enough in this land of ours and I trust, that the papers of the world will not be able to blazen forth that in this year of 1929, a woman has been hanged in Ireland.[118]

Later cases too exhibited a tendency for petitioners to cite gender in mitigation, evident in the 1946 case of Agnes McAdam for whom commutation was viewed as appropriate, 'particularly in view of the fact that the unfortunate prisoner is a woman'.[119] Such discourses were also evident in the letter of one senator who wrote that he respectfully submitted that 'a woman should not be hanged',[120] or from a Teachta Dála (TD, an elected member of parliament) who wrote that, 'as she is a woman I trust the sentence of death will not be carried out'.[121] Even in the 1956 case of Mamie Cadden, such rationales were still being proposed, for example the comments received from a constitutional scholar who urged commutation to avoid 'the shame and horror of bringing a human being – and a woman – to a barbarous death'.[122]

On this, admittedly stark, gender differential, O'Donnell argues that:

> When women are spared, as a category, this cannot be interpreted as a series of acts of mercy. It must be named for what it is, namely unfair discrimination. There is no just reason why all but one of the female murderers, but only around half of the male murderers, should have been spared.[123]

In this, he echoes the views of Justice Meredith, writing on the 1933 case of a capitally convicted man, that it was 'flagrantly unjust' if a rule existed under which women were automatically exempted from death.[124]

A further interpretation is that the clemency shown to women was a continuing manifestation of the inferior position of women in Irish society at this time. It just happened to be, in this specific instance, one through which women benefited. It is perhaps not so 'unjust' that women should be reprieved because they are 'women' if such category exemptions generally manifested to women's detriment. To argue otherwise would be to wish for the worst of both worlds. Elsewhere I have noted the extent to which the disproportionate granting of clemency to condemned women at this time 'cannot be read uncritically'.[125] As O'Donnell writes, there were undoubtedly cases of death-sentenced women in which the outcome, had they been male, would have been death.[126] In this way, we can say that chivalry was at work in the criminal justice system. However, when subject to feminist critique it is clear that chivalry was an exclusionary, rather than a benign, practice.[127]

From the mid-nineteenth century, as outlined by Linders and Gundy-Yoder, there had been sporadic debate on women and the death penalty.[128] Often, women's inherent weakness was foregrounded to justify differential treatment. All such rationales were grounded in essentialist understandings of gender. In the present case, some petitioners pleaded clemency citing the hardship of women's lives, particularly relating to the stigma of illegitimacy and motherhood. Some cited the importance of female subjectivity and suggested this as a frame of reference for understanding the actions of the condemned. The recourse to gender, and the uniqueness of women's lived experiences, find 'special connection … on the basis of their shared femininity',[129] an experience held to be beyond the understanding of men.

Alongside these themes, there were more political arguments that women should be exempt from executions imposed by laws in which they had no hand in making. Occasional strains of this argument were evident in the case of Jane O'Brien in which petitioners cited the lack of female representation on juries: 'as there was no woman on the Jury, it could not be maintained that the prisoner was tried by her peers'.[130] Commenting on the case of Elizabeth and Rose Edwards, Hanna Sheehy-Skeffington noted that no women had sat on the jury under the 'barbarous male code'.[131] These arguments had been first associated with the campaign for women's suffrage. Such arguments seem convincing, even at this remove. For instance, at the 1859 National Woman's Rights Convention, it was held that 'a citizen cannot be said to have a right to life, who may be deprived of it for the violation of laws to which she never consented'.[132]

The increasingly hostile environment for women, which manifested in Ireland with some force in the decades after independence, imposed onerous burdens on women which were peculiar to women. In the cases of infant murder, as explored in Chapter 6, the unyielding legal and social landscape created a perfect storm through which vulnerable women attempted to navigate a path. Women's displacement from the public sphere, and the restrictive barriers to full citizenship they faced in the years after independence, were the soil from which 'excessive' clemency grew.

Conclusion

Clemency for women *because* they were women was hardly unique to Ireland;[133] however, it was notably dominant as a rationale for reprieve through these years. Elsewhere, I have argued that paternalism directed the outcomes for condemned women.[134] Paternalism is an arrangement of power which holds one population inferior in rationality.[135] This was a deeply embedded and gendered ideology in post-colonial Ireland. Valiulis demonstrated that Irish lawmakers worked to 'portray women as dependent and childlike, incapable of assuming responsibility, of making decisions – the antithesis of the ideal of the Irish male citizen'.[136] Punitiveness works to 'Other' and entrench social differences for some groups. For women condemned to death in Ireland, in contrast, the leniency they experienced worked to further 'Other' them. This found its corollary in their post-reprieve experiences. Just as paternalism saved many from the gallows, it condemned others to lives of confinement.

Notes

1. Ann Lloyd, *Doubly Deviant, Doubly Damned* (London, Penguin, 1995); Frances Heidensohn, *Women and Crime*, 2nd edition (Basingstoke: Palgrave Macmillan, 1996).
2. For example, Barry S. Godfrey, Stephen Farrall and Susanne Karstedt, 'Explaining gendered sentencing patterns for violent men and women in the late-Victorian and Edwardian period', *British Journal of Criminology*, 45:5 (2005) 696–720.
3. Stacy Hynd, 'Deadlier than the male? Women and the death penalty in colonial Kenya and Nyasaland, c.1920–57', *Stichproben – Vienna Journal of African Studies*, 7:12 (2007) 13–33.
4. Anette Ballinger, *Dead Woman Walking: Executed Women in England and Wales, 1900–1955* (Dartmouth: Ashgate, 2000).
5. Lynsey Black, '"On the other hand, the accused is a woman": women and the death penalty in post-independence Ireland', *Law and History Review*, 36:1 (2018) 139–72.
6. For a discussion of the appropriateness of using the term 'prerogative of mercy' in the Irish context, see Ian O'Donnell, *Justice, Mercy, and Caprice: Clemency and the Death Penalty in Ireland* (Oxford: Oxford University Press, 2017), pp. 49–53.
7. The Executive Council of the Irish Free State was the equivalent of the British cabinet.
8. Under the 1922 Constitution of the Irish Free State, the Governor General was responsible for the reprieve of condemned persons. The office of the Governor General had replaced that of the Lord Lieutenant, and the role of Governor General was itself replaced by Article 13.6 of the 1937 Constitution which transferred the powers to the newly established Office of the President.
9. Mark Coen and Niamh Howlin, 'The jury speaks: jury riders in the nineteenth and twentieth centuries', *American Journal of Legal History*, 58:4 (2018) 505–34.

10 O'Donnell, *Justice, Mercy, and Caprice,* p. 98. Disparity by gender was also not unique to Ireland. In Britain from 1900 to 1949, 83 per cent of women and 33 per cent of men convicted of murder were recommended to mercy by the jury. Home Office, *Report of the Royal Commission on Capital Punishment,* cited in Coen and Howlin, 'The jury speaks', n. 171.

11 O'Donnell explores one case in which judicial intervention seemed to overstep the separation of powers, Ian O'Donnell, 'An interfering judge, a biddable executive, and an unbroken neck', *Irish Jurist,* 60 (2018) 112–22.

12 NAI, Department of Justice 18/2770.

13 NAI, Department of Justice 234/2599. Letter from Justice O'Byrne, 30 July 1929.

14 NAI, Department of Justice 18/11757A. Letter from Justice Dixon, 21 December 1949.

15 NAI, Department of Justice 18/3562 and B 18/3562. Letter from Justice McLoughlin, 28 December 1956.

16 NAI, Department of Justice 18/6678B. Letter from Justice Haugh, 19 May 1946.

17 Lizzie Seal, 'Imagined communities and the death penalty in Britain, 1930–1965', *British Journal of Criminology,* 54:5 (2014) 908–27.

18 Douglas Hay, 'Property, authority and the criminal law', in D. Hay, P. Linebaugh, J. G. Rule, E. P. Thompson and C. Winslow (eds), *Albion's Fatal Tree: Crime and Society in Eighteenth-Century England* (London: Allen Lane, 1975).

19 Nicola Lacey, *Women, Crime and Character: From Moll Flanders to Tess of the D'Urbervilles* (Oxford: Oxford University Press, 2008).

20 David M. Doyle and Liam O'Callaghan, *Capital Punishment in Independent Ireland: A Social, Legal and Political and History* (Liverpool: Liverpool University Press, 2019).

21 NAI, Department of Justice 234/1491. Garda report.

22 NAI, Department of Justice 18/2737A. Letter from Garda Commissioner, 14 June 1932.

23 NAI, Department of Justice 18/2737A. Garda report, 11 June 1932.

24 NAI, Department of Justice 18/885A. Garda report, 2 April 1935.

25 NAI, Department of An Taoiseach S.5904. Petition on behalf of Annie Walsh.

26 NAI, Department of Justice 234/2599. Garda report, received 3 July 1929.

27 NAI, Department of Justice 234/2599. Letter from Cecil Lavery, 25 July 1929.

28 Doyle and O'Callaghan, *Capital Punishment in Independent Ireland.*

29 NAI, Department of An Taoiseach S.5904. Petition on behalf of Annie Walsh.

30 NAI, Department of An Taoiseach S.8653; Department of Justice 3/18/2737.

31 Relative to other cases occurring around this time, these cases received more public notice.

32 NAI, Department of Justice 234/2599. Letter from Justice O'Byrne, 30 July 1929.

33 NAI, Department of Justice 18/11108 (Edward O'Connor). Letter from Justice Davitt, 28 October 1948, cited in Doyle and O'Callaghan, *Capital Punishment in Independent Ireland*, p. 93.

34 NAI, Department of Justice 18/2737A. Letter from Archbishop of Dublin Edward Byrne, 25 June 1932.

35 'Letters: Appeal for Prisoner', *Irish Press* (21 June 1932), p. 6.

36 NAI, Department of Justice 234/2599. Letter from Thomas O'Doherty, Bishop of Galway, 29 July 1929.

37 Doyle and O'Callaghan note that in the 1928 case of Gerard Toal, the local parish priest, who had been Toal's former employer, cautioned against commutation. In this case, there was evidence that the condemned man had also attempted to poison his former employer. Doyle and O'Callaghan, *Capital Punishment in Independent Ireland*, p. 144.

38 NAI, Department of Justice 234/1297. Letter, 22 June 1926.

39 NAI, Department of Justice 234/2599. Letter from Massachusetts, US, 8 October 1931.

40 NAI, Department of Justice 18/9074A. Letter from Senator Seamus Johnston, 9 April 1946.

41 NAI, Department of Justice 18/2769A. Memorandum from Michael J. Lennon, 1 March 1924.

42 NAI, Department of Justice 170/7622. Letter, 15 November 1948.

43 Lizzie Seal, *Capital Punishment in Twentieth-Century Britain: Audience, Justice, Memory* (Abingdon: Routledge, 2014).

44 Doyle and O'Callaghan likewise comment on the lack of general anti-death penalty sentiment, *Capital Punishment in Independent Ireland.*

45 Gerard O'Brien, 'Capital punishment in Ireland, 1922–1964', in N. M. Dawson (ed.), *Reflections on Law and History* (Dublin: Four Courts Press, 2006), p. 240.

46 Doyle and O'Callaghan, *Capital Punishment in Independent Ireland.*

47 NAI, Department of Justice 18/2769A.

48 NAI, Department of Justice 234/1297. Letter, 25 June 1926.

49 NAI, Department of An Taoiseach S.5571. Letter from Justice Johnston, 12 December 1927. Underlining in original.
50 NAI, Department of Justice 170/7622. Letter from Justice Gavan Duffy, 2 May 1949.
51 NAI, Department of Justice 234/2599. Handwritten petition of Annie Walsh, 30 July 1930.
52 NAI, Department of Justice 18/3110A. Letter, 12 December 1938. Underlining in original.
53 NAI, Department of Justice 18/3110A. Letter, 13 December 1938.
54 NAI, Department of An Taoiseach S.11040. Letter from 'A Citizen of Waterford', 10 December 1938. Underlining in original.
55 NAI, Department of Justice 170/7622. Letter, 28 November 1948.
56 See also John Carter Wood, '"Those who have had trouble can sympathise with you": press writing, reader responses and a murder trial in interwar Britain', *Journal of Social History*, 43:2 (2009) 439–62; Lizzie Seal, 'She killed not from hate, but from love': motherhood, melodrama and mercy killing in the case of May Brownhill, *Women's History Review*, 27:5 (2018) 669–87; Lizzie Seal, 'Issues of gender and class in the Mirror Newspapers' campaign for the release of Edith Chubb', *Crime Media Culture*, 5:1 (2009) 57–78.
57 NAI, Department of Justice 170/7622. Letter, 27 November 1948.
58 Occasionally, the reverse was also true. In 1928, Julia O'Neill was prosecuted for murder alongside her partner James McHugh. While the murder charge against O'Neill was withdrawn, McHugh was convicted and hanged. Doyle and O'Callaghan outline the arguments made in McHugh's case that O'Neill was the true instigator, *Capital Punishment in Independent Ireland*, p. 156.
59 NAI, Department of Justice 170/7622. Letter, 28 November 1948.
60 NAI, Department of Justice 18/885A. Letter from Canada, enclosing newspaper clipping, 20 May 1935.
61 NAI, Department of Justice 18/885A. Letter, 31 March 1935.
62 NAI, Department of Justice 234/3118. Letter, 22 March 1931. Underlining in original.
63 NAI, CCA 56/1944.
64 *Attorney General v Ellen Keogh* [1944] 1 IR 309. NAI, CCA 56/1944. Judge's charge to the jury.
65 NAI, Department of Justice 18/7448.
66 NAI, Department of Justice 18/7448A. Letter from Ellen Keogh, 30 May 1944.
67 NAI, Department of Justice 18/7448A. Department document, undated.

68 NAI, Department of Justice 18/2769A. Letter from Ernest W Proud, 29 February 1924.

69 NAI, Department of Justice 18/3562. Letter from Justice McLoughlin, 28 December 1956.

70 NAI, Department of Justice 234/1744. Note from Justice Sullivan, 17 December 1924.

71 NAI, Department of Justice 234/1744.

72 NAI, Department of Justice 234/1744. Report prepared by T. A. Finlay, 24 March 1925.

73 NAI, Department of Justice 234/2599.

74 NAI, Department of Justice 18/885A.

75 NAI, Department of Justice 170/7622. Letter, 28 November 1948.

76 Lizzie Seal, 'Ruth Ellis and the public contestation of the death penalty', *Howard Journal of Criminal Justice*, 50:5 (2011) 492–504, p. 492.

77 O'Brien suggested that this involved a form of selective memory which omitted the fact that most of those executed prior to independence had been ordinary criminals. O'Brien, 'Capital Punishment in Ireland'.

78 Seal, 'Imagined communities and the death penalty in Britain', p. 913.

79 Rian Sutton, 'A "matter for the consideration of the executive alone": the court of public opinion and narratives of mercy in the clemency cases of Elizabeth Gibbons and Chiara Cignarale', *Irish Jurist*, 60 (2018) 123–33.

80 John Carter Wood, *The Most Remarkable Woman in England: Poison, Celebrity and the Trials of Beatrice Pace* (Manchester: Manchester University Press, 2012).

81 Seal, 'Ruth Ellis and the Public Contestation of the Death Penalty', p. 494.

82 Seal, *Capital Punishment in Twentieth-Century Britain*, p. 99.

83 This organisation was founded in 1937 by Rosamond Jacob and John Henry Webb, Dublin-based Quakers. O'Brien writes that the history of the organisation was short and unsuccessful, O'Brien, 'Capital Punishment in Ireland'.

84 NAI, Department of An Taoiseach S.16116. Letter from Senator Owen Sheehy-Skeffington, 1 January 1957.

85 Wood, *The Most Remarkable Woman in England*.

86 NAI, CCA 16/1946. Telegram to Lord Chief Justice, 11 March 1946.

87 NAI, Department of Justice 234/3118. Letter, 22 March 1931.

88 NAI, Department of Justice 18/885A. Letter from Canada, enclosing newspaper clipping, 16 May 1935.

89 Seal, 'Imagined communities and the death penalty in Britain'.

90 O'Brien, 'Capital Punishment in Ireland', p. 232.
91 Thirty letters for a condemned person in the 1930s was substantial, and by the 1950s this could reach the hundreds. Seal, 'Imagined communities and the death penalty in Britain'.
92 Seal, 'She killed not from hate, but from love'.
93 NAI, CCC Limerick 1925–1928; Department of Justice H1004/275.
94 'The Clonbrook Tragedy', *Leinster Express* (10 January 1903), p. 5.
95 'Five under Death Sentences', *Fermanagh Herald* (18 July 1925), p. 6.
96 NAI, Department of Justice 234/2599. Letter from Justice O'Byrne, 30 July 1929.
97 O'Brien, 'Capital Punishment in Ireland'.
98 Of 35 persons sentenced to death under the Cumann na Gaedheal government between 1922 and 1932, the recommendations to mercy by the jury were ignored in 15 cases. In each of these 15 cases, the judge had disagreed with this recommendation. O'Brien, 'Capital Punishment in Ireland'.
99 NAI, Department of Justice 18/2737A. Memorandum on Jane O'Brien, 13 July 1932.
100 'Co. Limerick Murder', *Cork Examiner* (6 August 1925), p. 6.
101 For an account of how the executions of Thompson in 1923 and Ellis in 1955 influenced public debate on capital punishment, see Seal, 'Ruth Ellis and the public contestation of the death penalty'; Seal, *Capital Punishment in Twentieth-Century Britain*.
102 Newspaper reporting on murder trials throughout the 1920s was more substantial in cases of women convicted for the murder of adults compared to those convicted for the murder of infants. Within the sample, the cases of Hannah Flynn, Mary Moynihan, Hannah O'Leary, Annie Walsh (1925) and Annie Walsh (1929) demonstrated greater newsworthiness. Cases occurring later in the sample also attracted more column inches.
103 'Irish Woman to be Hanged To-day', *Irish Independent* (5 August 1925), p. 5.
104 'Co. Limerick Murder', *Cork Examiner* (6 August 1925), p. 6.
105 Ballinger, *Dead Woman Walking*, p. 204.
106 NAI, Department of Justice 18/2737A. Petition on behalf of Jane O'Brien.
107 NAI, Department of Justice 18/2737A. Letter from MJ O'Connor Solicitors, 13 July 1932.
108 David M. Doyle and Ian O'Donnell, 'The death penalty in post-independent Ireland', *Journal of Legal History*, 33:1 (2012) 65–91.
109 O'Donnell, *Justice, Mercy, and Caprice*.

110 O'Donnell, *Justice, Mercy, and Caprice*, p. 41.

111 O'Donnell, *Justice, Mercy, and Caprice*, p. 41.

112 O'Donnell, *Justice, Mercy, and Caprice*, p. 43.

113 Hannah O'Leary, Jane O'Brien, Mary Daly, Francis Cox and Mamie Cadden. O'Donnell, *Justice, Mercy, and Caprice*.

114 NAI, S7788A. Proposed legislation to amend the law relating to (1) insanity as a defence to criminal charges and (2) infanticide.

115 NAI, Department of Justice 234/2016. Memorandum, 15 December 1927.

116 NAI, Department of Justice 18/3110A. Letter from Justice O'Byrne, 10 December 1938.

117 'Letters to the Editor', *Irish Times* (18 May 1935), p. 6.

118 NAI, Department of Justice 234/2599. Letter, 29 July 1929.

119 NAI, Department of Justice 18/9074A. Letter from Assistant County Surveyor's Office, Ballybay, 8 April 1946.

120 NAI, Department of Justice 18/9074A. Letter from Senator Seamus Johnston, 8 April 1946.

121 NAI, Department of Justice 18/9074A. Letter from Mrs B. M. Rice TD, 8 April 1946.

122 NAI, Department of Justice 18/3562. Letter from J. M. Kelly, Pembroke College Oxford, undated.

123 O'Donnell, *Justice, Mercy, and Caprice*, p. 221.

124 NAI, Department of Justice, H234/6221B, cited by O'Donnell, *Justice, Mercy, and Caprice*, p. 221.

125 Black, 'On the other hand the accused is a woman', p. 140.

126 O'Donnell, *Justice, Mercy, and Caprice*, pp. 213–21.

127 Elizabeth F. Moulds, 'Chivalry and paternalism: disparities of treatment in the criminal justice system', *Western Political Quarterly*, 31:3 (1978) 416–30.

128 Annulla Linders and Alana van Gundy-Yoder, 'Gall, gallantry and the gallows: capital punishment and the social construction of gender 1840–1920', *Gender and Society*, 22:3 (2008) 324–48.

129 Seal, 'Ruth Ellis and the public contestation of the death penalty'.

130 NAI, Department of Justice 18/2737A. Petition on behalf of Jane O'Brien.

131 'Letters to the Editor', *Irish Independent* (24 May 1935), p. 10. Ireland should not be considered an outlier in the matter of women's participation on juries. Logan has noted that although the Sex Discrimination (Removal) Act 1919 allowed for women on juries, gender equality on juries was not achieved in England and Wales until 1974. This delay was caused by the rules for jury qualification which were linked to

property ownership, the use of peremptory challenges and the discretion of the judge to request single-sex juries. Anne Logan '"Building a new and better order?" Women and jury service in England and Wales, c.1920–70', *Women's History Review*, 22:5 (2013) 701–16.

132 Elizabeth Cady Stanton, Susan B. Anthony and Matilda Joslyn Gage, *History of Woman Suffrage*, Vol. 1, *1846–1861* (New York: Arno/*New York Times*, 1881/1969), cited in Linders and Gundy-Yoder, 'Gall, gallantry and the gallows', p. 339.

133 For instance, only one woman was sentenced to death in England and Wales following significant reform of the law on capital homicide in 1957. This was Mary Wilson, who was reprieved by the Home Secretary who argued that the execution of a woman would shock the public. Lizzie Seal, *Women, Murder and Femininity: Gender Representations of Women who Kill* (Basingstoke: Palgrave Macmillan, 2010).

134 Black, 'On the other hand, the accused is a woman'.

135 Moulds, 'Chivalry and paternalism'.

136 Maryann Gialanella Valiulis, 'Power, gender, and identity in the Irish Free State', *Journal of Women's History*, 6:4/7:1 (1995) 117–36, p. 124.

3

Insanity

This chapter examines discourses of insanity, particularly focusing on the 12 cases of women found unfit to plead or guilty but insane, as well as the cases of Elizabeth Doran and Mamie Cadden, who were found insane following their conviction for murder. The chapter considers the meanings of insanity, both 'popularly' and in the criminal trial. I outline some 'common-sensical' approaches to determining insanity, such as heredity and the importance of situating the defendant within the wider family, alongside the branding of women as 'weak-minded' and the association of female biology with disease. Throughout, discourses of pathology reflected intensely classed and gendered presumptions.[1] The sections that follow consider arguments in the literature that offending women were disproportionately subject to discourses of pathology, and place these claims in an Irish context.

The diagnoses and observations through the cases were made from the male perspective.[2] The paper trail left by medical professionals is a male discourse, created by men with the intention of explaining and treating women. In this, the medical discourse differed little from the legal discourse. While such research can illuminate 'the lives of the individuals unfortunate enough to have committed a crime and be deemed insane',[3] the lives that emerge are always partial.

The period of interest is characterised by some as a time of continuity rather than change in responses to mental illness. Developments in treatment philosophies did not necessarily translate into on-the-ground change in Irish asylums.[4] Many of the liberalising reforms of the Mental Health Act 1945 found little traction until the 1960s.[5] These decades *are* however characterised by rising rates of institutionalisation.[6] From 1851 to 1901, Irish asylum populations tripled.[7] In 1951, psychiatric institutions held 21,720 patients; Brennan calculated the rate of psychiatric institutionalisation in 1956 as 749.35 per 100,000.[8] The epidemic of institutionalisation reflected the poverty and marginalisation of swathes of Irish society more than it reflected endemic levels of insanity.

A further change through these decades was the professionalisation of psychiatry. Doyle and O'Callaghan argue that experts increasingly vied for influence in the courtroom from the 1940s.[9] The greater volume and scientific lustre of these opinions particularly affected reprieve decisions, although as O'Hanlon suggested, psychiatric evidence 'was often regarded with doubt and suspicion by judges and public alike'.[10] This suspicion was hinted at in a government memorandum of 1944, in which it was stated, not entirely accurately, that 'insanity as a defence has been very frequent in murder trials in recent years and has given rise to much criticism'.[11]

The institution for persons judged criminally insane was the Central Criminal Lunatic Asylum in Dublin.[12] On its establishment, it had twice as many beds for men as women, and only 21 per cent of admissions from 1850 to 1900 were female.[13] The crimes for which patients were admitted showed a stark gender profile too: women were much more likely to be admitted following the killing of a child, while men were more likely to have killed an adult (often their wives).[14] Looking at the mid-twentieth century, Brennan likewise observed a willingness to accept insanity in cases of inexplicable and violent familial killings perpetrated by men.[15] In contrast to the men found insane, I have previously argued that offending women deemed insane in this period were judged as 'difficult' rather than 'dangerous'.[16]

Insanity in the criminal trial

Legal insanity was largely governed by the M'Naghten rules.[17] Insanity outcomes could manifest in a number of ways. Defendants for whom there was some doubt as to mental state could avoid trial entirely if found unfit to plead by a jury. In these cases, the judge directed the defendant be kept in strict custody and taken care of until the pleasure of the government be made known concerning her.[18] Defendants found unfit to plead could later be declared capable of pleading and brought to trial, but a 1944 memorandum stated that 'If they regain sanity they are usually released.'[19] The Attorney General would then enter a *nolle prosequi* in respect of the original proceedings.

In other cases, defence counsel could argue during the trial that the defendant had been insane at the time of the crime. If accepted by the jury, and the burden was on the defence to demonstrate insanity on the balance of probabilities, the verdict was guilty but insane. When this 'special verdict' was handed down, under the Trial of Lunatics Act 1883, the judge would likewise direct that the person be kept in strict custody and taken care of until the pleasure of the government was made known concerning her. As with those found unfit to plead, if such persons regained sanity, 'they are usually released, provided the Minister for Justice is satisfied that there is no danger of their reverting to violent crime'.[20]

Brennan's review of domestic murder trials from 1930 to 1945 finds that insanity-related disposals were the most common outcomes in such cases, comprising around 40 per cent of verdicts.[21] Brennan considered that this 'raises the prospect that unfitness to plead and the insanity defence operated as devices to secure a more lenient outcome in capital cases'.[22] Cases which exhibited greater violence and less premeditation, and which were not easily classifiable as manslaughter, were more likely to end with an insanity disposal. On the question of whether such outcomes were justified on either the law or the evidence, she concluded that the facts were often interpreted in ways conducive to such a result regardless. As O'Hanlon wrote, it seemed likely that in charging a jury, many judges drew the parameters of legal insanity wider than the M'Naghten rules allowed.[23]

There was an awareness that the rules governing criminal insanity were far from reflecting the complexity of mental states.[24] This was evident in many cases of women convicted of murder, in which juries found it difficult to gauge culpability. The jury in the trial of Mary Kiernan initially returned a verdict of 'guilty but not responsible for her actions'. Justice O'Byrne advised that if they believed Kiernan had not known what she was doing at the time she killed her infant they must find her guilty of murder but insane. The jury instead found Kiernan guilty of murder. The jury in Deborah Sullivan's trial broke from deliberations to seek guidance on the same issue and Justice O'Byrne directed that counsel had not adequately established the insanity defence.[25] When petitioning on behalf of death-sentenced women, legal actors often urged consideration of insanity. Following Hannah Flynn's conviction for murder her counsel communicated to the Department that the verdict should have been guilty but insane, citing the 'well nigh impossible' reverse burden of proof needed to secure this verdict.[26] Flynn's solicitor wrote that 'there is no doubt that she is, in the popular meaning of the word, insane'.[27]

The idea that there was a 'popular meaning' of insanity was evident throughout, as various non-expert forms of understanding were used. One way of grappling with insanity was to situate it as hereditary. Beyond the search for familial explanations, sub-psychiatric discourses were also evident. These can broadly be divided into two categories: intellectual capacity and an understanding of childbirth as a catastrophic event which provoked disturbance of the mind. These two strands are invariably interlinked, as the label 'weak-minded' was liberally applied to infant murder cases. As Rattigan found, to be unmarried and pregnant was tantamount to a diagnosis of weak-mindedness.[28] In many cases, these narratives may have saved women from a murder conviction.[29] As suggested in Chapter 1, there were considerable vagaries of outcome in infant murder prosecutions. In almost all such cases, sub-psychiatric discourses were present, but these did not provide protection for all. The following sections explore hereditary insanity, 'weak-mindedness' and the effects of childbirth.

Hereditary insanity

Insanity was understood as hereditary. In cases of a death sentence, it became a pressing matter to locate a family history of 'abnormality'. This informed private correspondence and Garda reports, and allowed for details that could not be introduced at trial. A Garda report on Mamie Cadden revealed that they had found 'no history of insanity in the Cadden family, but there is a first cousin ... a patient in Castlebar Mental Hospital for the past ten years'.[30] That such relatives could be located was hardly surprising as Ireland reached its peak of institutionalisation in the mid-1950s.[31] The use of networks of local knowledge to construct identity was evident. The importance of family reputation was pertinent within a schema of identity which relied strongly on notions of heredity.

Other death-sentenced women were also understood within this framework. Mary Anne Keane's family were described as having 'a very bad mental history'.[32] The Garda report revealed:

> It is known that an aunt and an uncle of Mary Anne Keane died in an asylum, and that members of her own family ... were also committed. It is believed that accused was an inmate of an asylum at some time or other .... Accused was always looked upon as being more or less simple.[33]

In the case of Agnes McAdam too, local persons spoke to the unusual temperament of both Agnes and her family. Her solicitor, admitting that her abnormality fell short of insanity, stated that she 'is definitely not a normal person, and for that matter no member of her family is, though legally neither she nor they could be adjudged insane'.[34] One petitioner said he was 'creditably informed that there is a streak of insanity in the family'.[35]

That searches for abnormal family members were commonplace is evident in the report on Kate Owens which found that 'There is no insanity or other hereditary disease in the family as far as is known.'[36] Enquiries into the family of Mary Daly were more successful, reporting that one relative:

> used to go about begging alms. He slept in out-houses, and wore two or three overcoats. He used to visit Catholic Churches and pray for considerable periods. He was religiously 'touched'.[37]

These documents demonstrate not only the positioning of the individual within the family as a means of creating identity but also the powerful networks of local knowledge which informed the government's consideration of commutation in capital cases.

'Weak-mindedness'

One strand of sub-psychiatric discourse was the branding of women as 'weak-minded' and of 'low mentality'. This suggestion allowed the diminishment of agency and justified leniency in the form of lesser verdicts and lesser punishments.[38] It was a frequent claim on behalf of women who had been convicted of murder. Arguing for the reprieve of Elizabeth Hannon it was stated that her 'mentality is below average'.[39] Following Hannah Flynn's conviction for murder she was recommended to mercy by the jury 'on account of her low mentality'.[40]

In a petition on behalf of Hannah O'Leary and her brother Con, both of whom had been condemned to death, their 'abnormality' was stressed: '[They are] not to be judged by ordinary standards and are of a low form of mentality, and during their lives have at various times exhibited indications of mental disorder.'[41] The prison medical officer concluded that Hannah O'Leary was 'a dull, stupid-looking woman and from close personal observation and questioning of her, I would describe this prisoner as a person of more or less defective reasoning power'.[42]

For these death-sentenced women, sub-psychiatric discourses did not influence verdict but wielded power when considering clemency.[43] The boundary between 'weak-mindedness' and the capacity for criminal responsibility must be considered in such cases. Throughout the files, there were professional judgements to the effect that a woman's mental capacity rendered her 'abnormal'. However, in the overwhelming majority of these cases, this did not prevent the woman's trial or, in some cases, conviction. In many cases, particularly infant murder, the presumed link between sexual promiscuity and weak-mindedness was so entrenched as to be almost presumed. Nevertheless, when judging fitness to plead, it was insufficient that a woman was viewed as having 'low mentality'. This was demonstrated in the case of Kate Owens, whom the medical officer of Grangegorman Mental Hospital found to be 'weak minded' but also declared 'capable of understanding the charge against her and of giving instruction for her defence'.[44] Likewise, for Annie Walsh (1925) the judgement of her as 'a low mental type'[45] did not prevent her execution. Following a meeting with Walsh, one civil servant from the Department of Justice reported: 'Her mental faculties I would rate as much below the average ... though I have no reason to think she was incapable of controlling her actions'.[46]

Discourses of 'low mentality' were prevalent beyond cases of death-sentenced women too. Kate Kiely, 35 and unmarried, pleaded guilty to the manslaughter of her infant in 1935. In sentencing her, Justice Johnson referenced the 'plague of infanticide which was over-running the country' but felt disposed to be lenient due to her mental capacity.[47] Mary McBride, although described by a doctor as 'barely normal', pleaded guilty to the manslaughter of her illegitimate infant in 1940.[48] Mary Murphy pleaded likewise in 1941; although the medical officer recorded that 'The mentality of this prisoner is low', he had also found that 'She quite understands the difference between right & wrong.'[49]

Judgements about weak-mindedness were so widespread that to allow them to inform notions of culpability would have entailed a radical change in conviction patterns. Instead, prior to conviction, the women, as legal subjects, were presumed sane regardless of judgements on their mental calibre. For women convicted of murder, informal judgements on their mental state were then utilised to extend leniency. In the case of acquitted women or those convicted of lesser offences, similar arguments shaped pleas for lenient sentencing.

Some cases provoked more comment than others. The apparent lack of motive in the case of Agnes McAdam caused significant speculation. Agnes was ultimately convicted of the murder of her neighbour by poisoning. The defence contended that: 'If motive and murder are twin brothers the only possible explanation of a killing is that it is the act of a lunatic, because it is only a lunatic that will wantonly take the life of another without some impelling reason or motive.'[50] Without motive, the crime was unsettling; to defuse this, there were frequent references to her 'abnormality'. It was suggested that Agnes was a person of nervous disposition.[51] The prison medical officer reported that she was 'dull mentally and very slow to answer questions', concluding that her 'stream of mental activity is sluggish, that she is weak-minded and by reason of this her judgment and reasoning powers are defective'.[52]

The labelling of women as 'weak-minded' negated the reality that many of these women had held positions of employment prior to arrest, earned their own keep and led independent lives as far as was possible within the confines of their existence. In many cases, weak-mindedness was a presumption, one based in a deeply classed understanding of mental capacity and character. This is explored further in Chapter 8.

Effects of childbirth

Throughout the cases, sub-psychiatric discourses relating to birth and biology were most evident in infant murder cases, in which women's actions were framed as stemming from mental disturbance caused by childbirth.[53] Despite this, there was little willingness to admit most infant murder cases within the legal understanding of insanity.[54] Of single women charged with infanticide offences from 1922 to 1950, only 1.9 per cent were deemed unfit to plead and 1.5 per cent were found guilty but insane.[55] In some cases, the women's actions could be construed as entirely rational, but rather than interrogating the structural context, sub-psychiatric discourses emphasised individual-level factors. While the parameters of legal insanity did not generally permit unmarried women accused of infant murder, Farrell found that it did find greater use in cases of married women or women who killed older children.[56] This finding is borne out in the present study.

Although discourses of pathology associated with childbirth were rarely sufficient to establish legal insanity, they were important in mitigation. Justice Johnston recommended Elizabeth Hannon's reprieve because:

> Prisoner appeared to him from her demeanour in the dock and her general appearance to be a woman of weak intellect. He is of opinion that her intellect was further clouded by the distressing circumstances attending the birth of the child.[57]

As elaborated in Johnston's comment, arguments of biology were inseparable from assumptions of weak-mindedness. The label of 'weak-minded' was situated in the perceived inability to resist sexual intercourse. Elsewhere, 'weak-mindedness' had led to state-sponsored sterilisation. While this was hardly a viable policy for Catholic Ireland,[58] US research has demonstrated that it was overwhelmingly poor women judged to be promiscuous who were sterilised under these eugenics-inspired programmes.[59] Comments on Mary Somerville's 17-year-old daughter provide insights into these views in Ireland. Somerville had been death-sentenced for the murder of her illegitimate grandchild; notes on her file recorded that 'It is interesting to observe the apparent simplicity with which the girl [her daughter] was seduced ... an interesting commentary of itself of the type of people involved.'[60]

The use of pathologised discourses to disavow agency was adopted as a strategy by the women themselves. Mary Kiernan said her head 'went wrong',[61] claiming: 'I did not know what I was doing at the time'.[62] Elizabeth Hannon, meanwhile, stated 'I could not be in my right mind'.[63]

In the case of Mary Anne Keane, it was noted that 'it is not an uncommon thing for women to become mentally unbalanced after confinement'.[64] Two rationales were proposed for Catherine Ahearne's offence of infant murder: the physical consequences of giving birth unaided, or 'alternatively she was so much upset by the circumstances attending the birth that she could not reasonably be held responsible for her actions at the time'.[65] A medical expert in the case of Margaret Finn testified that she could have been suffering from 'mania' brought on by childbirth.[66] Pregnancy was therefore rendered as a cataclysmic event which interfered with the capacity of rational thought. In these framings, it is possible to discern nods to the shame of illegitimacy. There was clear appreciation that the *context* of illegitimate pregnancies caused distress, although it was not subject to deeper analysis.[67]

A number of unmarried women who were prosecuted for the murder of an infant were reported to have attempted suicide after the killing. Following the killing of her infant, Johanna O'Donnell attempted to cut her own throat with a razor; she ultimately pleaded guilty to attempted suicide.[68] Margaret Moore attempted to do likewise while 'almost bereft of her senses'.[69] In the case of Margaret Rabbitt, the medical officer 'had a fear she might commit suicide if left in her home with her mother'.[70] That the strain of illegitimacy could also be a cause of mental anguish for the father is evident in a 1935 case outlined by Rattigan in which a man took his own life after his girlfriend had become pregnant.[71]

In two cases in which women were convicted of the murder of an adult and sentenced to death, childbirth again played a role in mitigation. Frances Cox's murder of her brother was framed, post-conviction, by reference to her recent childbirth. However, at trial she was constructed as a rational actor who killed for personal gain. The prison medical officer reported Frances to be 'calm and rational in speech and behaviour', noting that 'She has maintained her interest in her home and is quite aware of the market value of stock etc.'[72] Gardaí held to this view of her also. However, Frances's legal counsel submitted a petition for clemency which proposed various grounds of compassion, including one that the Minister for Justice considered 'very important':

> Miss Cox gave birth to a child (which she killed) on 18th May and … the poisoning was done between that and the 29th May. The solicitor states that during that period Miss Cox must have been suffering from the effects of child-bearing (at which she received no attention from anyone) and from the effects of suppressed lactation, and he suggests that there is a strong probability that she was suffering from mental derangement at the time.[73]

When Frances's possible release from prison was considered in 1957, the 'mental strain' of childbirth was likewise proposed as rendering her 'not entirely responsible for her actions'.[74] In the case of Mary Daly, the fact that she had given birth some months prior to the murder of Mary Gibbons was also incorporated as a rationale for leniency: 'the motive is so inadequate and her conduct so inexplicable as to make her appear to have been for the moment insane'.[75]

There were various cases in which pregnancy and childbirth may have helped defendants escape murder convictions. Julia O'Neill and her romantic partner James McHugh were prosecuted in 1926 for the murder of Julia's elderly neighbour William Dollison. O'Neill and McHugh had first discussed the elderly man's pension, before venturing next door to demand he hand over the money. In this confrontation, McHugh had beaten Dollison to death. James McHugh was convicted and hanged.[76] Julia, meanwhile, pleaded guilty as an accessory after the fact. Julia O'Neill was a widow, but at the time of the killing she was pregnant with McHugh's child, giving birth in Mountjoy Prison in May 1926.[77] Her defence counsel 'pleaded for clemency on the grounds of her condition of health at the time of the crime. She came there under the influence of a stronger mentality, and was not altogether responsible for her actions.'[78]

In some cases, it seemed likely that these arguments were persuasive for juries in infant murder cases too, such as in the case of Margaret Hogan, found not guilty of the murder of her illegitimate infant in 1931. Medical evidence offered by the defence presented her actions as entirely beyond her responsibility: 'she suffered such mental and bodily anguish that she was unconscious of what she was doing and was irresponsible apart from that'.[79] In one 1932 case, medical evidence was given that in some cases mental disturbance in childbirth amounted almost to dementia.[80]

Female biology was also cited as a cause of mental disturbance beyond the experience of childbirth. The menopause was proffered as a means of understanding women's behaviour. In the case of Agnes McAdam, the judge remarked: 'the prisoner ... may be going through the difficult period in a woman's life'.[81] A petition on behalf of Jane O'Brien likewise declared that 'The Jury had their own view as to the possible emotions of a woman of such years', referring later to the 'pathological and physiological' effects of her age.[82] Female biology was understood primarily as illness and always as a predisposition to physical and mental weakness. Giving evidence in one case, a maternity nurse stated that the patient 'did not show any signs of disease apart from her natural illness consequent on her confinement'.[83] Isabella Snow, convicted of the manslaughter of her illegitimate infant in 1924, was admitted to hospital 'suffering from pregnancy';[84] meanwhile Nellie O'Brien, convicted of infanticide in 1953, went to the doctor as, in her own words: 'I did not get unwell.'[85] Menstruation, pregnancy and menopause were all variously framed as sickness.

Unfit to plead and guilty but insane

Through the 292 cases of women prosecuted for murder, nine women were found unfit to plead, and a further three were found

Table 3.1 Unfit to plead or guilty but insane

Name	Year	Offence	Outcome
Emily Devey	1925	Murder of her four-month-old infant	Guilty but insane
Mary O'Brien	1926	Murder of nine-month-old nephew	Unfit to plead
Anne McGarry	1928	Murder of husband	Unfit to plead
Margaret Hand	1928	Murder of adult woman	Unfit to plead
Kate Moran	1930	Murder of her twin infants	Guilty but insane
Annie Connolly	1930	Murder of her newborn infant	Unfit to plead
Kate Duffy	1933	Murder of husband	Unfit to plead
Mary Gertrude Faherty	1937	Murder of her four-month-old infant	Unfit to plead
Esther Marks	1938	Murder of her 12-month-old infant	Unfit to plead
Margaret Flannery	1943	Murder of newborn infant	Unfit to plead
Elizabeth Rogers	1945	Murder of newborn infant	Guilty but insane
Bridget Daly	1960	Murder of husband	Unfit to plead

guilty but insane (Table 3.1). All but one of these women had killed within their families. Three of the four women who had killed adults had killed their husbands. Of the eight women brought to trial for infant murder, all but one had killed their own infants.

Insanity disposals were not the only means by which certain women found themselves subject to psychiatric confinement. While Mary Kate Meehan was considered fit for trial and pleaded guilty to the manslaughter of her infant niece in 1948, Justice Kingsmill Moore passed a sentence of six months' imprisonment suspended on the condition she enter a mental hospital.[86] Christina McCarthy likewise pleaded guilty to infanticide, but in passing sentence the judge said this was a case more suited to institutionalisation than punishment and ordered her to enter Ennis District Hospital.[87] The 1954 case of Mary Agnes Staunton further demonstrates the contingency of legal insanity. Staunton was brought to trial on six counts of infant murder, pleading guilty to six counts of infanticide, and receiving a sentence of three years' penal servitude.[88] Witnesses gave evidence of Staunton's disturbed state of mind prior to her arrest, including paranoid delusions. In June, she had complained of hearing voices and confessed the killings. Following this confession, she was first taken to Verville Retreat, a private psychiatric hospital in Dublin, before being certified as insane and admitted to Carlow Mental Hospital where she received 'electrical treatment'. Cross-examining one of her doctors, Staunton's solicitor attempted to make the argument for insanity, asking: 'Would you go as far as to say that if she did give birth to children having regard to her mental history that the balance of her mind was disturbed at the time of their birth?' Her plea of guilty to murder in the Central Criminal Court was also concerning. Startled, the judge adjourned to give her the opportunity of pleading not guilty. Her counsel, Seán MacBride, confessed that this behaviour 'created a grave doubt' in his mind as to her mental state.[89] Regardless, Staunton's ultimate disposal was to prison.

Women who killed adults

Of the women who killed adults and received an insanity disposal, only Margaret Hand had not killed her husband. Margaret was a patient of Ballinasloe Mental Hospital, brought to trial in 1928 for the murder of a fellow patient, 50-year-old Honor Coen. As was hardly surprising, Margaret was found unfit to plead.[90] Hand had attacked Coen in the day room of the asylum and medical evidence showed the attack had exacerbated an already weak heart.[91]

The three women who had killed their husbands were likewise found unfit to plead. Anne McGarry, described as 'an elderly woman', was prosecuted for the murder of her octogenarian husband Roger.[92] He had died from extensive head wounds, inflicted while he slept. The *Irish Times* reported that Anne 'made a rambling deposition, in which she stated that she did not know her husband was dead until Thursday last'.[93] At her trial on 24 February 1928, counsel for the prosecution noted that Anne had been admitted to Sligo Mental Hospital the previous year 'as a homicidal maniac'.[94]

In 1933, 50-year-old Kate Duffy was found unfit to plead when tried for the murder of her husband Michael.[95] Seventy-year-old Michael was shot on 3 July 1933 and died some days later.[96] When arrested, Kate was found to be 'wild and hysterical'.[97] When charged with murder, she responded: 'I did not murder him. Is he dead?'[98] The victim's voice is evident in these records too, while in hospital her husband claimed: 'She did not mean it. She was always a good wife to me.'[99] Kate's children testified that their parents had always been on the best of terms, and that their mother had recently been ill with influenza. Under observation in Mountjoy Prison, Kate continued in a distressed condition, attempting to kill herself by severing an artery. She was subsequently transferred to Grangegorman Mental Hospital. Dr Hackett gave evidence that he believed her insanity could be temporary and attributable to the bout of influenza.[100]

The final case in this category is Bridget Daly. In 1960, 40-year-old Bridget was prosecuted for the murder of her husband James.[101] She had killed him with a double-barrelled shotgun in the kitchen of their home. In early 1959, Bridget had been a patient of St Patrick's Mental Hospital in Dublin. Her brother recalled the decision to send her to the hospital for treatment:

> He thought she was not normal in her health – that she wanted nerve treatment. He formed that opinion partly from what her husband told him, and partly from what he saw himself. She was erratic in her speech and abnormally worried.[102]

Bridget's doctor reported that, prior to her hospitalisation:

> She told me that Eamonn Andrews was talking about her on TV and that Radio Eireann had a daily broadcast on her. She said she could not understand why she should be persecuted like this, as she had never done anything to anyone.[103]

On return from hospital, her brother initially found her 'well improved'. However, on 8 May 1960, her brother and husband again became concerned about her mental state and decided that she should be readmitted. The day after this decision was made, she shot and killed her husband. While on remand, Bridget was admitted to St Brendan's Hospital (formerly Grangegorman Mental Hospital). The medical officer in Mountjoy had found her para-noidal and delusional, noting that: 'She replied to questions with a torrent of words, seldom pausing for breath and wandering from one topic to another.'[104]

In three of these cases, there was convincing evidence of insanity, in the prior (or current) hospitalisation of the accused. In no case were arguments made by the defence to deny the killing had taken place in the manner suggested by the state. In the case of Margaret Hand, her status as a psychiatric patient ensured she would be found insane. For Anne McGarry and Bridget Daly, both had previously been psychiatric in-patients and their behaviour demonstrated ongoing mental disturbance. Kate Duffy's case speaks to entirely shocking and unexpected behaviour, as her children and even her husband attested. In this case, her recent bout of influenza was suggested as a possible physical ailment provoking her mental aberration. From these cases, it seemed that women may have found it more difficult to successfully argue insanity in cases where they had killed men, compared to men who had killed women, echoing conclusions from Prior and Brennan.[105] Of the three women who had killed their husbands, the prior hospitalisation of two of them suggests that a high standard was necessary to successfully plead insanity.

Women who killed children

Among the women found unfit to plead or guilty but insane who had killed children, Mary O'Brien was the only woman who did not kill her own child. In 1926, she was sent to trial for the murder of her nine-month-old infant nephew and found unfit to plead.[106] O'Brien lived with her brother, his wife and their children. She had drowned her nephew in a pond and no motive was suggested. Mary's brother and sister-in-law said she had been fond of the children, but that she had 'always been delicate'. There is evidence that Mary soon appreciated the gravity of her actions, and a neighbour reported finding her later that same day sitting in a nearby field: 'she said she would stop there till she died. She also made a remark that she was going to Hell.'[107]

Of the seven women who killed their own children, they represented a different profile to the broader sample of cases of women prosecuted for infant murder as four were married at the time of the killing. Notwithstanding the small sample, the overrepresentation of married women suggests greater willingness to accept insanity disposals for married women. Of these four women, two cases presented seemingly inexplicable moments of violence while two cases occurred in circumstances in which the killing could be viewed as a response to crisis.

In October 1925, Emily Devey was found guilty but insane for the murder of her four-month-old infant.[108] Devey, aged 41, lived with her husband in a tenement building in Dublin. On 11 July 1925, she had thrown the infant from the window of the building. Hearing a commotion, the landlady rushed upstairs to find Emily standing with her older child in her arms. The landlady reported that Emily 'looked very frightened'. As a married woman, Emily's situation was unlike most of the women charged with infant murder. Her husband was at a loss to explain her behaviour: 'They were on the best of terms, and were not financially embarrassed. He never noticed her strange.' However, a fellow resident of the house recalled that Emily had complained of nerves and sleeplessness. The consensus was that Emily had been 'greatly devoted to her two children'. The prison medical officer gave his view that at the time of the offence, Devey had been insane. At her trial, Justice O'Shaughnessy directed the verdict of guilty but insane.[109]

The case of Esther Marks offered a similarly inexplicable example of maternal violence. Esther was 36 and lived in Dublin with her husband and three children. In 1938, she was prosecuted for the murder of her one-year-old daughter and found unfit to plead.[110] In the early morning of 26 May, Esther had left her house with the infant, the body of which was later found in the canal. Attending the house, a guard found Esther in an hysterical state: she 'complained that there was something wrong with her head, she was screaming loud'. Esther's husband Harry explained to the guard that Esther had previously been in hospital with her nerves. Her doctor deposed that he had been treating Esther for neurasthenia for 11 months. In her statement Esther said: 'I am not well. I am suffering from loss of sleep. I am ill.' As with the case of Emily Devey, insanity offered a means of understanding shocking actions. Similarly to Kate Duffy, a physical ailment was proposed as a contributing factor, and the prison medical officer recorded on 31 May that Esther was suffering from a goitre which could have provoked mental abnormality. There was therefore some suggestion of physical ailment as a cause, along with her doctor's diagnosis of neurasthenia. In November 1940, a *nolle prosequi* was entered on the murder charge.

The next two cases involved married women who killed their infants in circumstances that they experienced as crises. In 1938, 35-year-old Mary Gertrude Faherty was prosecuted for the murder of her four-month-old daughter and found unfit to plead.[111] She was separated from her husband, and living with her parents and two children. Mary had been deeply affected by her husband's departure in July 1936, especially after the birth of her daughter in February 1937. On 18 June 1937, she killed this infant by throwing disinfectant on her. Her mother and father had noticed her altered in the weeks prior to the killing. The injury was reported to the guards by Mary herself, and the sergeant on duty deposed that:

> She said she was not feeling well – that her nerves were gone and that she was anxious to go into a home and to have her two children put into a home. She said a mental hospital was the only place for her, that there was insanity in the family.

In her statement Mary expressed remorse, stating that she was 'nervous' and 'always worried'. Further in her statement she spoke in more detail about what led to the killing:

> For some time back I have been feeling bad & I felt very bad when my husband did not come for the Christening. For the past 3 weeks I have been strange in my manner & I felt I could not rear my children and at times I felt inclined to drown my baby.[112]

Elizabeth Rogers likewise killed her infant in circumstances likely to produce considerable strain. In 1945, 25-year-old Elizabeth was found guilty but insane of the murder of her newborn infant. She had set fire to the infant's cot in Dublin's Rotunda Hospital.[113] Elizabeth had been admitted to hospital on 20 January and gave birth that same day. In the early morning of 25 January, a fellow patient had seen Elizabeth near the fire carrying a lighting paper and moving to kneel by the infant's cot. At trial, her counsel stated that 'she had worry and troubles which produced the state of mind which resulted in the child's death'. Counsel for the prosecution revealed that Elizabeth had married on 30 November 1944, and 'suggested as a motive that the attendant shame following the birth of a child conceived out of wedlock might prompt a mother to destroy the child'.[114] As Kelly noted, the birth of a baby 'too soon' after marriage was deeply shameful.[115] Elizabeth also had an older illegitimate child, born to her in 1938, and this child was in the care of foster parents. The courtship with her husband had broken off when he learned of this child, but they had reconciled, and she had become pregnant in August 1944, three months before her marriage. During the trial, medical evidence was given on puerperal insanity, including the possibility that 'illegitimate pregnancy might be a cause of such anxiety, but usually there was something in the personal make-up as a contributory cause'.[116]

Although Elizabeth Rogers and Mary Gertrude Faherty had been found insane, there were clear motivations which moved them to kill. Despite being married, neither was in an enviable position. Rogers had become pregnant while unmarried, while Mary Gertrude Faherty was separated from her husband. Although 'rational' explanations for the killings existed, insanity seems to have been a more likely outcome because they were married women.

Three women had killed their illegitimate children. In these cases, there are clear and compelling motivations to kill, raising the question of what further evidence was suggestive of insanity. In 1930, 32-year-old Kate Moran was found guilty but insane in the murder of her twin daughters.[117] Kate had been working in England, where she had given birth, but returned home after the death of her father. One witness recalled speaking with Kate at a Dublin railway station and urging her to take the infants to a home. When they arrived at the South Dublin Union, Kate changed her mind, preferring to travel home to Westmeath. Guards later found the bodies in Moran's garden.[118] In this case, the motive seemed clear. The unmarried Kate Moran had killed her infants to avoid detection on her return to Ireland.[119]

Annie Connolly was prosecuted for the murder of her illegitimate infant and found unfit to plead in 1930.[120] Annie was an Irish speaker, and could not follow proceedings in English. When charged she said: 'I was so bad I did not know what I was doing.' On the face of it, it seems strange that she was found unfit to plead. Her crime mirrored hundreds of others committed by desperate women in similar situations. Without further information, it is impossible to speculate on the behaviour that led to this outcome. Her status as an Irish speaker may have placed her at a serious disadvantage in terms of legibility to legal and medical professionals.

Margaret Flannery, aged 33, was tried for the murder of her illegitimate infant in 1943 and found unfit to plead.[121] On her admittance to prison she was recorded as 'a mental defective'. When she had first complained of feeling ill, she was attended by the local maternity nurse, Nurse Connolly, and the medical officer of the area, both of whom noted her insanitary living conditions. Nurse Connolly deposed that Margaret slept 'on a bed of straw on the floor', and 'appeared to be abnormal'. In her statement of 28 June, Margaret said: 'When I came home [from staying with an acquaintance who was ill] in February I was in the family way but I never knew that I was in that condition. I knew I had intercourse with men but I did not think I had become pregnant.' The case raises questions of the border between weak-mindedness and insanity.

There were certainly other cases which seemed to present similar circumstances to those of Margaret Flannery. Jane Middleton, convicted of manslaughter, was considered 'sub-normal in intelligence' and her father had feared she would become deranged following the birth of her child as her own mother had.[122] Norah Browne was 'definitely incapable by reason of mental defect, of fully appreciating the gravity of the crime she is charged with',[123] but she too was convicted of manslaughter. Edith Armstrong was first found unfit to plead and the prison medical officer reported: 'She is not, in my opinion, certifiable as a Lunatic, but she is mentally defective.' Thompson was subsequently convicted of concealment of birth.[124] These cases demonstrate the contested nature of insanity, and the contingency by which certain women, and not others, were certified as insane.

Post-conviction insanity

Among the 21 women convicted of murder and reprieved from a sentence of death, two were subsequently found insane: Elizabeth Doran and Mamie Cadden. At the point at which they were found to be insane, they were transferred to the Central Criminal Lunatic Asylum. Although Doran was released after spending some years there, Mamie Cadden was to die in this institution.

Elizabeth Doran had been convicted of the murder of her infant in June 1926; less than two months later, on 24 July, she was certified as insane and transferred from Mountjoy Prison to Dundrum.[125] Doran had killed her illegitimate infant, but she was not the 'typical' case.[126] At 40, she was older than most of the women before the courts on this charge. Doran was also a widow, and had three adult sons. Her counsel had not attempted an insanity defence, but a doctor gave evidence that she 'was abnormal and of a low order of intelligence'.[127] Following her conviction, however, her behaviour gave rise to concern:

> Some days ago this Prisoner became very noisy shouting day & night, beating the walls violently & recently has developed dirty habits. She was sane on committal & she suffers from delusional insanity.[128]

Although certified as insane, Doran was judged 'probably curable'.[129] Two years after her committal, a report to the Inspector of Mental Hospitals concluded that 'though free from delusions, [Doran] is both mentally and morally of a decidedly low type'.[130] These judgements betrayed moral and class commentary: 'low' invoked both sexual 'looseness' and Doran's status as a member of the 'labouring class'. As Doran had given birth to an illegitimate infant, judgements about her morality had already been evident in Garda reports, such as in the statement that she was 'very depraved'.[131]

In Dundrum, it was recorded that: 'She is actively suicidal, and has made several determined efforts to do away with herself, and states that she will persist in her attempts until discharged from here.'[132] Doran later rationalised this behaviour: 'She says that her former attempts at suicide were due to this anxiety. I think that if she were discharged on probation she would be able to get on fairly well at her home.'[133] In May 1931, after almost five years, Doran was conditionally discharged from Dundrum, aided by the support of her sons. On release, the Department of Justice requested that local Garda submit quarterly reports on her. The resulting reports were universally positive:

> [Doran] has been kept under close observation but nothing has come to notice to show that it is unsafe to have her at large. She is enjoying good health and works daily as a charwoman for shop-keepers in Carnew. She is still residing with her three sons ... is leading a regular life, is attending to her religious duties and is on friendly terms with her neighbours. She is seen and spoken to frequently by the Gardaí and her mental condition appears quite normal.[134]

In November 1933, the final Garda report reiterated that as all reports 'show her to be behaving normally, perhaps they might be discontinued'.[135] The informal nature of surveillance was also evident within one Garda report which recorded that the Superintendent of Dundrum actually 'sees her daily going to and from work' and 'frequently engages in conversation with her and he has always found her to be perfectly normal in her manner'.[136]

Elizabeth Doran's case demonstrated the instrumental value of family support in securing release. Without her sons' petitioning, it is doubtful she would have been released. Particularly instructive was the Garda report that her sons were 'generally sensible, well conducted young men'.[137] Ultimately, Doran's family network, which promised care and concern, was crucial in her release. The case also illustrates the importance of markers of working-class respectability and the powerful combination of work, religion and assimilation into the community which allowed officials to withdraw surveillance.

Mamie Cadden spent one year and ten months in Mountjoy Prison following conviction before being certified as insane and transferred to Dundrum, where she died on 20 April 1959.[138] Although her defence had not argued insanity, she was branded as a 'mad, bad old woman' by her own counsel.[139] Prior to trial, the prison medical officer expressed doubts about her mental state, concluding that 'it is a very difficult matter to arrive at a proper estimation of her mentality'.[140]

These considerations shaped arguments for her reprieve also, and her solicitor petitioned that:

> She is of an abnormal mentality and while it is not suggested that this amounts to the degree of insanity exempting her from criminal responsibility, it occasioned considerable thought and anxiety to her advisors as to whether she was legally fit to plead. It is suggested that this abnormal mentality deprives her of the normal appreciation of her moral and criminal responsibilities.[141]

Cadden's abnormality manifested as aggression and paranoia, including 'outbursts from the dock', which had persuaded her legal team against putting her on the stand.[142] Many of Cadden's outbursts, including a letter she had sent to her landlord in 1956, were full of anger and abusive language,[143] and the prison medical officer noted her especial antipathy to 'those who administer Justice and also Catholic clergymen'.[144] It was her disruptive behaviour in prison, and the deterioration of her condition, which eventually led to her certification:

> She is deluded, has ideas of persecution and after a short while becomes rambling and incoherent in speech. She states that the Catholic chaplain entered her cell aimed a gun at her and threatened to kill her. She states she is in prison 'through the underhand working of the Catholics'. She becomes abusive and obscene in language when [describing] her persecutions. She is degraded in habits, defecates in her bed and on the floor and is violently resistive to necessary nursing attention. She has attacked members of the staff on several occasions.[145]

Despite concern about her mental state, the efforts made to convict Cadden of the capital charge suggest that her status as a known abortionist and repeat offender motivated prosecution.[146] The 'monsterisation' of Cadden appears to have justified a harsher criminal justice response and need for an expressive punishment.[147]

Conclusion

The women prosecuted for murder were subject to parsimonious pathologising, when pathology is considered through the formal lens of legal insanity in the criminal trial. Across the cases, it was clear that certain women were more likely to receive such a judgement, namely women who were married. However, while insufficient to ground findings of insanity, insinuations as to women's mental capacity were everywhere in evidence. Informal assumptions of 'weak-mindedness' and of biologically provoked mental disturbance coloured attempts to explain women's actions. These were highly gendered and classed understandings of mental capacity, locating women within their reproductive capabilities, within their class positions and within their families. Throughout, claims of 'low mentality' could be read as references to both poverty and perceived sexual deviance.

Notes

1 Catherine Cox, *Negotiating Insanity in the Southeast of Ireland* (Manchester: Manchester University Press, 2012).
2 Áine McCarthy, 'Hearths, bodies and minds: gender ideology and women's committal to Enniscorthy Lunatic Asylum, 1916–1925', in Diane Urquhart and Alan Hayes (eds), *Irish Women's History* (Dublin: Irish Academic Press, 2004).
3 Pauline M. Prior, 'Prisoner or patient? The official debate on the criminal lunatic in nineteenth-century Ireland', *History of Psychiatry*, 15:2 (2004) 177–92, p. 177.
4 Cox, *Negotiating Insanity*.
5 Elizabeth Malcolm, '"Ireland's crowded madhouses": the institutional confinement of the insane in nineteenth- and twentieth-century Ireland', in Roy Porter and David Wright (eds), *The Confinement of the Insane: International Perspectives, 1800–1965* (Cambridge: Cambridge University Press, 2003); Brendan D. Kelly, 'The Mental Health Treatment Act 1945 in Ireland: an historical enquiry', *History of Psychiatry*, 19:1 (2008) 47–67.
6 Eoin O'Sullivan and Ian O'Donnell, 'Coercive confinement in the Republic of Ireland: the waning of a culture of control', *Punishment & Society*, 9:1 (2007) 27–48.
7 Mark Finnane, *Insanity and the Insane in post-Famine Ireland* (London: Croom Helm, 1981), p. 130.
8 Damien Brennan, *Irish Insanity, 1800–2000* (London: Routledge, 2013), pp. 26–7.

9 David M. Doyle and Liam O'Callaghan, *Capital Punishment in Independent Ireland: A Social, Legal and Political History* (Liverpool: Liverpool University Press, 2019).

10 Roderick J. O'Hanlon, 'Not guilty because of insanity', *Irish Jurist*, 3 (1968) 61–77.

11 NAI, S7788A. Proposed legislation to amend the law relating to (1) insanity as a defence to criminal charges and (2) infanticide. However, by the 1940s the numbers of insanity acquittals had dropped considerably, Pat Gibbons, Niamh Mulryan and Art O'Connor, 'Guilty but insane: the insanity defence in Ireland, 1850–1995', *British Journal of Psychiatry*, 170:5 (1997) 467–72.

12 This asylum opened in 1850, under the Central Criminal Lunatic Asylum (Ireland) Act 1845.

13 Pauline M. Prior, *Madness and Murder: Gender, Crime and Mental Disorder in Nineteenth-Century Ireland* (Dublin: Irish Academic Press, 2008); Oonagh Walsh, '"A lightness of mind": gender and insanity', in Margaret Kelleher and James H. Murphy (eds), *Gender Perspectives in Nineteenth-Century Ireland: Public and Private Spheres* (Dublin: Irish Academic Press, 1997).

14 Prior, *Madness and Murder*.

15 Karen Brennan, 'Murder in the Irish family, 1930–1945', in Niamh Howlin and Kevin Costello (eds), *Law and the Family in Ireland, 1800–1950* (London: Palgrave, 2017).

16 Lynsey Black, 'The pathologisation of women who kill: three cases from Ireland', *Social History of Medicine*, 33:2 (2020) 417–37.

17 *R v M'Naghten* (1843) Cl & F 200. Insanity was understood as a defect of reason caused by a disease of the mind, under which someone did not know the nature and quality of the act, or did not know the act was wrong. Although an Irish court held (*Attorney General v O'Brien* [1936] IR 263) that the M'Naghten rules were not an exhaustive definition of insanity, including its failure to embrace 'irresistible impulse', this was not definitively adopted into Irish law until 1974 (*Doyle v Wicklow County Council* [1974] IR 55). Further, diminished responsibility was only introduced into Irish law in the Criminal Law (Insanity) Act 2006.

18 Or the Governor General prior to 1937.

19 NAI, S7788A. Proposed legislation to amend the law relating to (1) insanity as a defence to criminal charges and (2) infanticide.

20 NAI, S7788A. Proposed legislation to amend the law relating to (1) insanity as a defence to criminal charges and (2) infanticide. Although O'Donnell notes that for many this meant very lengthy periods of

confinement. Ian O'Donnell, *Justice, Mercy, and Caprice: Clemency and the Death Penalty in Ireland* (Oxford: Oxford University Press, 2017).

21 Brennan, 'Murder in the Irish family'.

22 Brennan, 'Murder in the Irish family', p. 172.

23 O'Hanlon, 'Not guilty because of insanity'.

24 Doyle and O'Callaghan, *Capital Punishment in Independent Ireland*.

25 NAI, Department of An Taoiseach S.5886. Memorandum, 17 June 1929.

26 NAI, Department of Justice 18/2769A. Memorandum, 1 March 1924.

27 NAI, Department of Justice 18/2769A. Letter from Ernest W. Proud, 29 February 1924.

28 Clíona Rattigan, *'What Else Could I Do?': Single Mothers and Infanticide, Ireland 1900–1950* (Dublin: Irish Academic Press, 2012).

29 Although, as shown in Chapters 4 and 5, such arguments could have adverse consequences for women when it came to sentencing and punishment.

30 NAI, Department of An Taoiseach S.16116. Superintendent Wymes' summary of the facts and evidence, 13 November 1956.

31 Damien Brennan, *Irish Insanity*; Eoin O'Sullivan and Ian O'Donnell, *Coercive Confinement in Ireland: Patients, Prisoners and Penitents* (Manchester: Manchester University Press, 2012).

32 NAI, Department of Justice 18/3540. 12 June 1929.

33 NAI, Department of Justice 18/3540. 24 May 1929.

34 NAI, Department of Justice 18/9074A. Letter from James McGeough, 8 April 1946.

35 NAI, Department of Justice 18/9074A. Letter, 8 April 1946.

36 NAI, Department of An Taoiseach S.13383A. Memorandum.

37 NAI Department of Justice 170/7622. Garda report, 15 November 1948.

38 As Chapter 4 demonstrates, these considerations were hugely impactful on sentencing.

39 NAI, Department of Justice 234/2016. 15 December 1927.

40 NAI, Dublin Commission, Kerry, 5 February 1924.

41 NAI, Department of Justice 18/2770. Petition, 25 July 1925.

42 NAI, Department of Justice 18/2770. Letter from General Prisons Board, 17 July 1925.

43 This is explored further in Chapter 2.

44 NAI, Department of An Taoiseach S.13383A. Memorandum.

45 NAI, Department of Justice H1004/275.

46 NAI, Department of Justice, H1004/275. Letter, 17 July 1925.

47 'Infanticide Case', *Irish Press* (29 June 1935), p. 2.

48 NAI, SBCCC November 1933 to 22 April 1941; SFCCC, Donegal 1939–1940.

49 NAI, SBCCC, State Books February 1928 to November; SFCCC, Dublin 1941.

50 'Woman Denies Tampering with Cakes for Social' *Irish Times* (15 February 1946), p. 2.

51 NAI, CCA, 16/1946. Evidence of Patrick J. McAdam.

52 NAI, Department of An Taoiseach S.13804A. Memorandum, prison medical officer, 24 February 1946.

53 O'Donovan argued that pathologised rationales were proposed as an acceptable means of allowing for the difficult socio-economic circumstances of women. Katherine O'Donovan, 'The medicalisation of infanticide', *Criminal Law Review*, May (1984) 259–64. Within the archives there was some reluctance to commit to the clear and unequivocal pathologisation of infant murder, noted in the comments of the Secretary at the Department of Justice, Stephen Roche. Roche wrote, on the English Infanticide Act of 1938: 'I think that its meticulous pathological phrases about "the effect of birth" and "the effect of lactation consequent on birth" would sound strange in the Dáil.' NAI, Department of An Taoiseach S.7788A.

54 Elaine Farrell, *'A Most Diabolical Deed': Infanticide and Irish Society, 1850–1900* (Manchester: Manchester University Press, 2013). It was accepted that 'puerperal insanity' was rare, although it was acknowledged that it was more likely for women who were 'weak-minded', who had a family history of insanity, or who experienced a traumatic event (such as childbirth in difficult conditions). For women who were judged to be suffering from puerperal insanity, there was also an understanding that it was transitory.

55 Rattigan, *'What Else Could I Do?'*, pp. 205–6.

56 Farrell, *'A Most Diabolical Deed'*.

57 NAI, Department of An Taoiseach S.5571. Memorandum, 15 December 1927.

58 Although, as shown in Chapters 4 and 5, such women were subject to institutionalisation.

59 Johanna Schoen, 'Between choice and coercion: women and the politics of sterilization in North Carolina, 1929–1975', *Journal of Women's History*, 13:1 (2001) 132–56.

60 NAI, Department of An Taoiseach S.11040. Garda report, 17 November 1938.

61 NAI, Department of Justice 234/1491. Letter from Michael Lennon, 18 March 1927.

62 NAI, Department of Justice 234/1491. 31 January 1927.

63 NAI, Department of Justice 234/2016. 11 February 1930.

64 NAI, Department of An Taoiseach S.5884. 11 June 1929.

65 NAI, Department of An Taoiseach S.5891. Memorandum.

66 'Death Sentence on Girl', *Irish Independent* (4 March 1931), p. 5.

67 Occasionally, judges and legal actors passed harsh judgement on the hostility of the public to women who were pregnant and unmarried, see Chapter 6.

68 'Dead Child', *Cork Examiner* (29 October 1926), p. 5.

69 NAI, SBCCC, November 1933 to 22 April 1941; 'Unhappy Home', *Irish Press* (3 May 1938), p. 2.

70 NAI, SBCCC, 1941 to 1945; SFCCC, Galway 1942.

71 Rattigan, *'What Else Could I Do?'*, p. 27.

72 NAI, CCA 72/1949. Prison medical officer, 22 October 1949.

73 NAI, Department of An Taoiseach S.14689A. Memorandum, 21 December 1949.

74 NAI, Department of An Taoiseach S.14689B. Memorandum, 4 March 1957.

75 NAI, Department of Justice 170/7622. Letter from Justice Gavan Duffy, 2 May 1949.

76 Doyle and O'Callaghan, *Capital Punishment in Independent Ireland*, pp. 156–8.

77 'Murder Charge', *Evening Echo* (27 October 1926), p. 1.

78 'Ghastly Crime', *Evening Herald* (27 October 1926), p. 2.

79 'Body in Suit Case', *Irish Press* (20 November 1931), p. 12.

80 'Young Girl's Ordeal', *Irish Times* (4 June 1932), p. 3.

81 NAI, Department of Justice 18/9074A. Letter from Justice Gavan Duffy, 16 February 1946.

82 NAI, Department of Justice 18/2737A. Petition on behalf of Jane O'Brien. The deliberate intention of Jane O'Brien's crime was so antithetical to notions of femininity that it was cited as evidence of innocence by defence.

83 NAI, Department of An Taoiseach S.5884. Deposition of Margaret Campbell, 11 April 1929.

84 'The Death of an Infant', *Drogheda Independent* (29 September 1923), p. 3.

85 NAI, SFCCC, Limerick 1946–55. Statement of Nellie O'Brien, 29 August 1953.

86 NAI, SBCCC, February 1946 to 1952.

87 NAI, SBCCC, January 1953 to December 1956.
88 NAI, SBCCC, January 1953 to December 1956.
89 'Trial of Kildare Woman Adjourned', *Irish Independent* (9 February 1954), p. 8.
90 NAI, SBCCC, November 1927 to June 1935.
91 'Blow of Form', *Connacht Tribune* (27 November 1928), p. 13.
92 NAI, SBCCC, November 1927 to June 1935.
93 'Sligo Man's Shocking Injuries', *Irish Times* (15 November 1927), p. 8.
94 'Husband Butchered', *Evening Herald* (24 February 1928), p. 1.
95 NAI, SBCCC, November 1933 to 22 April 1941.
96 'Louth Shooting', *Evening Herald* (4 July 1933), p. 1.
97 'Co. Louth Shooting Tragedy', *Evening Herald* (2 August 1933), p. 1.
98 'Poor Dad', *Evening Herald* (5 July 1933), p. 2.
99 'Co Louth Shooting Tragedy', *Evening Herald* (2 August 1933), p. 1.
100 'Unfit to Plead', *Evening Echo* (23 November 1933), p. 1.
101 NAI, SBCCC (Counties) 1957 to 1961.
102 'Wardstown Fatality Case Re-opened', *Meath Chronicle* (26 March 1960), p. 1.
103 'Wife Accused of Murdering Husband', *Irish Press* (30 March 1960), p. 9.
104 NAI, SFCCC, Meath 1957–1960s. Prison medical officer, 23 May 1960.
105 Prior, *Madness and Murder*; Brennan, 'Murder in the Irish family'.
106 NAI, SBCCC (Change of venue cases for all counties) June 1925 to December 1926.
107 'Charge of Murder', *Waterford News and Star* (14 May 1926), p. 8; 'Baby in Pond', *Cork Examiner* (30 April 1926), p. 12.
108 NAI, SBCCC, June 1925 to June 1927.
109 'Child's Tragic Death in Dublin', *Irish Independent* (14 July 1925), p. 5; 'Eccles Street Tragedy', *Evening Herald* (26 October 1925), p. 3; 'Mother's Insane Act', *Cork Examiner* (27 October 1925), p. 5.
110 NAI, SFCCC, Dublin 1939–40.
111 NAI, SBCCC, November 1933 to 22 April 1941.
112 NAI, SFCCC, Mayo 1937.
113 NAI, SBCCC, 1941–45; SFCCC, Dublin 1945.
114 'Sleep-Walking Submission in Murder Charge', *Irish Times* (11 May 1945), p. 1.
115 Laura Kelly, 'Sexual knowledge and family planning practices in Ireland, c.1950–80: an oral history', 17 September 2020, CHOMI, University College Dublin.

116 'Sleep-Walking Submission in Murder Charge', *Irish Times* (11 May 1945), p. 1; 'Woman Found Guilty of Murder, but Insane', *Irish Times* (12 May 1945), p. 1.
117 NAI, SBCCC, November 1927 to June 1935.
118 'Infants' Bodies Found', *Westmeath Independent* (1 February 1930), p. 5.
119 O'Donnell notes that Moran was discharged to the care of nuns after 32 months. O'Donnell, *Justice, Mercy, and Caprice*, p. 238.
120 NAI, SBCCC, November 1927 to June 1935.
121 NAI, SBCCC 1941–45; SFCCC, Mayo 1942.
122 NAI, SFCCC, Sligo 1945.
123 NAI, SFCCC, Kerry and other counties (Carlow) 1945. Report extract, 14 June 1944.
124 NAI, SFCCC, Donegal 1937–38.
125 NAI, GPB/PEN/3/216; Department of Justice 234/1297.
126 NAI, SFCCC Wicklow 1926.
127 'Woman Sentenced to Death', *Cork Examiner* (4 June 1926), p. 9.
128 NAI, Department of Justice 234/1297.
129 NAI, Department of Justice 234/1297.
130 NAI, Department of Justice 234/1297. Letter to the Inspector, 21 March 1929.
131 NAI, GPB/PEN/3/216. Garda report, 3 July 1926.
132 NAI, Department of Justice 234/1297. Letter to the Inspector, 21 March 1929.
133 NAI, Department of Justice 234/1297. Minute sheet to Secretary of the Department of Health, 26 March 1931.
134 NAI, Department of Justice 234/1297. Garda report, 3 August 1932.
135 NAI, Department of Justice 234/1297. Letter from Garda Síochána to Department of Justice, 2 November 1933.
136 NAI, Department of Justice 234/1297. Garda report, August 1931.
137 NAI, Department of Justice 234/1297. Garda report on Thomas Doran, 12 March 1931.
138 NAI, Department of Justice 18/3562. Notification of Discharge, Removal, Death or Escape of a Person Admitted from Gaol as a Criminal Lunatic, 21 April 1959. Her mental condition at the time of her death was listed as arteriopathic dementia.
139 'Murder Trial', *Irish Independent* (31 October 1956), p. 1.
140 NAI, Department of Justice 18/3562. Prison medical officer, 29 August 1956.
141 NAI, Department of An Taoiseach S.16116. Telegram from Stanley A. Siev, 4 January 1957.

142 NAI, Department of An Taoiseach S.16116. Telegram from Stanley A. Siev, 4 January 1957.
143 One letter Cadden sent to the Revenue Commissioners in April 1956 read: 'No <u>Dirty "Underground Communist"</u> can do that. "<u>Irish Landlords</u>" If he comes in here to <u>throw me out</u>, I will <u>shoot</u> him <u>dead</u> and also put the <u>Butcher Knife</u> to the Handle in his <u>Pot Belly</u>.' NAI, Department of An Taoiseach S16116. Underlining in original.
144 NAI, Department of Justice 18/3562. Memorandum, 1 January 1957.
145 NAI, Department of Justice 18/3562. Medical Certificate.
146 These efforts included use of the legal doctrine constructive malice. Cadden had been convicted in 1939 of child abandonment, and in 1945 of attempting to procure a miscarriage. For these offences, she had spent 12 months and five years in prison respectively. In memoranda, Cadden was described as 'of bad character'. The judge in her 1945 trial had stated: 'Of all the persons, men and women who have stood in the dock before me during my eighteen years on the Bench, I think this woman is easily one of the worst.' Elsewhere it is noted that Cadden 'is undoubtedly a really "bad lot"'. Compounding this, the prison medical officer branded her as 'amoral'. NAI Department of Justice 18/3562.
147 Subsequent accounts suggest there was significant animosity towards Cadden, with Reddy writing that crowds yelled 'Hang her', see Tom Reddy, *Murder Will Out: A Book of Irish Murder Cases* (Dublin: Gill and Macmillan, 1990). Ciaran Byrne wrote in a more recent newspaper piece, that 'outside a mob chanted: "Hang the bitch"'. See, Ciaran Byrne, 'The Year a Hangman was Made Redundant', *Irish Independent* (1 October 2011), p. 177. Contemporaneous newspaper reporting recorded that significant crowds attended the trial and verdict, and that some women in the public gallery sobbed when sentence was passed. 'Death Sentence is Imposed on Miss Cadden', *Irish Press* (2 November 1956), p. 5; 'Miss Cadden Found Guilty of Mrs O'Reilly's Murder', *Irish Times* (2 November 1956), p. 6.

4

Sentencing and punishment

This chapter explores the sentences passed on women convicted of offences that fell short of murder, and considers the rationales of punishment that informed sentencing. The discretionary system of sentencing and punishment overflowed the limits of the state's formal criminal justice apparatus, spilling into the realm of religious control, as considerable numbers of women were sent by the courts to religious institutions. For the women so confined, these institutions could be 'sticky' or porous, and their use was characterised by a lack of transparency and deference to religious authority. The Irish criminal justice system in these years, by its commitment to informality and discretionary forms of decision-making, manufactured both leniency and punitivism.[1] The chapter explores why, for certain women, religious confinement was preferable to imprisonment. Definite hierarchies of punishment existed, and for many legal actors religious institutionalisation represented greater leniency than imprisonment. However, the requirement to spend time in a religious institution did not amount to 'freedom' as was occasionally reported in the press.[2]

Sentencing at a glance

Ireland was, and remains, a highly discretionary sentencing regime. The mandatory sentence of death for persons convicted of murder was handed down to only 22 women. As a result, as Table 4.1 shows, for women convicted of non-capital offences, typically manslaughter or concealment of birth, there was considerable judicial discretion in sentencing.

Table 4.1 All sentences, 1922–64

Sentence imposed	Number
Death	22
Penal servitude (not suspended)	11
Imprisonment (not suspended)	36
Religious institution (suspended sentence or probation)	86
Recognisance/suspended sentence	40
Discharged	12
Fine	1
To be detained in custody at the pleasure of the Governor General	1
Total	209

Eleven women were sentenced to penal servitude (not suspended), so called to distinguish it from the shorter sentence of 'imprisonment'.[3] Disproportionately, women sentenced to penal servitude had been convicted for their role in the killing of an adult or child (aged over one year). These sentences ranged from the minimum period of three years to terms of seven years. Two women had killed adults and one had killed a four-year-old child. A further eight women were initially charged with infant murder. Penal servitude was, in the tariff of punishments, a harsh sentence for this offence; however, each case appeared to present aggravating factors. Rosanna Mahon, who pleaded guilty to the manslaughter of her daughter's infant in 1937, was described in the *Examiner* as a midwife, a level of knowledge which may have rendered her more culpable.[4] Similarly, Kathleen Gilbourne, who pleaded guilty to the manslaughter of the infant of Julia Dunne in 1948, was a 'handy-woman', which made her particularly morally blameworthy. She was ultimately convicted of manslaughter, and eight offences under sections 58 and 59 of the 1861 Offences Against the Person Act (relating to the procurement of abortion), receiving two sentences of seven years' penal servitude, to run concurrently.[5] In 1954, Mary Agnes Staunton pleaded guilty to the infanticide of six newborn infants, receiving a sentence of three years' penal servitude.[6] Maggie McGrory pleaded guilty to the manslaughter of her infant and was sentenced to three years' penal servitude in 1947. Her case is remarkably similar to the many other cases of unmarried women who received lesser punishments, save for one detail. She had given birth in Stranorlar County Home in Donegal, and after killing her son on the Donegal side of the border, she had crossed into Northern Ireland, requiring Gardaí to request the assistance of the Royal Ulster Constabulary.[7] Johanna Walsh pleaded guilty to the manslaughter of her four-month-old infant in 1945. The fact that her son was older at death was no doubt compounded by evidence that she intended to leave the country for England, and had attempted to have her travel permit renewed. She was sentenced to five years' penal servitude.[8]

Of course, there are those cases which do not seem to offer aggravating features, such as that of Margaret Dillon, who pleaded guilty to the manslaughter of her infant in 1940 and received a sentence of four years' penal servitude.[9] Margaret alleged that she had become pregnant as a result of rape, but her failure to report this to Gardaí was criticised by Justice Martin Maguire. Passing sentence, he noted, 'it was a serious case. She had been well cared for in the county home before and after the birth of the child, and the child was well and healthy when she took her away from the home.'[10] The fact of the child's birth in a county home may also have been a mark against her. In the 1926 case of Nora Kearney, Justice Johnston's view that the jury should instead have found her guilty of murder, rather than manslaughter, may have persuaded him to impose a harsher sentence.[11] Ellen Keogh, who pleaded guilty to the manslaughter of her infant in 1944, was sentenced to three years' penal servitude. Ellen had initially been found guilty of murder, but this conviction had been quashed.[12] At her retrial, there may have been a sense that she had benefited from a lucky escape. Thirty-six women were sentenced to imprisonment (not suspended) for periods ranging between two months and two years. Imprisonment as a punishment crumbled in the 1940s; despite similar numbers of women coming before the courts, only four women received a non-suspended sentence of imprisonment in this decade.

Meanwhile, many women gave a recognisance and were free to leave court once certain undertakings were given. Nineteen women undertook to be of good behaviour and keep the peace. Additional conditions were imposed on nine others, including requirements to reside with named persons, such as their parents. Twelve women received a suspended sentence of imprisonment with additional conditions, ten of which included entering into a recognisance. Only one woman received a fine. This was 67-year-old Margaret Hillis, convicted of incitement after she had encouraged her unmarried daughter to kill her infant after its birth in Monaghan County Home. Prosecuting, Dudley White petitioned Justice Johnston that it would be a 'public scandal' if she were discharged from court, and suggested a fine of £100 or 12 months' imprisonment. Johnston fined her £50 and noted that, but for her age, he would have sent her to prison.[13]

For Mabel Matthews, her sentence may have concealed a disposal to a religious institution. In 1945, Matthews was found guilty of the manslaughter of her 61-year-old partner Timothy Carroll. Matthews and Carroll met ten years previously and had been living together for two years. According to Carroll's brother, Carroll had a drink problem, and many witnesses in the lodging houses where they had resided gave evidence of loud fights when both had been drinking, including physical violence inflicted by Matthews on the victim. When her case came due, a *nolle prosequi* was entered on the murder charge and she was instead tried for manslaughter. She was sentenced on 2 July, and was, according to her sentence, discharged from court with a suspended sentence of 18 months' imprisonment with hard labour, giving a recognisance in the sum of £50 and agreeing to keep the peace for two years. Matthews's employer also acknowledged herself bound, in the sum of £50, for the observance of Matthews.[14] However, correspondence suggested that Matthews may have gone instead to Thorndale House, a Salvation Army institution in Belfast. A letter from the management of this institution stated: 'I am quite willing to take this woman into our Home to give her a chance to make good, if you can get a travel permit for her.'[15] Thorndale House was an industrial home and a mother and baby home from the 1920s to the 1970s. The Industrial Home operated 'as a probation home for women sent by the police, courts and social services'.[16] It is unknown if Matthews went to Thorndale House, or if the surety given by her former employer sufficed instead.

Twelve women were discharged from court immediately without punishment. All had initially been charged with infant murder, and all pleaded guilty to lesser offences (seven to concealment, four to manslaughter, one to infanticide). Their ages ranged from 18-year-old Mary Anne Kingleaun to 66-year-old Jane Hynes. Seven of the 12 cases occurred in the 1920s, suggesting that the chances of a woman being discharged without punishment dwindled over time. In some cases, judges felt that the prisoner had spent a sufficiently long time in prison awaiting trial. In the 1925 case of Mary Anne Kingleaun and Michael Connor (both of whom were convicted of the concealment of Kingleaun's infant), it was brought to Justice Hanna's attention that both had been in custody for 12 months. Hanna remarked that, 'It is a very serious thing to keep a man twelve months in jail awaiting trial. I am not complaining about anybody, but it is a state of affairs we are bound to do our best to remedy.'[17]

In the case of 66-year-old Jane Hynes, who pleaded guilty to the concealment of birth of her daughter's infant, she was released immediately without punishment. It is likely that her age, and the defence arguments as to the respectability of the family, as well as the claim that the father of the infant victim had agreed to marry Jane's daughter Margaret, secured her immediate release.[18] Margaret, although sentenced to two months' imprisonment, was also released, her sentence backdated to run from two months prior to sentencing.[19] Bridget Conboy was discharged immediately after undertaking to place herself in the care of her father. Nora Meehan, who pleaded guilty to the manslaughter of her daughter's infant, was sentenced to nine months' imprisonment, but this was commuted immediately by the Minister for Justice after enquiries were made into her duties at the railway company where she worked.[20] This case occurred in 1942, and her disposal may have been motivated by wartime considerations. A further woman who was discharged without punishment, Josephine O'Sullivan, was married with three children, and had become pregnant while her husband was employed in England.[21] In one case, discharge from court was not a straightforward release, Margaret Jane McDermott was discharged on agreeing to go to Pembroke Road.[22]

Some women discharged from court immediately and with nominal or no punishment were gifted such leniency because of their marriage (recent or impending) to the putative father of the infant victim. In these cases, marriage offered a barrier to detention in either a religious institution or prison. Generally, these women entered into a recognisance, undertook to keep the peace and were discharged immediately. In the case of Mary Hanley, convicted of concealment of birth in 1931, her solicitor forwarded evidence of marriage with the comment: 'I take it that this ends the above matter.'[23] One newspaper headline in the 1937 case of Margaret Stokes proclaimed: 'Court Offer of Marriage Accepted: Woman Released'.[24] These cases elaborate the intensely patriarchal meanings of the family based on marriage, in which the offending women's behaviour was resolved by being subsumed into the family unit.

Mary Cole was convicted of the murder of two children in 1928. Because she was just 15, she was not sentenced to death, but was instead ordered to be detained in custody at the pleasure of the Governor General. Shortly after conviction in March, a memorandum on her case noted that the Minister for Justice 'has never been quite satisfied' with her being held in prison. Probation officer Kathleen Sullivan approached the Minister with a view to having 'this wretched girl' placed in Our Lady's Home. It was believed that, at Henrietta Street, she 'will be under proper reformative influences and at the same time the community will be protected from a person of the gravest criminal tendencies'.[25] Cole was still there in June 1932, at which point it was reported that she 'Should not be discharged until arrangements are made for her future.'[26]

The most common sentence women received was a period of detention in a religious institution. Of 209 women convicted and sentenced (for whom outcome was known), 86 were ordered to spend some period of time in religious detention. This could be a condition of a suspended sentence or as a probation condition. These women generally entered into a recognisance (in which they guaranteed to abide by certain conditions and pledged a specific sum of money as surety) and gave an undertaking to keep the peace and be of good behaviour for a number of years. All 86 women had been prosecuted for the murder of an infant. As Table 4.2 shows, punishment behind the walls of religious institutions increased after 1922, becoming particularly dominant in the 1940s; this was also the decade in which the number of jury trials collapsed. In the

Table 4.2 Year-by-year sentences, 1922–64

Year	Death	Penal servitude	Imprisonment	Religious institution	Recognisance or suspended sentence	Discharged	Other	Unknown
1922	0	0	0	0	0	0	0	0
1923	0	0	0	0	1	0	0	0
1924	2	0	0	1	2	0	1	3
1925	2	0	0	0	1	1	0	2
1926	2	3	5	2	4	2	0	2
1927	1	0	4	3	1	3	0	3
1928	0	0	3	3	1	0	1	2
1929	4	0	2	4	1	1	0	4
1930	1	0	1	2	2	0	0	0
1931	1	0	1	1	4	0	0	0
1932	1	0	0	3	0	1	0	0
1933	0	0	5	4	0	0	0	0
1934	0	0	0	2	3	0	0	0
1935	2	0	4	2	1	0	0	0
1936	0	0	1	2	0	0	0	0
1937	0	1	1	4	1	0	0	0
1938	1	0	1	3	1	0	0	0
1939	0	0	0	2	1	0	0	0
1940	0	1	0	4	0	0	0	0
1941	0	0	0	10	0	0	0	0

Year								
1942	0	0	1	1	5	1	0	0
1943	0	0	1	1	6	1	0	1
1944	0	0	0	2	5	1	1	0
1945	0	0	0	2	4	1	1	0
1946	0	0	0	0	6	0	0	1
1947	0	0	0	3	2	0	1	0
1948	0	0	1	3	2	0	1	0
1949	0	0	0	1	2	0	0	2
1950	0	0	0	0	1	2	1	0
1951	0	0	0	0	0	0	0	0
1952	0	0	0	0	0	0	0	0
1953	0	0	1	1	1	0	0	0
1954	0	0	0	0	0	0	1	0
1955	0	0	0	1	0	0	0	0
1956	0	0	0	0	0	0	0	1
1957	0	0	0	1	0	0	0	0
1958	0	0	0	0	0	0	0	0
1959	0	0	0	0	0	1	0	0
1960	0	0	0	0	0	0	0	0
1961	0	0	0	0	0	0	0	0
1962	0	0	0	0	0	1	0	0
1963	0	0	0	0	0	0	0	0
1964	0	0	0	0	0	0	0	0

1940s, for women charged with infant murder, the criminal justice process became a well-oiled machine for the manufacture of guilty pleas and religious detention.

Exploring sentencing

Considering sentencing, certain aggravating and mitigating factors emerged. In infant murder cases, aggravating factors included the commission of a previous offence of a similar nature. In 1929, Margaret Walsh pleaded guilty to concealment and her previous conviction was remarked on:

> Mr Justice O'Byrne said the accused had in 1925 pleaded guilty to a similar charge, and was given a chance, no punishment being inflicted. He felt for a considerable time that he would sentence her to jail, but taking into consideration the various representations made and the accused's surroundings, he had made up his mind to give her another chance.[27]

Justice O'Byrne decided again 'to give her another chance' and sent her to High Park for 18 months instead of prison.[28] O'Byrne's deliberations revealed the hierarchy among possible disposals, with imprisonment held as a severer sentence than detention in a religious institution. Walsh again appeared before the courts in 1933, pleading guilty to concealment on 4 December. On her third conviction, she received a sentence of 12 months' imprisonment.[29] Walsh had graduated from discharge, to religious home, to imprisonment.

True to the moral panic of the time, having given birth to previous illegitimate infants was also construed as a noteworthy and occasionally aggravating factor, albeit an offence against morality rather than law. Although not necessarily contributing to harsher sentences, it was considered worthy of remark with regard to character. In Mary Flynn's 1934 trial, a Garda witness gave evidence that: 'Her general character was good, but on a previous occasion she had borne a child for whose maintenance she had been paying.'[30] Flynn pleaded guilty to manslaughter and received a suspended sentence of 12 months' imprisonment on condition that she enter into a recognisance and agree to put herself in the care of a named individual. However, there are instances when evidence of previous illegitimate births motivated judges to impose harsher punishment. At the Central Criminal Court sitting commencing in June 1935, Justice Johnston engaged in a comparative exercise of offence severity. Kate Kiely pleaded guilty to the manslaughter of her infant and received a sentence of six months' imprisonment with hard labour. At the same sitting, Bridget Burke also pleaded guilty to the manslaughter of her infant, and was sentenced to three calendar months' imprisonment suspended if she entered into a recognisance and went to the Legion of Mary hostel in Limerick for three months.[31] Passing sentence on Burke, Johnston noted that despite 'the awful plague of infanticide ... he was disposed to take a lenient view'.[32] Sentencing both women on the same day, Johnston 'said that this [Burke's] was a different case from the previous [Kiely's]'.[33] Thirty-five-year-old Kate Kiely was already a mother to three illegitimate teenage children. From the facts presented, there was little to distinguish between the circumstances of the births and deaths of the infant victims but Kiely's repeated illegitimate pregnancies may have militated against her in sentencing. This broader milieu, of the fevered concern around morality, illegitimacy and infant murder, also constituted a background aggravating factor, as judges declared their intention to sentence with an eye to deterrence.

Mitigating factors considered by the judge included the marriage of the convicted women. This is clear from those women whose recent or impending marriages secured their immediate discharge from court. Marriage held a particular protection against disposal to a religious institution, and married women were much less likely to be sentenced to spend time in religious detention. Of the 86 women sent to religious homes, 78 were unmarried, two were separated, and just one was married.[34] The sole married woman was Kate Reilly, who pleaded guilty to the manslaughter of her infant in 1937 and was sent to Donnybrook for 12 months. Justice Gavan Duffy imposed this sentence because of the evidence which showed Reilly had been mentally unwell at the time of the offence and he may have viewed it as a more lenient setting for a period of care.[35] While married women were less likely to be religiously detained, there were cases in which families had broken down, and in which women had lost the protections of privacy that family bestowed. Kathleen Ogal pleaded guilty to manslaughter in 1942, and was sentenced to a two-year suspended sentence, agreeing instead to enter High Park laundry for one year. Kathleen was a married woman with children, but her marital family had disintegrated to such an extent that her husband now lived with his mother, and her two daughters were living with their father and grandmother.[36] Kathleen had first attained, and then lost, the trappings of marriage and maternity.

Motherhood could also mitigate sentence. In 1957, Lena Mulligan pleaded guilty to infanticide. She was a married woman but appeared to be living separately from her husband or living as a widow. She had seven living children, and reports agreed 'that the accused woman's other children were well looked after'.[37] She was given a suspended sentence and entered into a recognisance.

Marriage was less of a protective factor against imprisonment. Of the 36 women sentenced to a term of imprisonment (not suspended), they were more likely to be married when compared to the cohort of women sent to religious homes. Of 36, three had been first prosecuted with the murder of an adult, one with the murder of a child, and 32 with infant murder. Taking the 32 cases of women prosecuted for infant murder as more directly comparable, 23 of the 32 imprisoned were unmarried, six of those imprisoned were married while one was a widow.[38] For these women, it was also less likely that the infant victim had been their own child, and grandmothers and aunts were more common among the cohort of women sent to prison.

Case by case, other mitigating factors also emerged. The prospect of 'suitable employment' was suggested to Justice Hanna in the 1927 case of Bridget Conboy, such that she should avoid a custodial sentence, and she was discharged from court on the undertaking that her father would look after her.[39]

Despite the discretion afforded judges, certain sentencing logics developed over particular court sittings, as presiding judges refined and calibrated punishment. Justice Sullivan, through the sitting of the Central Criminal Court commencing on 17 November 1931, presided over three cases of women charged with infant murder, all of which were heard on the same day. All three women pleaded guilty to concealment and were ordered to give a recognisance in the sum of £20, to keep the peace for two years and to put themselves in the care of a family member.[40] This is an example of a discrete court sitting in which the judge engaged in localised attempts to synchronise sentencing according to a logic operational across a small number of cases.

In the 1933 case of Bridget McCormack, Justice Meredith also calibrated his punishments to the tariff of that particular court sitting. After an absence of ten minutes, the jury found McCormack guilty of the manslaughter of her infant and recommended her to mercy. Meredith concluded that he could not impose a lesser sanction than three years' penal servitude. In this instance, the foreman of the jury spoke out against the severity of the sentence. Meredith recommended that any remission of sentence 'would have to be obtained through the usual State channels'.[41] A number of weeks later, though, Meredith reconsidered. He remarked on the jury recommendation to leniency, stating that, at the time, he could not see his way to reducing the sentence.

> Since then a large number of similar cases had come before him, and the jury in several of them made recommendations of mercy. He had reconsidered the present case and had come to the conclusion that the sentence he had imposed was out of line with other sentences in similar cases. He had gone into the matter and found that he could reduce a sentence during a session. He proposed to reduce the sentence of three years to one of twelve months' imprisonment.[42]

This desire to achieve consistency within a generally discretionary field occasionally resulted in seemingly arbitrary decisions that disregarded a jury's verdict, as happened in the Central Criminal Court sitting of 19 February 1929, with Justice Johnston, who heard the separate cases of Bridie Fitzpatrick and Johanna Donovan on 22 March.[43] Prosecuting counsel Carrigan and Justice Johnston attempted to balance the outcomes of these cases, with one crucial detail that bears some discussion – Johanna Donovan had been found not guilty. Bridie Fitzpatrick's case was heard first, and she pleaded guilty to the manslaughter of her infant. Johanna Donovan's case was heard subsequently, and the jury returned a not guilty verdict. On this verdict, following Johnston's question to the jury as to whether they had considered manslaughter, Carrigan and

Johnston shared their disappointment at the failure of juries to bring in proper verdicts in infant murder cases: 'Carrigan … said it was futile to bring cases of that kind to that Court. Mr Justice Johnston said it was absolutely futile.'[44] As a result, Carrigan said that 'in view of that verdict, another prisoner, who had pleaded guilty to manslaughter in connection with a similar offence, should also [be] discharged. His Lordship granted the application.'[45] These actions suggest a number of conclusions; that neither Johnston nor Carrigan accepted the jury's acquittal of Johanna Donovan, that they viewed her as having committed the offence despite the verdict. On this basis, Johnston was willing to discharge Bridie Fitzpatrick from court because he perceived it as an injustice that she should receive punishment, when Johanna Donovan, whose actions amounted to the same offence, had not.

Hierarchies of punishment: considering prison and religious institutions

Judges weighed religious detention against imprisonment, often concluding that religious institutions were a lenient alternative to prison. This logic of punishment dominated sentencing discussion. Defence barristers often requested that judges consider religious institutionalisation. In the case of Bridget Cullinan, convicted of concealment in 1933, her barrister argued leniency, stating that she was 'willing' to enter an asylum. The judge agreed, expressing his 'deep sympathy with the prisoner'.[46] In the 1935 case of Bridie McNamee, in which she was convicted of concealment, her barrister urged a religious home over prison, but Meredith instead sentenced her to three months' imprisonment.[47] In practical terms, it is likely that the short prison term was the more lenient sentence than any period spent in a religious institution. The majority of women sentenced to religious detention were given terms from 12 months to two years – longer periods of time than those sentenced to terms of imprisonment (see Table 4.3).

A number of women were required to spend a period in religious detention for 'at least' a given time. One woman was required to spend between 6 and 12 months, 'as the nuns may decide'.[48] Only

Table 4.3 Sentence lengths for imprisonment and religious institutions
(excluding penal servitude sentences)

Length of sentence	Prison	Religious institution
2–5 years	2	24
12–18 months	17	57
Less than 12 months	17	2
Unknown	0	2
Indeterminate	0	1
Total	36	86

one woman received a sentence of religious institutionalisation of less than six months.[49] Nevertheless, the notion of lenience persisted. When Elizabeth McAllen's barrister appealed for leniency after her 1934 conviction for concealment, he petitioned that she be sent to a religious institution rather than prison. The judge demurred, stating that he suspected that 'six months in Mountjoy [prison] did that class of girl more service than the adoption of any other course towards them'. He would, however, await a probation report before passing sentence. Later that day, presumably on foot of this report, the judge recorded a suspensory sentence of six months' imprisonment on receiving an undertaking from her to stay for 12 months in Our Lady's Home.[50] For criminal justice actors, religious institutions seemed to offer greater chance of 'reform'. Sentencing Bridget Dinan to spend one year in the Sisters of Charity laundry in Cork in 1938, Justice O'Byrne declared that 'He intended to give her a chance of making good.'[51] Similarly, in the 1929 case of Christina Kearns, who pleaded guilty to manslaughter by neglect, 'Mr Justice Hanna said he did not believe in sending that kind of girl to prison. He would much prefer sending her to a home.'[52] Prison was not viewed as a suitable punishment for younger women, particularly those whose lives thus far betrayed no previous 'immorality'. The archives collected in the McAleese Report suggested that by the 1960s, prison was still not the preferred option for many women, evident in the need to make provision for religious institutions as places of remand for girls and women aged 16 to 21; yet this period also saw greater awareness that such women should have 'the same rights and privileges as prisoners'.[53]

The perception of leniency persevered despite awareness that a spell in a religious home, particularly a Magdalen laundry, could carry greater stigma than time spent in prison. As Luddy found, from the 1920s, some influential religious figures were cognisant of the fact that many women would prefer to enter prison than a laundry.[54] Similar thinking was evident in the 1913 case of Mary Ellen Murphy, convicted for her role in the Dublin 'lockout'. Murphy had been sentenced to one month in High Park Reformatory and her case was taken up by trade unionists James Connolly and Jim Larkin. Speaking in England, Larkin stated: 'Think of the statesmen that would send a pure clean-minded, clean-souled girl of 16 to spend a weeks' holiday with those who had forgotten their race, their sex and their soul.'[55] It hardly mattered that the institution itself clarified that she had been sent to the reformatory, not the laundry. The claims for leniency were elusive in many cases, as women entered a separate system of gendered control. For many women, it represented a more definite barrier against society, a surer means of exclusion and marginalisation than imprisonment.

Justice James Meredith was notable as a judicial voice who did not appear to favour religious detention. It is impossible at this remove to speculate as to why, although Doyle and O'Callaghan have noted that he hailed from a Protestant background (which may have made him more ambivalent about Catholic Church institutions), and that throughout his judicial career he expressed concerns about the death penalty and overly zealous police investigative techniques.[56] He had occasion to pass sentence in eight cases relating to infant murder from 1930 to 1935, and in each case he imposed a sentence of imprisonment. The offences for which the eight women were ultimately convicted included one offence of intent to prevent a coroner's inquest, three of concealment and four of manslaughter. Among the women sentenced were those who might reasonably have expected to avoid religious detention regardless of sentencer. This was so, for instance, in the 1933 case of Nora McInerney Snr, who was found guilty of the concealment of birth of her daughter's newborn infant. The jury added a strong recommendation to mercy when they returned their verdict and Meredith sentenced her to two months' imprisonment.[57] In this case, it is likely that McInerney's age and marital status made her an unlikely candidate for a religious home. Likewise, in the 1933 case of Margaret Walsh, Meredith may have been influenced by her status as a repeat offender. Meredith sentenced her to 12 months' imprisonment following her plea to concealment, although he dated this term to run from her committal to prison five months previously, effectively ensuring a brief sentence.[58] However, among the women before him, there were others who would likely have received a sentence of religious detention before a different judge. Meredith imposed a similar backdated sentence in the 1935 case of Annie Cox, who pleaded guilty to the manslaughter of her infant. The sentence was nine months' imprisonment, to run from her committal to prison five months previously.[59] In 1935, Bridie McNamee pleaded guilty to concealment, and received a sentence of three months' imprisonment. When McNamee's barrister suggested she be sent to a religious institution, Meredith responded that 'while he recognised the excellent work being done by the Sisters in these homes, he would send the accused girl to prison'.[60]

Why was prison considered an unsuitable punishment for so many women? Following independence, prison became an increasingly rare disposal for women (a trend which had begun prior to independence). The imprisonment rate for women, expressed per 100,000, was 6.8 in 1926, 3 in 1951 and just 1.6 in 1971, with daily average numbers of female prisoners falling from 100, to 43, to 23, in these years.[61] In 1970, the daily average population of women in prison was just 14.[62] This inevitably led to the closure of prison space for women, and by mid-century only sections of Dublin's Mountjoy Prison and Limerick Prison remained open to women and any plans for a new women's prison were 'placed on the longest of long fingers'.[63] While in 1914–15, women were 33 per cent of the prison population, in 1950 they were just 16 per cent.[64] As Rogan noted, 'Prison was not the place where women were detained in Ireland',[65] and most discussion of women's punishment in these decades occurred under the broader guise of religious confinement. One reason for the ill-favoured view of the prison was its criminogenic influence and its potential as a site of contagion. The women who formed the core of the female prison population in these decades were petty but prolific offenders: a 'hardened' recidivist cohort.[66] This explicit fear was referenced in the 1938 case of Bridget Dinan, in which the Sisters of Charity in Cork corresponded with her solicitor and agreed to accept Dinan if convicted. These letters were exchanged in July, and Dinan pleaded guilty to manslaughter in December. The letters revealed that one nun had been a regular prison visitor of Dinan's, and had identified a threat among her fellow prisoners:

> Indeed if there is to be any hope for her in the future the sooner this can be done the better as there is another much older woman there also whose example and conversation would have a very bad effect on Bridget. Though we do not as a rule like to take these girls before the case is tried we will make an exception of her on the condition we will not be held responsible if she escapes. I believe there is little to fear on that score. I only mention it.[67]

Probation officer E. M. Carroll, writing in 1941, outlined these issues clearly in a memorandum on the issue of women's prisons:

> Perhaps the greatest disadvantage of the system is that young girls, even while on remand, are able to meet and converse with hardened offenders 'doing time', whose vile influence is seen in the changed attitude of the newcomer, even after a few days. In my experience of Probation work, I have not yet found a first offender really benefiting from a prison sentence, but on the contrary have seen many young girls become embittered, hardened and morally decadent as the result of association with the depraved characters who form the normal population of our prisons ... soon the girl becomes an 'incorrigible' type.[68]

Brangan identified an ideology of pastoral penality within the Irish prison system, characterised by Catholic conservatism. Within this mindset, the humanity of the prisoner and their role as a member of their family was prioritised. With regard to male prisoners, Brangan noted that temporary release 'had been developed in a manner that could maintain the sanctity of the Irish family unit'.[69] The damaging effects of imprisonment were acknowledged. While the prison was acknowledged as a damaging environment for women, an alternative and gendered punishment regime existed in the guise of religious confinement.

Religious institutions as sites of punishment

Table 4.4 outlines the numbers of women sentenced to spend time in the various religious institutions. These institutions were of discrete types, some of which predated the state, while others were established after independence. Magdalen laundries were an eighteenth-century innovation, with Dublin's Leeson Street being the first in Ireland in 1765, a Protestant lay-run refuge envisioned

Table 4.4 Institutions to which women were sentenced, 1922–64

Institution name	Institution type	Women sent under sentence
Bethany Home	Mother and baby home	5
St Mary Magdalen's, Donnybrook, Sisters of Charity	Magdalen laundry	8
Sisters of Mercy, Galway	Magdalen laundry	2
Gloucester Street (Sean McDermott Street), Sisters of Our Lady of Charity of Refuge	Magdalen laundry	9
Good Shepherd Cork	Magdalen laundry	1
Good Shepherd Limerick	Magdalen laundry	10
Good Shepherd New Ross	Magdalen laundry	1
Good Shepherd Waterford	Magdalen laundry	2
Our Lady's Home, Henrietta Street, Sisters of Charity of St Vincent de Paul	Other	26
High Park, Sisters of Our Lady of Charity of Refuge	Magdalen laundry	15
Legion of Mary Hostel, Limerick	Other	1
Sean Ross Abbey	Mother and baby home	1
Sisters of Charity Cork	Magdalen laundry	1
St Patrick's Refuge, Sisters of Mercy	Magdalen laundry	4
Total		86

for the rescue of 'fallen women'.[70] Through the nineteenth century, as the institutional power of the Catholic Church surged,[71] existing laundries were taken over by Catholic religious orders, while new institutions were established. This trend was not unique to Ireland, and Finnegan wrote that by 1898 there 300 such sites in England alone containing some 6,000 inmates.[72] Mother and baby homes were a more specifically post-independence innovation, established in response to the crisis of 'illegitimacy' of the 1920s. Luddy detailed how this network established a tiered system of moral culpability, in which mother and baby homes were envisaged as sites for 'first offenders', while laundries could be used for the incorrigible.[73] Likewise, Our Lady's Home on Dublin's Henrietta Street had been operating since the 1800s, and had accepted women and girls from the courts for decades, a service for which they received state funding.[74] The Legion of Mary hostel in Limerick was established, similarly to laundries, for the reform of women working in prostitution.[75] As O'Donnell and O'Sullivan noted, the uniqueness of these institutions in Ireland was not in their existence but in the intensity of their use after independence.[76]

One of the starkest patterns in punishment in the years after independence was the increase in women being sentenced to spend time in religious institutions. The first such sentence was Annie Flynn, ordered to spend 18 months in Henrietta Street after pleading guilty to concealment at the Dublin Commission in February 1924.[77] These disposals gathered pace until the 1940s when they reached their zenith. Rattigan and Smith have noted this post-independence shift towards greater reliance on religious detention.[78] Rattigan's work traces the divergences in punishment between pre- and post-independence, and the preference for religious detention from the later 1920s, as well as the divergence between post-independence Ireland and post-1922 Northern Ireland when it came to sentencing patterns in 'infanticide' cases. As explored in Chapter 6, concerns about morality, illegitimacy and infant mortality from the late 1920s coincided with more punitive attitudes to women charged with infant murder in the Irish Free State. In this period, a specialised institutional network was established for the confinement of unmarried mothers, and public discourse worried relentlessly about moral laxity and its fatal consequences.[79] The sentencing pattern across the years speaks of ever greater reliance on religious institu-tionalisation, and the totalising of this mindset as the only solution to illegitimacy and infant death.

The pattern in punishment and sentencing shifted again after the Infanticide Act 1949. In the three decades preceding the 1949 reform, religious institutionalisation had become the relied upon disposal for women convicted of offences relating to infant murder. After 1949, this waned. Brennan has undertaken the first study of sentencing following the Infanticide Act, finding that detention in a religious institution became much rarer after 1950. While Rattigan has suggested that the 1949 Act brought little change in practice,[80] it would seem that very tangible shifts occurred in relation to sen-tencing. Of the sentences it was possible to verify, Brennan found that only 10 per cent of women were ordered to spend time in reli-gious institutions, arguing that, if accurate, 'this would be a striking change in practice' from the post-1922 decades.[81]

There were a number of routes by which women entered reli-gious homes from the criminal justice system. The Irish Human Rights Commission examined entry under sentence, on probation and on remand.[82] Others were sent to homes following temporary or early release from prison.[83] There was occasional comment on the inadequacy of the patchwork of provisions allowing for reli-gious detention. The 1936 Cussen Report advised establishing a statutory footing for their use within the criminal justice landscape. In response to this issue, the Criminal Justice (Female Offenders) Bill 1942 was proposed but never enacted. The 1936 report had identified the rationale for religious detention and outlined the issues with the system:

> Judges and Justices are reluctant to commit young girls to prison, but they have no legal power to order their detention otherwise. The difficulty is usually overcome by sending the offender to a Home con-ducted by a Religious Order, provided the girl consents to go there, and the Home agrees to accept her.[84]

Many women were given suspended prison sentences on the condition they enter a religious home.[85] The Irish Human Rights Commission found that the perceived element of 'choice' smoothed a lack of statutory underpinning: 'Using this approach of providing an "option", was most likely employed by the Courts to avoid any legal infirmity that might arise from detaining such women in laundries without legal authority.'[86] Women were also sent to laundries under probation orders. The 1907 Probation of Offenders Act empowered probation to be used after conviction had been secured and in lieu of imprisonment. In these cases, the offender was discharged on the condition that they enter into a recognisance and be of good behaviour for a period of time. The Criminal Justice Administration Act 1914 stipulated that a condition of residence could also be imposed. This condition was taken to include a period of residence in a religious home.

Both of these disposals involved the appearance of 'choice' and sentences were structured to imply the acceptance by the convicted woman of these conditions, although the operation of this in practice was ambiguous. Throughout, there appeared to be no instances of convicted women refusing the 'choice' of a religious institution, although a 1928 Circuit Criminal Court case in County Limerick (not included in the sample) suggested that this was possible. Jane Lynch pleaded guilty to concealment of birth, and it was recorded that 'She was put back for sentence, as she declined to go to a home under the charge of nuns.'[87] Nevertheless, it is likely that the coercive power of the legal system and the vulnerability of many of the convicted women made active resistance unfeasible.

The mesh of provisions facilitating detention in religious homes was partial and had accumulated in a piecemeal fashion, and those provisions which existed belied their discretionary and informal use. The private and voluntary nature of the institutions meant they were under no obligation to accept women from the courts. The 1936 Cussen Report listed this as one deficiency of the system:

> In our view this procedure is undesirable for obvious reasons, chief among them being the absence of specific power enabling the Judges and Justices to commit to these Homes. Further, the Courts have to rely on the generosity and co-operation of the Religious Orders conducting these Institutions who accept such cases without payment.[88]

The report further noted that religious orders received women from the courts without payment. Under the Criminal Justice Act 1960, religious homes would receive capitation payments for women aged

16 to 21 placed with them on remand (and the McAleese Report found that this was extended to women placed in religious institutions on probation as well, despite no statutory basis for this specific payment). Prior to this, there was no discrete provision allowing for payment for women sent to religious homes by the courts, although section 35 of the Public Assistance Act 1939 allowed for the payment by local authorities for individuals who met the requirements for public assistance. This mechanism was alluded to in the 1945 case of Jane Middleton, who pleaded guilty to the manslaughter of her infant and gave an undertaking to keep the peace and reside at the Bethany Home for two years.[89] Almost two years later, solicitors acting on behalf of the Bethany Home wrote to the Department of Justice requesting payment for her maintenance; the letter complained that 'no payment from any source has been received for her maintenance or for the clothing etc., supplied to her. It is understood that her people cannot afford to make any payment.'[90] The letter revealed that they had received guidance from the Department of Local Government and Public Health in 1946 that:

> the procedure in these cases was to approach the particular Assistance Authority with a view to the recognition of the Home under Section 35 of the Public Assistance Act, 1939, such authority to be that from whose district the inmate was admitted. The Home therefore wrote to the Sligo County Council but they could not see their way to contribute towards the girl's maintenance.[91]

Running out of options, the Bethany Home sought satisfaction from the Department of Justice. This correspondence suggested that religious institutions could receive payments for women sent from the courts, even prior to the 1960 legislation. Our Lady's Home, Henrietta Street, meanwhile, had received payment for women received on probation from the 1940s,[92] and Smith recorded that this institution had received funding from the state for its work since the late 1800s.[93] Relatedly, differential levels of transparency were associated with discrete institutional types. For instance, while Our Lady's Home received state funding and was open to inspection, Magdalen laundries continually resisted oversight or inspection,[94] a further issue itemised by probation officer Carroll in her appraisal of religious homes versus imprisonment as sites of punishment.[95]

As religious institutions were under no obligation to accept convicted women, 'go-betweens' were required to facilitate their use. Kathleen O'Malley, who pleaded guilty to concealment in 1947, entered into a recognisance and was ordered to enter the Good Shepherd laundry in Limerick for one year. Correspondence records the convent's acceptance of O'Malley:

> We shall be very pleased to receive this girl into our Home and we hope when the Case comes on, you shall mention this to the Judge. We presume some kind of Dention [*sic*] Order will be made out, so that she may remain some time in the Home, where everything possible will be done to help her.[96]

It is clear that preparatory work was undertaken in advance of a case being heard, to establish whether certain religious institutions were open to admitting women. Much of this was undertaken by probation officers. Although probation developed slowly in Ireland, and remained rooted in voluntarism and religious organisations for longer than in Britain, the small numbers of state probation officers were supplemented by voluntary probation officers, attached to St Vincent de Paul, the Legion of Mary and the Salvation Army.[97] Not only did probation officers facilitate negotiations between the courts and religious organisations, they also undertook to accompany women to the institutions. However, this appears to have been an ad hoc arrangement. In the 1938 case of Bridget Dinan, the County Registrar wrote to the Accounts Branch of the Department of Justice to report that Miss Carroll had accompanied Dinan to the Sisters of Charity Magdalen laundry in Cork, and remarked that, 'I was rather anxious about this as Miss Carroll is not bound to do any work for the Circuit or Central Criminal Courts, although I fear we call upon her very frequently and she responds most willingly.'[98]

Release from religious institutions: the sticky and the porous institution

As befits the intensely discretionary system of sentencing, the length of time that women remained in such detention varied considerably (in the few cases for which length of time could be ascertained).

In many cases, the conversations around periods of detention and possible release suggested that it would be desirable to keep detained women in the institutions for as long as possible. The superioress of the Sisters of Charity laundry in Cork noted that 'we are prepared to take Bridget Dinan ... into our Home – Magdalen Asylum – and we will do our best to keep her in safety even after her time has expired'.[99] The County Registrar duly responded that, 'I note that you are prepared to take the above-named girl into your Asylum and keep her there for a year or more, if necessary.'[100] These letters hinted at an expectation that laundries would detain women for as long as possible. The case of Lucy Byrne provides a devastating illustration of this. At her trial on 21 November 1929, Byrne pleaded guilty to concealment of birth. She was sentenced to six months' imprisonment, suspended on the condition that she enter into a recognisance, keep the peace and enter Donnybrook Magdalen Laundry for two years. Byrne remained in Donnybrook for decades, and died in hospital on 4 June 1978.[101] In 1941, probation officer E. M. Carroll cautioned that Magdalen laundries expected lifelong detention:

> The supervision is strict and the religious atmosphere and moral training provide a barrier against contamination not available in prison treatment. This religious training however is directed with the purpose of leading the subjects to a permanent renunciation of the world and to a life of penance in the particular institution, in accordance with its rules. All very laudable, but hardly appropriate for the type of girls undergoing a court sentence for a serious crime, seeing that with very rare exceptions none such would dream of remaining on in a Home voluntarily after the period of detention has expired.[102]

This was in contrast to other institutions, such as Our Lady's Home, which, Carroll noted, possessed the capacity to offer 'the advantage of a fresh start'. Not every woman was deemed eligible for Our Lady's Home however, and Carroll recorded its clientele as 'first time offenders provided they are not of immoral character ... the "better types" among girls charged with infanticide and kindred crimes'.[103]

In some instances, the heads of religious orders were afforded considerable authority to determine punishment, and in the case of Nora O'Connor, who pleaded guilty to manslaughter in 1927, it was recorded 'that she will go to High Park Convent and remain there until the superioress consents to her discharge'.[104] Discretion was also evident in the 1953 case of Nellie O'Brien, who was ordered to the Good Shepherd Home in Limerick after pleading guilty to infanticide 'and to remain there for not less than six months, and not more than 12 months as the nuns may decide'.[105]

The organisation of religious custody was operated along informal lines, which left little room for transparency, considering that many religious institutions were not subject to inspection and that considerable deference was shown to religious organisations. Edith Armstrong pleaded guilty to concealment in 1937 and agreed to enter the Bethany Home for a period of three years. Built into her sentence was a form of sentence review: 'and if after the expiration of two years detention therein the medical officers of said house shall consider her fit for discharge therefrom she may be discharged and the period of detention shortened'.[106] The lack of transparency was evident in many facets of religious detention, including in seemingly trivial occurrences such as in the 1938 case of Bridget Kelly, who was sent to Our Lady's Home for two years, and whose parents were 'most anxious to know the nature of the Order and also the address of the Institution in which the girl is'.[107] Once detained in a laundry, women were not entitled to receive visitors. These women were outwith the system of inspection and petitioning, and had no recourse to prison visiting committees or petitions to the Minister for Justice. As noted in Chapter 5, for many women detained in religious institutions after their release from prison, it was probation officer Elizabeth Carroll who raised the issue of release. The system allowed for porosity of borders and paternalistic early release for some as surely as it also mandated lengthy detention for others. What is clear at this remove, is that the Department of Justice delegated tremendous authority to religious organisations for the care of convicted women.

While for many women religious institutions were 'sticky' places, the borders of the religious homes could also be highly porous. While the archives are often lacking in clues as to a woman's release (or not) from a religious institution, there is information in some cases. The McAleese Report also sheds some light, by matching anonymised case studies to cases within the sample. Annie Dunne pleaded guilty to concealment of birth in 1926, and, in addition to giving a recognisance and agreeing to keep the peace, was sent to the Good Shepherd Home in Waterford for 12 months.[108] The McAleese Report records that Dunne entered the laundry, but was 'subsequently taken to Dublin by her sister'.[109] Elizabeth McNamara pleaded guilty to manslaughter in 1946, and was sentenced to six months' imprisonment suspended on her entering Gloucester Street laundry for 15 months.[110] Drawing on Department of Justice files, the McAleese Report records that after six months in the laundry, McNamara's father wrote to the Minister for Justice 'requesting that his daughter ... be released of the obligation to remain in Gloucester Street Convent for a term of 15 months'.[111] It was revealed that employment had been secured for McNamara. The Minister requested that the probation officer make enquiries. On first communication, the Good Shepherd congregation said McNamara should remain for a longer period of time; however, after a further period of three months, they recommended release, and McNamara was released two days later.

Release could also be temporary, as in the case of Mary Geraghty, who pleaded guilty to manslaughter in 1943 and was sentenced to three years' penal servitude suspended on the condition that she enter Our Lady's Home Henrietta Street for 18 months. On 30 March 1944, she gave the following undertaking after the death of her uncle:

> I, Mary Geraghty, at present staying at the Convent Henrietta Street, Dublin (Our Lady's Home) pursuant to undertaking entered into by me before the Central Criminal Court hereby undertake and promise if allowed to visit ... Co. Meath from to-day until Monday 3rd April 1944 for the purpose of attending the funeral of my Uncle ... and attending to legal matters to return to the Convent in Henrietta Street, Dublin, before the hours of 6pm on Monday 3rd April.[112]

For Mary Keady, who pleaded guilty to manslaughter in 1941, and was sentenced to three years' penal servitude suspended on the condition she enter Our Lady's Home, probation officer Elizabeth Carroll ensured her release when her father became gravely ill.[113] Questions of whether women experienced the 'sticky' or the 'porous' religious institution were dependent on women's social capital, often contingent on the active intervention of family members and a judgement that such family were respectable. The occasionally porous borders of these religious institutions can also be reflected in the transient use of such sites. Sarah Guiton, alias Carew, who pleaded guilty to the manslaughter of her infant in 1927, revealed that she had returned to Ireland from England in February and spent two weeks 'in a home in Gloucester St' before securing employment in Dublin.[114]

The limits of the religious institution as a site of punishment

Religious institutions were central to the criminal justice system in Ireland in these decades. Despite this centrality, some cases demonstrated the complexity of using religious institutions as sites of punishment, and of the 'fitness' of these institutions as alternatives to prison. In particular, the unwillingness or inability of these sites to respond to intransigent inmates represented serious breakdowns in the religious system of detention in two cases. In 1938, Margaret Moore was convicted of the manslaughter of her infant. She received a sentence of 12 months' imprisonment suspended on the condition that she enter St Patrick's Refuge, a Magdalen laundry in Dublin's Dun Laoghaire, for two years.[115] Moore's life was a catalogue of vulnerability. At the time of her trial, she was 20 years old. Her uncle, who was the father of the infant victim, had received a sentence of six months' imprisonment for concealment. Upon her uncle's early release, he called on Moore at the laundry, and while he was not permitted to see her, Moore became upset that her uncle was free while she remained confined. Fearful of what she might do, she was removed temporarily to a mental hospital. While in hospital, her uncle visited her, informing her that he was working to secure her release. On her return to the laundry, the nuns remained concerned and sent her to the Sancta Maria hostel, a Legion of Mary hostel. It was at this point that the probation officer, Elizabeth Carroll, returned from leave. Carroll immediately 'induced' Moore to leave the hostel and enter High Park laundry. However, Moore's place of punishment was now no longer in step with her sentence, and the County Registrar advised that 'something must be done to regularise the position'. At a meeting with Justice Conor Maguire, the sentencing judge, this issue was resolved by a sentence amendment. However, a potentially more pressing problem was that Moore now no longer wished to spend two years in *any* Magdalen laundry, and had asked instead to serve the suspended 12 months' imprisonment. Carroll wrote that: 'She persists in saying that she would prefer to do the 12 months suspensory sentence.' While Moore had been persuaded to enter High Park for a few nights as a temporary measure, 'She has been refusing to comply with the ordinary rules, and keeps on saying that she would prefer Mountjoy.'

The question of interest here is whether Moore could trigger the original sentence – whether she could 'choose' the suspended sentence. Carroll's response was to avoid this if at all possible. She asked that the term of detention in a laundry be amended from two years to 12 months, to render it less daunting. However, Carroll also wrote that 'there might be a chance of holding on [to] the girl at the end of that time for a further period'. Informally at least, there was a hope that Moore would be kept for longer than legally stipulated.

Religious institutions did not possess the same capacities as the prison for the control and containment of dangerous inmates. Nora Hannigan was convicted of concealment in 1931 and sentenced to two years in Donnybrook laundry.[116] Hannigan's case raised the question of what happened if women sentenced to religious homes broke the terms of their sentence. While in Donnybrook, Hannigan broke the peace, and the terms of her sentence, by 'endangering the life' of another inmate. The superintendent complained, 'We cannot be accountable' for Hannigan, and asked that she be removed 'without delay'. The first solution was Hannigan's transfer to another laundry. Her original sentence was duly amended to stipulate that she spend two years in Gloucester Street from the date of the amendment. In practical terms, this meant that Hannigan would spend an additional ten months in a laundry. In addition to this amendment, the judge also included a suspended sentence of two years' imprisonment. Three months after the amendment, Hannigan was again before the courts for breach of the peace. This time, the term of imprisonment was triggered, but her imprison-ment would run from the *original* date of sentence. The courts had been willing to extend Hannigan's stay in the laundry but were not willing to extend a stay in prison. Prison was a place to manage the difficult or the dangerous. Religious institutions, despite being an essential component in the state's response to women who had committed crimes of violence, were unable and unwilling to manage Hannigan's behaviour.

Conclusion

The cases of women prosecuted for murder and convicted of lesser offences demonstrate the intensely gendered punishment regimes prevailing in post-colonial Ireland. The sentencing of this cohort illustrates the shadow system of penality, operating with the explicit imprimatur of the formal state but often beyond the bounds of state oversight. The delegation of punishment to religious organisations was notable for particular cases, namely younger women who could be deemed to have committed an offence of morality. For such women, the 'sin' of sexuality rendered them subject to reli-gious control. Religious detention came to dominate as the decades passed, rising in importance as the idea of the prison as a site of punishment for women fell out of favour.

Notes

1 Diarmuid Griffin, *Killing Time: Life Imprisonment and Parole in Ireland* (London: Palgrave Macmillan, 2019).
2 'Limerick Girl Freed', *Irish Press* (5 November 1937), p. 3.
3 Penal servitude was provided for under the Penal Servitude Acts 1853 to 1891, and referred to periods of imprisonment of three years or more.
4 'Infanticide Charge', *Cork Examiner* (4 June 1937), p. 2.
5 NAI, SBCCC, February 1946 to 1952.
6 NAI, SBCCC, January 1953 to December 1956.
7 NAI, SBCCC, February 1946 to 1952; 'Murdered Baby Charge', *Irish Press* (18 August 1947), p. 1.

8 NAI, SBCCC, February 1946 to 1952; 'Dead Infant', *Limerick Leader* (16 June 1945), p. 5.
9 NAI, SBCCC, November 1933 to 22 April 1941.
10 'Child's Death', *Cork Examiner* (4 December 1940), p. 3.
11 'Body in River', *Evening Herald* (11 March 1926), p. 1.
12 NAI, CCA, 1944/56.
13 'Aged Woman's Trial', *Evening Herald* (24 October 1924), p. 1.
14 NAI, SBCCC, 1941–45.
15 NAI, SFCCC, Dublin 1945. Letter from Salvation Army, Thorndale House to Major Jeffears, 30 June 1945.
16 Leanne McCormick and Sean O'Connell, 'Mother and Baby Homes and Magdalene Laundries in Northern Ireland, 1922–1990' (Dublin: Inter-Departmental Working Group on Mother and Baby Homes, Magdalene Laundries and Historical Clerical Abuse, 2021), p. 41.
17 'Alleged Concealment of Birth', *Leitrim Observer* (13 June 1925), p. 3.
18 'Child's Death', *Evening Echo* (3 March 1927), p. 1.
19 NAI, SBCCC (change of venue cases for all counties) June 1925 to December 1926.
20 NAI, SBCCC, 1941–45.
21 NAI, SBCCC, February 1946 to 1952; SFCCC, Limerick 1946–55.
22 NAI, SBCCC (change of venue cases for all counties) June 1925 to December 1926. This may have been a reference to Cascia Nursing Home at 13 Pembroke Road, see JFM Research and Adoption Rights Alliance, 'Submission to the Working Group on Discrimination Against Women in Law and in Practice' (Dublin: JFMR/ARA, 2015).
23 NAI, SBCCC 1D-33-68, November 1927 to June 1935.
24 *Irish Press* (3 March 1937), p. 3.
25 NAI, Department of An Taoiseach, TSCH/3/S5744 1928. Memorandum, case of Mary Cole.
26 NAI, Department of Justice, 234/1744. Document, 17 June 1932.
27 'Concealment of Birth', *Irish Independent* (2 July 1929), p. 9.
28 'Concealment of Birth', *Irish Independent* (2 July 1929), p. 9.
29 'Prison Terms Imposed at Criminal Court', *Irish Press* (5 December 1933), p. 8.
30 'Case Against Domestic Servant', *Evening Herald* (13 March 1934), p. 5.
31 NAI, SBCCC, November 1933 to 22 April 1941.
32 'Infanticide Case', *Irish Press* (29 June 1935), p. 2.
33 'Women Sentenced', *Cork Examiner* (24 July 1935), p. 2.
34 The marital status of five women was unknown.

35 'Butlersbridge Tragedy', *Anglo-Celt* (6 November 1937), p. 12.
36 NAI, SBCCC, 1941–45; SFCCC, Tipperary 1942.
37 'Suspended Sentence for Mother', *Irish Times* (12 November 1957), p. 7.
38 In two cases it was not definitively known, but in these cases the infant victim was the woman's grandchild, and it was likely they were either married or widowed.
39 'Charge against Leitrim Girl', *Anglo-Celt* (26 February 1927), p. 5.
40 Hannah O'Brien, Cork; Mary Kealy, Kilkenny; Bridget Moylette, Mayo. See NAI, SBCCC, November 1927 to June 1935.
41 'Child Murder Charge', *Irish Times* (22 November 1933), p. 2.
42 'Girl's Sentence Reduced', *Evening Herald* (4 December 1933), p. 2.
43 NAI, SBCCC, November 1927 to June 1935, Tipperary and Limerick.
44 'Judge Criticises Verdict', *Irish Independent* (23 March 1929), p. 11.
45 'Judge Criticises Verdict', *Irish Independent* (23 March 1929), p. 11.
46 'An Infant's Death', *Evening Echo* (14 March 1933), p. 2.
47 'Infanticide Cases in Dublin', *Weekly Irish Times* (23 November 1935), p. 19a.
48 Nellie O'Brien, who pleaded guilty to infanticide in 1953. NAI, SBCCC, January 1953 to December 1956.
49 Bridget Burke pleaded guilty to manslaughter in 1935 and was ordered to spend three months in the Legion of Mary hostel in Limerick. NAI, SBCCC, November 1933 to 22 April 1941.
50 'Concealment of Birth', *Cork Examiner* (7 July 1934), p. 7.
51 'Girl Promises to Go to Cork Convent', *Irish Times* (7 December 1938), p. 2.
52 'Manslaughter through Negligence', *Weekly Irish Times* (30 November 1929), p. 9.
53 Letter from the Department of Justice to the Sisters of Our Lady of Charity of Refuge, Lower Sean MacDermott Street, 24 October 1960, cited in Inter-departmental Committee to Establish the Facts of State Involvement with the Magdalen Laundries, 'McAleese Report' (Dublin: Department of Justice and Equality, 2013), ch. 9, p. 221.
54 Maria Luddy, *Prostitution and Irish Society, 1800–1940* (Cambridge: Cambridge University Press, 2007), p. 133.
55 Peter Murray, 'A militant among the Magdalens? Mary Ellen Murphy's incarceration in High Park Convent during the 1913 Lockout', *Irish Labour History Society*, 20 (1995) 41–54.
56 David M. Doyle and Liam O'Callaghan, *Capital Punishment in Independent Ireland: A Social, Legal and Political History* (Liverpool: Liverpool University Press, 2019).

57 'Infant's Death', *Evening Echo* (28 November 1933), p. 2; 'Infanticide Charges at Dublin', *Nenagh Guardian* (2 December 1933), p. 2.

58 'Farmer Sentenced', *Irish Press* (5 December 1933), p. 8.

59 NAI, SBCCC, November 1933 to 22 April 1941.

60 'Infanticide Cases in Dublin', *Weekly Irish Times* (23 November 1935), p. 19a.

61 Eoin O'Sullivan and Ian O'Donnell, *Coercive Confinement in Ireland: Patients, Prisoners and Penitents* (Manchester: Manchester University Press, 2012).

62 Christina Quinlan, *Inside: Ireland's Women's Prisons, Past and Present* (Dublin: Irish Academic Press, 2011).

63 Mary Rogan, *Prison Policy in Ireland: Politics, Penal-Welfarism and Political Imprisonment* (London: Routledge, 2011), p. 118.

64 Quinlan, *Inside*.

65 Rogan, *Prison Policy in Ireland*, p. 118. Rogan writes that attention was only diverted to women in prison from the late 1960s and early 1970s.

66 Quinlan, *Inside*.

67 NAI, SBCCC, November 1933 to 22 April 1941. Letter from the Sisters of Charity, Cork, 9 July 1938.

68 Dublin Diocesan Archives, AB8/b/XXVIII/983. Memorandum prepared by E. M. Carroll, probation officer at Dublin Metropolitan Courthouse, and forwarded by the County Registrar of the Circuit Court to Archbishop McQuaid, enclosed in a letter, 9 July 1941.

69 Louise Brangan, 'Pastoral penality in 1970s Ireland: addressing the pains of imprisonment', *Theoretical Criminology*, 25:1 (2021) 44–65, p. 54.

70 Luddy, *Prostitution and Irish Society*.

71 Tom Inglis, *Moral Monopoly: The Rise and Fall of the Catholic Church in Modern Ireland*, 2nd edition (Dublin: UCD Press, 1998).

72 Frances Finnegan, *Do Penance or Perish: A Study of Magdalene Asylums in Ireland* (Oxford: Oxford University Press, 2004).

73 Maria Luddy, 'Moral rescue and unmarried mothers in Ireland in the 1920s', *Women's Studies*, 30:6 (2001) 797–817. Although not used as disposals for sentenced women, county homes (formerly workhouses under the Poor Law) were a third prong of this institutional response.

74 James M. Smith, *Ireland's Magdalen Laundries and the Nation's Architecture of Containment* (Manchester: Manchester University Press, 2008).

75 Luddy, *Prostitution and Irish Society*.

76 Ian O'Donnell and Eoin O'Sullivan, '"Coercive confinement": an idea whose time has come?', *Incarceration*, 1:1 (2020) 1–20.
77 'Munster', *Irish Independent* (7 February 1924), p. 8.
78 Clíona Rattigan, '*What Else Could I Do?': Single Mothers and Infanticide, Ireland 1900–1950* (Dublin: Irish Academic Press, 2012); Smith, *Ireland's Magdalen Laundries*.
79 Luddy, 'Moral rescue'.
80 Rattigan, '*What Else Could I Do?*'.
81 Karen Brennan, 'Murderous mothers and gentle judges: paternalism, patriarchy, and infanticide', *Yale Journal of Law and Feminism*, 30:1 (2018) 139–95, p. 161.
82 Irish Human Rights Commission, 'Assessment of the Human Rights Issues Arising in Relation to the "Magdalen Laundries"' (Dublin: IHRC, 2010).
83 McAleese Report; Lynsey Black, '"On the other hand, the accused is a woman": women and the death penalty in post-independence Ireland', *Law and History Review*, 36:1 (2018) 139–72.
84 Commission of Inquiry into the Reformatory and Industrial School System, 1934–36, 'The Cussen Report' (Dublin: Stationery Office, 1936), p. 48.
85 Numbering 46 of 86 women (of the 83 cases for whom full details are known).
86 Irish Human Rights Commission, 'Assessment of the Human Rights Issues', p. 15.
87 'County Criminal Business', *Cork Examiner* (13 February 1928), p. 5.
88 The Cussen Report, p. 48.
89 NAI, SBCCC, 1941–45.
90 NAI, SFCCC, Sligo, 1945. Letter from H. J. W. Downey & Sons Solicitors to the Department of Justice, 17 October 1947.
91 NAI, SFCCC, Sligo, 1945. Letter from H. J. W. Downey & Sons Solicitors to the Department of Justice, 17 October 1947.
92 Irish Human Rights Commission, 'Assessment of the Human Rights Issues'.
93 Smith, *Ireland's Magdalen Laundries*.
94 Luddy, *Prostitution and Irish Society*.
95 Dublin Diocesan Archives, AB8/b/XXVIII/983. Memorandum prepared by E. M. Carroll, probation officer at Dublin Metropolitan Courthouse, and forwarded by the County Registrar of the Circuit Court to Archbishop McQuaid enclosed in a letter, 9 July 1941.
96 NAI, SFCCC, Limerick, 1946–55. Letter from the Reverend Mother, Good Shepherd Convent, Limerick, 21 October 1947.

97 Deirdre Healy and Louise Kennefick, 'Hidden voices: practitioner per-spectives on the early histories of probation in Ireland', *Criminology & Criminal Justice*, 19:3 (2019) 346–63; Gerry McNally, 'Probation in Ireland: a brief history of the early years', *Irish Probation Journal*, 4 (2007) 5–24; McAleese Report, ch. 9.

98 NAI, SFCCC, Cork 1938. Letter from County Registrar to Accounts Branch, Department of Justice, 7 January 1939.

99 NAI, SBCCC, November 1933 to 22 April 1941. Letter, 2 December 1938.

100 NAI, SBCCC, November 1933 to 22 April 1941. Letters, 3 December 1938.

101 I am much indebted to the work of Claire McGettrick and the Magdalene Names Project for this information, http://jfmresearch.com/home/magdalene-names-project/ (accessed 17 September 2021). On sentence, see, NAI, SBCCC November 1927 to June 1935.

102 Dublin Diocesan Archives, AB8/b/XXVIII/983. Memorandum pre-pared by E. M. Carroll, probation officer at Dublin Metropolitan Courthouse, and forwarded by the County Registrar of the Circuit Court to Archbishop McQuaid enclosed in a letter, 9 July 1941.

103 Dublin Diocesan Archives, AB8/b/XXVIII/983. Memorandum pre-pared by E. M. Carroll, probation officer at Dublin Metropolitan Courthouse, and forwarded by the County Registrar of the Circuit Court to Archbishop McQuaid enclosed in a letter, 9 July 1941.

104 NAI, SBCCC (change of venue cases for all counties) June 1925 to December 1926.

105 NAI, SBCCC, January 1953 to December 1956.

106 NAI, SBCCC, November 1933 to 22 April 1941.

107 NAI, SFCCC, Monaghan 1937. Letter to County Registrar, Circuit Court Office, 6 January 1939.

108 NAI, SBCCC, June 1925 to June 1927.

109 McAleese Report, ch. 9, p. 277.

110 NAI, SBCCC, February 1946 to 1952.

111 NAI, Department of Justice, 18/9639B, cited in McAleese Report, ch. 9, p. 274.

112 NAI, SFCCC, Meath 1943.

113 NAI, SFCCC, Galway 1941.

114 'Alleged Infanticide', *Evening Herald* (6 May 1927), p. 3.

115 NAI, SFCCC, Dublin 1938.

116 NAI, SBCCC, November 1927 to June 1935.

5

Post-reprieve punishment of death-sentenced women

The extension of mercy to death-sentenced women, by commuting a death sentence to a sentence of penal servitude for life, was the overwhelming outcome for women convicted of murder. The paternalistic discourses which shaped debate on commutation and in sentencing for lesser offences dominated post-reprieve as well. Efforts were frequently made to have women serving sentences of penal servitude for life released from prison, either to their families or to religious institutions. This chapter examines the experience of imprisonment for reprieved women (listed in Table 5.1), occasionally heard in the women's own voices through their petitions from prison, and looks at the processes and rationales which saw women transferred to religious homes.

As outlined in Chapter 4, a range of institutions existed in which women and girls were detained. The past two decades have seen a period of reckoning on these practices of institutionalisation, and on the infliction of cruelty and abuse within these sites.[1] This has occasioned a number of inquiries which have sought, each within their narrowly defined parameters, to investigate particular facets of individual institutions. In this regard, the McAleese Report and the Mother and Baby Homes Commission of Investigation Final Report are particularly relevant to the lives of the 21 reprieved women as well as those women convicted of lesser offences discussed in Chapter 4.[2] Tempering the conservatism of these official reports, survivor testimony, oral history and academic work has offered searing accounts which show the lived experiences of persons who were confined in religious institutions.[3] Throughout this chapter, the words of both the confined women and those in positions of

Table 5.1 Women reprieved from sentence of death, 1922–64

Name	Convicted	Age	Location	Victim
Hannah Flynn	27 February 1924	28	Co. Kerry	Margaret O'Sullivan (former employer)
Mary Moynihan	12 December 1924	22	Co. Cork	Nora Horgan (employer)
Hannah O'Leary	30 June 1925	37	Co. Cork	Patrick O'Sullivan (brother)
Elizabeth Doran	3 June 1926	40	Co. Wicklow	Own infant
Mary Kiernan	28 October 1926	22	Co. Westmeath	Own infant
Elizabeth Hannon	12 December 1927	30	Co. Westmeath	Own infant
Mary Anne Keane	10 June 1929	23	Co. Roscommon	Own infant
Deborah Sullivan	13 June 1929	21	Co. Kerry	Own infant
Annie Walsh	21 June 1929	42	Co. Galway	Sonny Dan Walsh (husband)
Catherine Ahearne	25 June 1929	26	Co. Wexford	Own infant
Christina Russell	27 November 1930	28	Co. Dublin	Own infant
Margaret Finn	3 March 1931	25	Co. Clare	Own infant
Jane O'Brien	8 June 1932	52	Co. Wexford	John Cousins (nephew)
Elizabeth and Rose Edwards	28 March 1935	20 and 28	Co. Roscommon	Infant of Elizabeth
Mary Somerville	15 November 1938	50	Co. Monaghan	Infant grandchild
Kate Owens	22 November 1943	36	Co. Westmeath	Own infant
Agnes McAdam	15 February 1946	53	Co. Monaghan	James Finnegan
Mary Daly	29 April 1949	27	Dublin City	Mary Gibbons
Frances Cox	21 November 1949	30	Co. Laois	Richard Cox
Mamie Cadden	1 November 1956	64	Dublin City	Helen O'Reilly

authority offer yet another account of the use of semi-penal sites of confinement.

Reprieved women in prison

The 21 reprieved women continued to be held in Dublin's Mountjoy Prison following commutation. A Department of Justice memorandum specified that persons serving a sentence of penal servitude for life should not be considered for release until they had served the equivalent of 20 years (with an exception for women convicted of infant murder).[4] However, the 21 reprieved women spent hugely differing periods of time in prison before their release. In his work on life sentences and parole in Ireland, Griffin found that while the length of time spent in prison by a life-sentenced prisoner has increased significantly, particularly from the 1980s, there was an earlier trend of huge variation. Between 1925 to 1955, life-sentenced prisoners could spend anywhere between five months and 17 years in prison, with 5.75 years as the mean time.[5]

Considering time spent in prison after reprieve, Doyle and O'Donnell found a disparity between men and women. Reprieved women served a median period of three and a half years, compared to seven and a half years for men.[6] Gender disparity was embedded within the practice, as standard remission was a quarter for men and a third for women.[7] Within the figure for women, there was disparity between the time served for women convicted of the murder of an infant and those convicted of murdering an adult.[8]

As shown in Table 5.2, women who had murdered an infant spent shorter periods of time in prison. While one woman spent almost five and a half years in Mountjoy Prison,[9] most spent less. A 'working rule' in infant murder cases provided official imprimatur to a practice of holding such women in prison for two years.[10] Despite this, there was no certainty on how long such women would or should spend imprisoned. This was demonstrated by the Secretary at the Department of Justice who noted, in the case of Christina Russell, that due to the age of the infant at death she 'should suffer five full years imprisonment before we consider releasing her either wholly or to a Home'.[11] Discretionary

Table 5.2 Time spent in prison by women convicted of the murder of an infant

Name	Time spent in prison
Elizabeth Doran	51 days[1]
Elizabeth Hannon	2 years, 7 months, 5 days
Mary Kiernan	6 months, 3 days
Mary Anne Keane	1 year, 4 months, 26 days
Deborah Sullivan	4 months, 21 days
Catherine Ahearne	3 years, 11 months, 28 days
Christina Russell	3 years, 3 months, 21 days
Margaret Finn	2 years, 7 months, 1 day
Elizabeth Edwards	2 years, 5 months, 10 days
Rose Edwards	1 year, 8 months, 4 days
Mary Somerville	2 years, 1 month, 9 days
Kate Owens	5 years, 5 months, 11 days

[1] Elizabeth Doran was certified as insane and transferred to the Central Criminal Lunatic Asylum; she spent a further four and a half years in the asylum.

decision-making allowed for significant differences in imprisonment length.

Crucially, these figures do not represent periods spent confined in other institutions following transfer from prison. Although Elizabeth Doran spent less than two months in Mountjoy Prison after her conviction, she was certified as insane and transferred to the Central Criminal Lunatic Asylum. In total she spent almost five years in some form of confinement. A further six of the remaining 11 women convicted of infant murder went on to spend time in religious institutions.

Removing infant murder cases, the contrast between imprisonment periods experienced by reprieved men and women becomes less marked (shown in Table 5.3). The periods of time spent in prison for women convicted of killing an adult were more substantial than the median figure of three and a half years for all reprieved women.

Commenting on Hannah Flynn's lengthy imprisonment, the Department of Justice noted that there was 'no record of any cases since 1879 of women serving such a long time, the longest range from 7 to 14 years.'[12] However, while Flynn's case was unusual, it

Table 5.3 Time spent in prison by women convicted of the murder of an adult

Name	Time spent in prison
Hannah Flynn	18 years, 7 months, 26 days
Mary Moynihan	5 years, 7 months, 6 days
Hannah O'Leary	17 years, 2 months, 19 days
Annie Walsh (1929)	6 years, 7 months, 5 days
Jane O'Brien	9 years, 1 month, 14 days
Agnes McAdam	3 years, 7 months, 16 days
Mary Daly	4 years, 6 months, 25 days
Frances Cox	7 years, 4 months, 1 day
Mamie Cadden	1 year, 9 months, 6 days[1]

[1] Mamie Cadden was transferred to the Central Criminal Lunatic Asylum on 7 August 1958 and died there on 20 April 1959.

was not entirely isolated, evident in the similar length of time served by Hannah O'Leary and in the upper figure of 14 years cited. The periods of time spent in prison by women who murdered an adult ranged from fewer than two years, for Mamie Cadden, to more than 18 and a half years, for Hannah Flynn. Again, the figures for this group are misleading, and do not encompass the time spent in the Central Criminal Lunatic Asylum by Mamie Cadden, or those women who were transferred to religious institutions from prison.

While 21 women had their death sentence commuted to penal servitude for life, Annie Walsh (1929) was the only reprieved woman whose sentence was formally commuted further, and on 12 August 1932 her sentence was reduced to ten years' penal servitude, as was the sentence of her co-convicted Martin Joyce.[13] The distinction in the case of Annie Walsh (1929) may have reflected a more general, or 'masculine', means of extending commutation due to the presence of the male co-convicted, and was also justified by ongoing doubts about the pair's guilt.

Reprieved women's petitions

Processes of mercy continued post-reprieve as women petitioned for further relief from sentence. Many women situated themselves within their family, stressing their caring and domestic roles in the family home. Mary Moynihan said she was needed by her father, who was 'very sad and lonely and heart-broken over my trouble'.[14] Mary Kiernan wrote, 'My mother is widow [*sic*] and I am all the girl she has, and she is in a terrible way about me.'[15] Margaret Finn's mother also petitioned that she needed her daughter:

> I am a poor lone widow living alone in the side of the road. It would be a great comfort and charity for me if your gracious self was pleased to releace [*sic*] this my daughter for I am alone and destitute and saddly [*sic*] needs her help.[16]

Failing health was also cited; Hannah Flynn petitioned that 'I feel my health breaking with the long years of imprisonment and the weary longing to see my people again'.[17] The effect of imprisonment on mental health was also noted, such as Mary Moynihan's remark that: 'I feel terribly depressed when I think of the miserable life before me'.[18] Six months later, Moynihan wrote that 'imprisonment seems to be depressing me of late'.[19] Hannah O'Leary referenced the 'strain' of imprisonment.[20] Jane O'Brien petitioned that she was 'advancing in years' and wished to be released that she might 'be allowed an opportunity of finding a way of living, and of making a fresh start in life'.[21] Mary Somerville, meanwhile, wrote that she was 'failing in health of body and mind'.[22]

Separation was often tinged with the pain of bereavement.[23] The Governor of Mountjoy Prison revealed that Hannah Flynn's siblings had not told her of the death of her parents and were 'afraid to tell her the truth'.[24] Kate Owens mentioned her mother's poor health and wrote that she was eager 'to see and speak to her before she dies'.[25] Mary Moynihan also suffered the loss of her mother, something about which she harboured feelings of guilt: 'Since my conviction my poor Mother has died no doubt of a broken heart.'[26] Catherine Ahearne also blamed herself for her husband's emigration to Australia following her 'disgrace'. Catherine wished to be released to travel to Australia to be with him, claiming that 'it is more for his sake than my own that I ask to be allowed to go to him', as she feared he would lapse into alcoholism without her.[27]

Many petitions included pledges to lead a better life, such as this undertaking from Margaret Finn: 'I promise if I am given this one chance I shall turn over a new leaf and live a better life for the future.'[28] Mary Moynihan too claimed, 'I faithfully promise never never more to offend',[29] while Kate Owens assured that prison had 'taught her a good lesson'.[30]

Women did not universally express regret for their crimes. Mary Moynihan continued to implicate her lover, and the husband of the victim, in the murder: 'I was only 19 years of age at the time and was not altogether to blame.'[31] Moynihan relied on her youth in a number of her petitions, claiming that she was 'born and reared in the heart of the country and was entirely ignorant of the law'.[32] Moynihan was not the only woman who laid the blame elsewhere; Mary Anne Keane complained that: 'I have suffered enough with a bad husband for this past eight years.'[33]

The petitions offer a glimpse of the voices of the women themselves. They provide insight into how women viewed their circumstances. As documents, though, they present issues of agency and authenticity. In her microhistory of the case of Mary M.,[34] in which we are presented with a first-hand account of rape, Earner-Byrne points out that Mary presented a narrative that was 'morally unquestionable'.[35] The narratives evident in petitions share common themes, such as the attempt to reduce culpability. The content of petitions was necessarily mediated by their purpose, the intended audience and the position of their authors, and it is likely that petitions were significantly influenced by instruction from prison chaplains and others. This brings home the situated nature of discourse.[36] Petitions cannot uncritically be read as true 'bottom-up' accounts. Nevertheless, there is also evidence of individuality within them, for example in the obvious anger of some, such as Mary Moynihan and Mary Anne Keane, towards the men they blamed. The opportunity for petitions to be fully exploited is also evident in the carefully worded petition of Mary Somerville, a rare woman who seemed more able to resist the coercion of the system and who provided pitch-perfect repentance: 'I have shown to my spiritual director my true sorrow and penitence for my crime.'[37]

Release from prison

Familial circumstances were influential in decision-making on whether women would be released unconditionally from prison. Mary Kiernan served only six months in prison before release to her family. The Department of Justice had communicated to the Governor of Mountjoy: 'You will please suggest, in a discreet fashion ... that she should petition for a further mitigation of sentence.'[38] The construction of Mary Kiernan as 'respectable', as confirmed by the Garda report, may have gone in her favour.[39] Christina Russell was also released unconditionally; the support of her family throughout her imprisonment was evident from their frequent letters and visits, demonstrating that a support network was often viewed as necessary before women could be released.[40] Catherine Ahearne, also released unconditionally to her family, likewise benefited from significant family support, including the submission of her family's income and employment details, while her mother undertook to look after Catherine, claiming that 'there will be no difficulty in getting suitable and permanent employment'.[41] Elizabeth and Rose Edwards were supported by numerous petitions and letters from their parents expressing their desire to have them return home; Rose was unconditionally released after less than two years, while Elizabeth was also released to her family after an additional period spent in a religious institution.[42] Petitioners who could provide a concrete plan for the future were more likely to be successful in securing unconditional release from prison. Frances Cox cited her financial stability: 'I will not be destitute as I own the farm and have an income from the letting of it since my mother's death.'[43] Cox also benefited from undertakings given by a member of the Salvation Army.[44] Guarantees of employment, or a respectable and financially secure family, provided convincing justifications for unconditional release, but the ability to rely on such resources was far from universal.

Reflecting the view of prison elaborated in Chapter 4, the Department of Justice sought to release women from prison after an appropriate length of time. Brangan, writing on male imprisonment from the 1970s, observed a humane view of the prisoner and the desire to release men to their families where possible.[45] While there was no wish to see women in prison for prolonged periods either, their release was not a straightforward matter. Prison was a place for habitual criminals, which made first offenders 'embittered, hardened and morally decadent'.[46] When Christina Russell's death sentence was commuted to penal servitude for life, the Department noted that 'Her case with others similarly sentenced will be placed on the list for periodic review with a view to determining when they might be released.'[47] The Department occasionally contacted the Governor to enquire about the status of long-serving women; but equally it was stated that Hannah O'Leary *should* have been considered for release when she had served ten years of her sentence, an anniversary which came and went unmarked.[48] When Hannah Flynn was released from prison, the Catholic chaplain wrote:

> My only regret is that this good news came while I am on retreat, and so I could not take the pleasure of giving it to Hannah myself. We will have to release Margaret Dillon now – the only Female Convict left![49]

For Kate Owens, menopause finally secured her release from prison. As a persistent 'infanticide' offender, her ability to conceive informed perceptions of her 'risk'. Considering release, the medical officer stated that: 'There are some indications that she is nearing the menopausal stage of her career.'[50] Two years earlier, Owens's case had been dismissed:

> Nevertheless the prisoner's history tends to show that she has not the will power to resist her physical impulses and her release now might only result in a second conviction for child murder. I think the question of her release should be delayed for another two years: she is now about 41 years of age and perhaps by that time she may have passed the child-bearing age.[51]

As noted in Chapter 2, Garda reports often presented more punitive views than others in the criminal justice system. In the case of Hannah Flynn, until the husband of the victim passed away, Garda reports continually recommended that her release to her family would provoke only trouble.[52] Equally, Garda reports recommended detaining women for lengthier periods if substantial efforts had gone into the investigation, such as the extensive search for the body of the infant of Elizabeth Edwards.[53] Regarding Mary Moynihan, the prison chaplain claimed that the Minister for Justice, Kevin O'Higgins, had told him that 'in view of the extended investigations ... no action could be taken' on her early release.[54]

While some women were quickly freed from the formal grasp of criminal justice, others were instead confined in the grey area of religious institutionalisation. Prison was viewed as an unsuitable environment for many women, but this did not mean that unconditional release was necessarily appropriate. This differentiation is evident in the distinction made between Elizabeth and Rose Edwards. Rose was released unconditionally from prison, whereas Elizabeth was discharged to Henrietta Street to spend another year and three months there before eventual release. Elizabeth and Rose had been convicted of the murder of Elizabeth's illegitimate infant, but while the offence was the same for both, the 'sin' of illegitimacy was Elizabeth's alone.[55] The 'two-tier' nature of release was demonstrated by a letter from Miss Boland, a member of Mountjoy Prison's Visiting Committee, on behalf of Christina Russell. Boland asked if the 'authorities might allow [Christina] to go to a Convent for some time, perhaps, if they will not release her altogether'.[56]

Confinement in religious institutions

Of 21 reprieved women, 11 were conditionally discharged from prison to religious institutions (listed in Table 5.4). Additionally, Kate Owens was discharged to a paid situation with the Sisters of Charity, St Monica's, after almost five and a half years in prison.[57]

Some had expressed their willingness to enter a religious institution in their petitions from prison. For some who initially asked to be released to their family, their petitions became more modest over time. In May 1942, Flynn wrote that she would 'be willing to accept any terms with regard to Licence to finish my 20 years if I were allowed out'.[58] Discussions of what was to be done with Flynn include the note: 'I may add that she herself does not want to go to a convent.'[59] In October, Hannah relented: 'I am willing to go to the Good Shepherd Convent, Limerick and remain there.'[60] Mary

Table 5.4 Women conditionally discharged to religious institutions

Name	Institution	Institution type
Hannah Flynn	Good Shepherd Convent, Limerick	Magdalen laundry
Mary Moynihan	Our Lady's Home, Henrietta Street, Sisters of Charity of St Vincent de Paul	Other
Hannah O'Leary	Sisters of Charity, Cork	Magdalen laundry
Elizabeth Hannon	Our Lady of Charity Refuge, High Park, Dublin	Magdalen laundry
Mary Anne Keane	St Mary Magdalen's, Donnybrook, Sisters of Charity	Magdalen laundry
Deborah Sullivan	Our Lady's Home, Henrietta Street, Sisters of Charity of St Vincent de Paul	Other
Margaret Finn	St Mary Magdalen's, Donnybrook, Sisters of Charity	Magdalen laundry
Jane O'Brien	Our Lady's Home, Henrietta Street, Sisters of Charity of St Vincent de Paul	Other
Elizabeth Edwards	Our Lady's Home, Henrietta Street, Sisters of Charity of St Vincent de Paul	Other
Mary Somerville	Bethany Home, Dublin	Mother and baby home
Agnes McAdam	Good Shepherd Convent, New Ross, Wexford	Magdalen laundry

Moynihan also petitioned to be released to her family, but from 1930 her petitions included her willingness to enter a 'Home'. All Moynihan's petitions until this point had been refused, but in 1930 the Department of Justice, for the first time, began to consider her release seriously.[61] Jane O'Brien declared her willingness to enter a convent if that was the wish of the Department: 'In the event of a favourable hearing for this petition, I am ready to reside for a period in Henrietta Street Convent, and to give a promise of good behaviour.'[62]

Petitions were encouraged by religious visitors to prison. It was stated that Kate Owens had 'for some time past been visited regularly by the Sisters of Charity', and that there was one Sister 'who was deeply interested in her'.[63] Chaplains working in the prisons similarly urged women to petition for release to a 'Home' and worked behind the scenes to facilitate transfers, providing liaison between governors, the Department, probation officers and the institutions.[64] Mary Moynihan received considerable support from the Catholic chaplain who claimed he had 'never believed and do not now believe that Mary Moynihan was guilty of murder by actual participation in the act or by conspiracy prior to it'.[65] In a Lombrosian vein, the chaplain argued that in his 11 years working with convicts he had concluded that 'she is not the criminal type at all'. The chaplain argued that continued exposure to 'women, many of whom are a little mad, and nearly all completely bad', would provoke only 'despairing callousness' in Moynihan. Another Catholic chaplain cited similar reasoning in the case of Elizabeth Hannon, arguing that her release to a religious institution would provide 'whatever hope of permanent improvement' there was. He further outlined his view that she was not 'evily inclined' but was that 'type so frequently met with in prison who are led to evil without any great difficulty'.[66]

The work of Protestant chaplains was evident from the case of Mary Somerville; the Church of Ireland chaplain petitioned the Department for her release 'to one of our Protestant Homes for a period to be determined by you'.[67] Occasional interest from influential religious leaders was shown, such as Archdeacon Cathal McCarthy who corresponded directly with the Minister for Justice on Jane O'Brien's release to Henrietta Street, deemed appropriate because 'it is a place to which persons are sometimes committed by court and especially one of the Sisters there has been visiting Jane weekly for years & is her trusted friend'.[68] Hannah O'Leary found a place with the Sisters of Charity in Cork through the efforts of the Discharged Female Prisoners' Aid Society.[69]

The procedure of conditional discharge which saw women released to religious institutions was vague. A licence was issued to women, conditional on their willingness to enter an institution, and the obligation to report any change of address to the local

Garda station was duly remitted.[70] The procedures were ad hoc and women could not be compelled to remain in the institution if they chose to leave. The government's only solution in this scenario was to entirely cancel the licence and return the women to prison, but this mechanism was generally not used.[71] The absence of legal coercive power was due to the fact that the licences were not formally worded as conditional on entry to an institution; to achieve this, each licence would have to be brought before both Houses of the Oireachtas, the Irish Parliament, which the Department considered 'undesirable' in order to avoid 'harsh, tyrannical or absurd conditions'.[72] This lack of formal coercive power did not diminish the unofficial coercion, which was noted by the Department in their comment that women were 'unlikely' to leave.

Transfer was also conditional on the acquiescence of the particular institution. The Reverend Mother of the Good Shepherd Convent in Limerick had at first refused to take Hannah Flynn.[73] Flynn was declined by a number of institutions, prompting the Department to despair: 'I don't see that we can do anything in this case.' The Department outlined their unsuccessful attempts to have Flynn placed in an institution:

> The authorities at Our Lady's Home, Henrietta Street, who undertake the care of female prisoners on discharge, have definitely declined to take her, and enquiries by the Governor from all Institutions, including the Good Shepherd Convent, Limerick, have been equally unsuccessful.[74]

The archives revealed how a number of institutions could be approached to ascertain which would accept the woman, or which provided the most suitable 'fit'.[75] In the case of Margaret Finn, a plan of action was outlined whereby first the Magdalen laundry at Donnybrook, and then High Park, would be approached.[76]

The women were understood according to a binary of criminals versus sinners. Women convicted of infant murder were considered less 'criminal' but more morally culpable. Indeed, 'The notion of moral criminality was ingrained in most public debates on the issue of illegitimacy.'[77] There were associated gradations of condemnation attached to each institution; Henrietta Street was considered suitable for women who had not 'fallen'. Probation officer

Kathleen Sullivan[78] wrote in 1930 that Henrietta Street was 'open to girls who have erred in other directions, but who have not led a life of vice'.[79] Probation officer E. M. Carroll noted in 1941 that Henrietta Street was for the 'better types'.[80] Mary Moynihan was first accepted into the Sisters of Charity at Donnybrook in Dublin, a Magdalen laundry,[81] but probation officer Sullivan viewed this institution as unsuitable:

> This latter Convent is a Home for Penitents, and I should not like a girl, who was under twenty when [she went] to Mountjoy, and who had not associated with women of evil life, to be placed among such women, if a convent of a different type is willing to receive her. The Convent in Henrietta Street does not receive women of the unfortunate class, and for this reason is, in my opinion, more likely to have a reformative effect on Mary Moynihan than a Magdalen Home would have.[82]

Women deemed in need of moral reform, and whose home circumstances did not speak favourably to unconditional release, found themselves in a further period of confinement post-prison in this mesh of religious institutions. The gendered nature of this regime was clear from the case of Edward O'Connor. In 1948, O'Connor was convicted of the murder of his illegitimate infant in circumstances similar to many women who committed the same offence. Doyle and O'Callaghan note the judge's comments on O'Connor as 'of a rather low order of intelligence, rather weak in character and not likely to stand up to any crisis'.[83] These comments would not be out of place in the cases of female defendants. And yet, O'Connor was released on licence from his commuted sentence after three years. It seems likely that a woman so sentenced, and deemed to be of a weak intellect, would have spent some time in a religious institution prior to her ultimate release.

Time spent in religious institutions

Magdalen laundries offered a starker alternative to Henrietta Street. Carroll noted that such institutions held an expectation of lifelong confinement, 'with the purpose of leading the subjects to permanent renunciation of the world and to a life of penance'.[84] This is clear from the outcomes for women transferred from prison to a laundry compared with those women transferred to institutions such as Henrietta Street. Table 5.5 demonstrates that the length of confinement varied considerably in each case. Table 5.6 shows the total time reprieved women spent confined in various sites of confinement.

From Table 5.6, the disparity in the length of time reprieved women spent coercively confined becomes apparent. Hannah Flynn was convicted at the age of 28, and spent the rest of her life either in prison or in a religious institution. Mary Kiernan in contrast spent only six months in prison before she was released.

There are difficulties in establishing release dates for women transferred to religious institutions. Although conditional discharge to religious institutions was recorded by the Department of Justice, the eventual release or death of the women was not. Further information was gleaned from the McAleese Report, which presented anonymised case studies, three of which could be identified as reprieved women.[85] The lack of access to the archives of religious orders renders investigation of the fates of individual woman difficult. For instance, an enquiry sent to the Department of Justice in 1965 on the case of Agnes McAdam, who was released from prison to a laundry in 1949, received the response: 'the subject of your enquiry was released several years ago to the care of a religious community. It is not known to the Department if the person is still alive.'[86] O'Donnell, from reviews of death records, ascertained that McAdam had remained in the laundry for over 13 years, before being transferred to a nursing home where she died.[87]

Release from religious institutions

Women were informed that the date of their eventual release from a religious institution was largely dependent on their own conduct.[88] Probation officer Sullivan often reminded the Department of this pledge. Such assurances were also sometimes invoked by the women themselves, such as Mary Anne Keane, who reminded Sullivan that she had been promised eventual release from Donnybrook

Table 5.5 Time spent in religious institutions

Name	Entry	Exit	Institution
Hannah Flynn	23 October 1942	After 30 years, released to county hospital where she died	Magdalen laundry
Mary Moynihan	18 July 1930	Paid situation in St Philomena's children's home, Stillorgan, Dublin, summer 1932	Our Lady's Home
Hannah O'Leary	18 September 1942	Died in the Sisters of Charity, Cork, after 21 years[1]	Magdalen laundry
Elizabeth Hannon	17 July 1930	Died there approximately 30 years later	Magdalen laundry
Mary Anne Keane	4 November 1930	Unknown; Keane was still there in July 1936	Magdalen laundry
Deborah Sullivan	2 November 1929	Paid situation in St Anne's, Northbrook Road, Dublin, December 1932	Our Lady's Home
Margaret Finn	3 October 1933	Died there an unknown number of years later	Magdalen laundry
Jane O'Brien	21 July 1941	Unknown	Our Lady's Home
Elizabeth Edwards	6 September 1937	Released to family December 1938	Our Lady's Home
Mary Somerville	23 December 1940	Left 14 February 1941	Mother and baby home
Agnes McAdam	30 September 1949	Transferred to a nursing home to die 13 and a half years after admittance[2]	Magdalen laundry

[1] O'Donnell, *Justice, Mercy, and Caprice*, p. 233.
[2] O'Donnell, *Justice, Mercy, and Caprice*, p. 234.

Table 5.6 Total time confined in prison and religious institutions
from date of conviction

Name	Approximate length of confinement from date of conviction
Hannah Flynn	48 years, 7 months
Mary Moynihan	7 years, 7 months
Hannah O'Leary	38 years
Elizabeth Doran	4 years, 11 months
Elizabeth Hannon	32 years
Mary Kiernan	6 months
Mary Anne Keane	Unknown (at least 5 years, 7 months)
Deborah Sullivan	3 years, 5 months
Catherine Ahearne	3 years, 11 months
Annie Walsh (1929)	6 years, 7 months
Christina Russell	3 years, 3 months
Margaret Finn	Unknown (at least 4 years, 7 months)
Jane O'Brien	Unknown (at least 9 years, 1 month)
Elizabeth Edwards	3 years, 8 months
Rose Edwards	1 year, 8 months
Mary Somerville	2 years, 3 months
Kate Owens	5 years, 5 months
Agnes McAdam	17 years
Mary Bernadette Agnes Daly	4 years, 8 months[i]
Frances Cox	7 years, 4 months
Mamie Cadden	2 years, 6 months

[i] The case of Mary Daly presents some uncertainties. A documentary on her case suggested she spent ten years in a religious home post-prison, but there is nothing to confirm this in the Department of Justice archives which instead cite a date for release on indefinite licence of 23 November 1953. The information that she spent ten years in a convent is from *Idir Mná* (season 2, episode 3) (Ireland: Midas Productions Ltd, 2009), which aired on Tuesday 12 October 2010 on TG4. The documentation bearing the date of the indefinite licence is in NAI, Department of Justice 171/7781. Penal Record of Convict.

laundry.[89] Despite this, factors extraneous to the women's conduct were key to release. Securing a second release, this time from religious control, was contingent on issues of family support and suitability, and judgements as to individual mental capacity (tinged inevitably by judgements on morality).

Family

'Wantedness' and concerns for future care informed decisions. As with unconditional release from prison, support structures were essential to escaping religious confinement. Mary Moynihan received letters and visits from her family throughout her time in prison, and the goodwill experienced by Moynihan continued through her period of confinement in Henrietta Street, from where she was released in 1932.[90] Elizabeth Edwards was also supported by her family members who continually petitioned that she might be released from Henrietta Street:

> Regarding my unfortunate daughter, Elizabeth Edwards who suffered so much then being sentenced to death, if nothing more it was enough to ruin her health and nerves for life, I'm now asking you in your kindness of heart to allow her home to me for this holy feast Xmas, when all members of family are anxious to be together.[91]

In contrast, Hannah O'Leary remained in prison for almost two decades before discharge to a religious institution because no one could be found who would undertake to care for her: 'The question of her release on licence has been considered from time to time but nothing could be done in the matter as she had neither home nor relatives and no Institution was willing to take her.'[92] The same concerns followed O'Leary to the Sisters of Charity laundry in Cork. Agnes McAdam, meanwhile, was transferred from prison to a religious institution as her family refused responsibility for her.[93]

Even when family actively supported a woman's return, the judgement that such family were unsuitable could prolong confinement in both prison and a religious institution. This occurred in the case of Hannah Flynn, who, in common with Hannah O'Leary, was discharged to a religious institution after almost two decades in prison. Unsuitability was often a coded reference to poverty, perceived immorality or abnormality. Hannah Flynn's family were the subject of unflattering reports by the local Garda: 'All members of the family are willing to receive Hannah, but as they still appear to be sub-normal mentally, it is thought they would not be suitable to take care of the prisoner.'[94] This was reinforced by a personal acquaintance of the Governor, who wrote that while he 'should be very sorry to deprive anybody of their liberty ... home, such as it is, is not the best place for Hannah Flynn'.[95] The perceived immorality of Margaret Finn's mother, whose character was described as 'not very exemplary', prevented her unconditional release from prison and later from the Sisters of Charity laundry at Donnybrook. Despite the petitioning of Finn's mother, Margaret's illegitimate brother was cited as evidence of her family's unsuitability.[96] Compounding this, Finn's mother was also reported to be 'not in possession of any land save two small gardens'.[97] Mary Anne Keane's release from a religious institution was conditional on her husband's agreement to take her back, but his refusal to accept his wife prolonged Keane's confinement.[98]

Infantilisation

For those for whom no release was forthcoming, they were subject to intensely paternalistic discourses which infantilised and pathologised them. The obliviousness of some of the women to discussions about their future is clear in the correspondence on Hannah O'Leary and Hannah Flynn, in which the Department communicated to the Governor that, 'The prisoners should not be permitted to obtain any inkling that the question of their release on licence is under consideration.'[99]

While sub-psychiatric discourses smoothed the extension of clemency to death-sentenced women, these diagnoses also served to caution against release. Elizabeth Hannon's possible release from a religious institution was not recommended on the grounds that she was 'almost a mental defective'.[100] Probation officer Kathleen Sullivan observed that: 'They [the nuns] consider her very much below normal in intellect and think she would not be very safe in the world.'[101] In the case of Mary Anne Keane, her classification as below average intelligence prevented her release from religious confinement; probation officer Sullivan noted that Keane was 'a woman of low mentality. It would not be possible to place her in a situation such as domestic servant.'[102] Sullivan, writing on both Hannon and Keane, remarked that they were 'safer where they are' as neither was 'fit to face the world'.[103] The judgements of the religious congregations were also instrumental in decisions on release.

Again, on Elizabeth Hannon: 'the authorities in High Park do not recommend an early release as she has settled down and appears content. ... [S]he never speaks about the future or asks about her eventual release.'[104]

Allied to a dim view of some women as unable to care for themselves, it was also believed that these women would be unable to hold positions as domestic servants, effectively leaving them with no means of support. Their future productivity was therefore linked to release. In contrast, Mary Moynihan had a glittering 'career' through both prison and Henrietta Street and the Catholic chaplain in Mountjoy Prison believed she 'would lead a useful life if released while still young'.[105] Moynihan's productivity meant she was offered a situation following her release from Henrietta Street and she went to St Philomena's children's home in Dublin in August 1932.[106] Deborah Sullivan too accepted a situation in St Anne's in Dublin and was released from Henrietta Street in December 1932.[107] Both women accepted these positions to avoid returning home. In Deborah Sullivan's case, it was stated that, 'She does not want to face the neighbours around her home.'[108] Kate Owens similarly accepted a position while in prison, the position of maid in St Monica's Home, as her 'conduct and industry have been excellent throughout her sentence'.[109] The Sisters of Charity wrote to the Department that they were 'very interested' in Owens, and that St Monica's had 'seventy widows there at present, and a person of Kate's stamp would suit admirably'.[110] Kate Owens was still residing in St Monica's in 1951, but by 1956 she had moved on, and reported to the Garda that she had 'a very nice place here ... I am nearly two years here and the people I work for don't know anything of my past'.[111] Owens was subsequently relieved of the duty to report change of address to the Garda.

Mary Somerville was a rare case of determined agency, of a reprieved woman who navigated her way out of religious confinement. Somerville was an older woman who had farmed her own land prior to arrest. While in prison, she petitioned for release with a comprehensive account of her future plans.[112] She was duly released to the Bethany Home on 23 December 1940, which she left on 14 February 1941 having made the necessary arrangements. Somerville wrote to the Department to inform them, leaving a forwarding address in Northern Ireland: 'Just a line to let you no [*sic*] I am now leaving Bethany Home and is going to see my son. ... I am going to make my home there. ... Yours truly, Mary Somerville.'[113] In 1942, Somerville wrote again from her residence in Northern Ireland, and asked, and was refused, a free pardon.[114] Somerville's age, her ability to fend for herself and the nature of the institution no doubt combined to ease her path to freedom.

Informal religious detention

The literature on laundries and related institutions speaks to harsh and punitive regimes. A report from Henrietta Street on Elizabeth Edwards' progress illustrated the benevolent/punitive dichotomy of institutionalisation; the probation officer wrote that the 'Rev Mother said she would like her opinion to be expressed that the girl has now been sufficiently punished'.[115] It had been suggested that Elizabeth Edwards assume a different name on entry to Henrietta Street, which the Department had refused.[116] The need for secrecy was stated prior to Agnes McAdam's entry to the Good Shepherd laundry in Wexford by the Superioress, who wrote to the chaplain: 'Please Father, will you impress on her the necessity of keeping her secret? No one here will ever know anything about her except self and the Sister in charge of the girls.'[117] Other women, such as Mary Anne Keane, were unhappy in the religious institution. It was noted in 1936 that Keane was 'very unsettled in the Convent and desires to be liberated on licence'.[118] Despite the informality and discretionary nature of detention, the implicit coercive power, as experienced by women who were already marginalised, was overwhelming. The McAleese Report stated that women referred by the criminal justice system, 'were made aware of why they were there and – in the case of court referrals – how long they were required to stay',[119] but this was not the case for women transferred from prison.

The informal and discretionary processes which governed transfer can be seen in a comment from Stephen Roche, the Secretary at the Department of Justice, in relation to Christina Russell, who was being considered for release from prison either to a religious institution or to her family: 'I always approach a case of this kind with the helpless sort of feeling that there is no reliable standard for one's guidance.'[120] The discretionary nature of confinement, and the tacit acceptance that women remained in the institutions by virtue of informal coercion, was made clear in the following comment on Elizabeth Edwards' continued confinement:

> I am still of opinion that she might safely be permitted to return home, & we have in any event no power to keep her in the Home if she leaves of her own volition as residence in the Home was not a condition of her licence.[121]

Probation officer Sullivan was of the opinion that the provision of a future release date would aid rehabilitation:

> It does seem desirable that the Rev Mother of Convents to which prisoners undergoing a life sentence are sent should be in a position to hold out some tangible hope of release. It is perhaps difficult to bind yourself at this stage to any very short term, but I think the prisoner could be assured that there was no question of holding her for life, and that if she were well conducted and showed definite signs of reform she might expect to be released at the end of a few years.[122]

Sullivan and the Reverend Mother of Henrietta Street both held this view; however, the Reverend Mother also required that women serving sentences of penal servitude who were sent to her would be required to stay for a minimum period. Sullivan wrote that:

> [T]here has always been a tacit understanding with Henrietta Street and other convents that no one would be sent to them unless they were to remain a year or eighteen months. This period is necessary to form good habits and to give any training. Apart from this, a constant coming and going among the inmates is unsettling.[123]

Probation officer Sullivan emerges from the archives as an occasional advocate for the women. She regularly reminded the Department that they had been promised hope of eventual release. Despite a corpus of informally articulated notions regarding the proper disposal of women serving sentences of penal servitude, there were no official guidelines on how they would achieve eventual unconditional release. Therefore, just as the Eucharistic Congress of 1932 was used to petition for the reprieve of death sentences, it also provided motivation for probation officer Sullivan to petition for the release of women from religious confinement. Sullivan contacted the Department in relation to four women – Mary Moynihan, Deborah Sullivan, Elizabeth Hannon and Mary Anne Keane – who were at that time detained in various institutions. In response to her appeal, Secretary Roche wrote, 'All four women are deserving of pity and help rather than of further punishment.'[124] The ad hoc nature of transfer to and release from religious institutions rendered such opportunistic petitioning necessary as there was no officially accepted 'end date' to the periods of confinement.[125]

A Department of Justice document which considered the fate of Mary Anne Keane suggested the rarity with which some women left the institutions:

> Going back as far as 1928 I can trace only one case in which a convict released on licence to a 'Home' was afterwards allowed to leave the 'Home' and take up a situation outside. In the other cases the women were sent to other Homes or Convents as domestic servants, etc.[126]

This illustrates the difficulty of leaving the network of religious institutions entirely – their 'sticky' rather than 'porous' quality – as demonstrated by the paths of those who went on to employment still within the system of religious institutions. The attitude of the Sacred Heart Home in Roscommon, which unsuccessfully undertook to effect reconciliation between Mary Anne Keane and her husband, spoke volumes on the attitude held by some, particularly perhaps those women convicted of infant murder:

> Why cannot she remain with the nuns there, and try to be happy under the circumstances. She should be grateful to have escaped execution and now try to make reparations to God for her dreadful deed.[127]

Conclusion

For women reprieved from a sentence of death, their negotiations for clemency did not cease once they were free of the condemned cell. The petitioning of women from prison, while they cannot be read uncritically, provide rare examples of the women's voices. In this light, petitions illustrate the position of women within their families and reveal the emotional and physical strains of imprisonment. Further, the petitions demonstrate sparks of resistance and anger, which serve to acknowledge the lived experience of imprisonment and confinement, and the subjectivities of reprieved women.

Reprieved women's experiences of imprisonment differed significantly from reprieved men. Ballinger has referenced the 'life after punishment' experienced by reprieved women confined in semi-penal sites; it is suggested herein that 'punishment' did not end at the prison door for such women.[128] In Ireland, release from prison often worked to conceal gendered punishment regimes which captured women for life. The transcarceration of women from prison to religious institutions contributed to the fall in the rates of women's imprisonment post-1922, as imprisonment came to be viewed as inappropriate for women. Farrell found that throughout the nineteenth century, women were assisted to emigrate from convict prisons.[129] This was abandoned in favour of religious confinement post-1922, certainly for women viewed as unsuitable for release to the community. This contrasts with the experiences of men post-1922, who were encouraged to emigrate following release from a term of penal servitude.[130]

Notes

1 Mary Raftery and Eoin O'Sullivan, *Suffer the Little Children: The Inside Story of Ireland's Industrial Schools* (Dublin: New Island, 1999); James M. Smith, *Ireland's Magdalen Laundries and the Nation's Architecture of Containment* (Manchester: Manchester University Press, 2008); Eoin O'Sullivan and Ian O'Donnell, *Coercive Confinement in Ireland: Patients, Prisoners and Penitents* (Manchester: Manchester University Press, 2012).

2 Inter-departmental Committee to Establish the Facts of State Involvement with the Magdalen Laundries, 'McAleese Report' (Dublin: Department of Justice and Equality, 2013); Mother and Baby Homes Commission of Investigation, 'Mother and Baby Homes Commission of Investigation Final Report' (Department of Children, Equality, Disability, Integration and Youth, 30 October 2020).

3 Raftery and O'Sullivan, *Suffer the Little Children*; Smith, *Ireland's Magdalen Laundries*; O'Sullivan and O'Donnell, *Coercive Confinement in Ireland*.

4 NAI, Department of Justice 18/2769A. Note from Mountjoy Prison, 6 November 1936.

5 Diarmuid Griffin, *Killing Time: Life Imprisonment and Parole in Ireland* (London: Palgrave Macmillan, 2019).

6 David M. Doyle and Ian O'Donnell, 'The death penalty in post-independent Ireland', *Journal of Legal History*, 33:1 (2012) 65–91.

7 Ian O'Donnell, *Justice, Mercy, and Caprice: Clemency and the Death Penalty in Ireland* (Oxford: Oxford University Press, 2017).

8 Lynsey Black, '"On the other hand, the accused is a woman": women and the death penalty in post-independence Ireland', *Law and History Review*, 36:1 (2018) 139–72.

9 Kate Owens was a 'persistent offender' and had previously been convicted of concealment of birth.

10 Reference to the 'working rule' made in the files: NAI, Department of Justice 234/2016; Department of Justice 234/2603; Department of Justice 234/3332.

11 NAI, Department of Justice 234/3332. Letter from Stephen Roche, 17 November 1933.

12 NAI, Department of Justice 18/2769A. Note from Mountjoy Prison, 6 November 1936.

13 NAI, Department of Justice 234/2599.

14 NAI, Department of Justice 234/1744. Petition of Mary Moynihan, 19 July 1928.

15 NAI, Department of Justice 234/1491. Petition of Mary Kiernan, 31 January 1927.

16 NAI, Department of Justice 234/3118A. Letter from Kate Finn, 12 July 1933.

17 NAI, Department of Justice 18/2769A. Petition of Hannah Flynn, 5 July 1931.

18 NAI, Department of Justice 234/1744. Petition of Mary Moynihan, 22 January 1930.

19 NAI, Department of Justice 234/1744. Petition of Mary Moynihan, 28 June 1930.

20 NAI, Department of Justice 18/2770A. Petition of Hannah O'Leary, 14 March 1934.

21 NAI, Department of Justice 18/2737A. Petition of Jane O'Brien, 8 July 1941.

22 NAI, Department of Justice 18/3110A. Petition of Mary Somerville, 14 December 1940.

23 Visiting regulations allowed varying number and lengths of visits according to sentence type and how long had been served.

24 NAI, Department of Justice 18/2769A. Note from Mountjoy Prison, 14 May 1942.

25 NAI, Department of Justice 18/6678A. Petition of Kate Owens, 22 May 1947.

26 NAI, Department of Justice 234/1744. Petition of Mary Moynihan, 22 January 1930.

27 Just as the Department of Justice granted Catherine permission to leave prison to join her husband in Australia, contact with Laurence Ahearne was broken. It was later reported that he had been admitted to hospital suffering from alcohol-related ill-health. NAI, Department of Justice 234/2603.

28 NAI, Department of Justice 234/3118A. Petition of Margaret Finn, 28 September 1931.

29 NAI, Department of Justice 234/1744. Petition of Mary Moynihan, 19 July 1928.

30 NAI, Department of Justice 18/6678A. Petition of Kate Owens, 26 May 1948.

31 NAI, Department of Justice 234/1744. Petition of Mary Moynihan, 19 July 1928.

32 NAI, Department of Justice 234/1744. Petition of Mary Moynihan, 4 November 1927.

33 NAI, Department of Justice 18/3540. Petition of Mary Anne Keane, 19 September 1930.

34 Lindsey Earner-Byrne, 'The rape of Mary M: a microhistory of sexual violence and moral redemption in 1920s Ireland', *Journal of the History of Sexuality*, 24:1 (2015) 75–98.

35 Earner-Byrne, 'The rape of Mary M.', p. 79.

36 Anne Worrall, 'Discourse analysis', in Eugene McLaughlin and John Muncie (eds), *The Sage Handbook of Criminology* (Thousand Oaks, CA: Sage, 2005).

37 NAI, Department of Justice 18/3110A. Petition of Mary Somerville, 14 December 1940.

38 NAI, Department of Justice 234/1491. Letter to Governor of Mountjoy Prison, 27 January 1927.

39 NAI, Department of Justice 234/1491. Garda report, undated.

40 NAI, Department of Justice 234/3332. Note from Governor of Mountjoy Prison, 1 June 1933.

41 NAI, Department of Justice 234/2603. Letter from M. J. O'Connor & Co. Solicitors, 10 June 1933.

42 NAI, Department of Justice 18/885A.

43 NAI, Department of Justice 18/11757A. Petition of Frances Cox, 21 November 1956.

44 NAI, Department of Justice 18/11757A. Memorandum from Governor of Mountjoy Prison, 3 December 1956.

45 Louise Brangan, 'Pastoral penality in 1970s Ireland: addressing the pains of imprisonment', *Theoretical Criminology*, 25:1 (2021) 44–65.

46 Dublin Diocesan Archives (DDA) of Archbishop John Charles McQuaid. AB8/b/XXVIII/983. Memorandum prepared by E. M. Carroll, probation officer at Dublin Metropolitan Courthouse, forwarded in a letter, 9 July 1941.

47 NAI, Department of Justice 234/3332. Minute Sheet, January 1931.

48 NAI, Department of Justice 18/2770A. Letter from Mountjoy Prison to Minister for Justice, 1 January 1938, enclosing details of female convicts undergoing a sentence of penal servitude for life who have served ten years of their sentence, in compliance with a Circular of 426 of 19 August 1894.

49 NAI, Department of Justice 18/2769A. Letter from John Kelly, Holy Cross College, Clonliffe to Governor of Mountjoy Prison, 30 September 1942. This was likely a reference to Margaret Dillon, who was sentenced to four years' penal servitude in December 1940 for the manslaughter of her infant.

50 NAI, Department of An Taoiseach S.13383B. Memorandum, 12 April 1949.

51 NAI, Department of Justice 18/6678A. 10 November 1947.

52 NAI, Department of Justice 18/2769A. Report prepared by P. Connolly, 27 July 1942.

53 NAI, Department of Justice 18/885A.

54 NAI, Department of Justice 234/1744. Letter from John Fitzpatrick, Junior Roman Catholic Chaplain to Minister for Justice, 6 November 1927.

55 NAI, Department of Justice 18/885A.

56 NAI, Department of Justice 234/3332. Letter from Miss Boland to Judge McElliot, 13 November 1933.

57 NAI, Department of Justice 18/6678A.

58 NAI, Department of Justice 18/2769A. Petition of Hannah Flynn, 12 May 1942.

59 NAI, Department of Justice 18/2769A. Report prepared by P. Connolly, 27 July 1942.

60 NAI, Department of Justice 18/2769A. Petition of Hannah Flynn, 8 October 1942.

61 NAI, Department of Justice 234/1744.

62 NAI, Department of Justice 3/A18/2737. Note, 15 July 1932.

63 NAI, Department of Justice 18/6678A. Memorandum, 12 April 1949.

64 The possessive domain of chaplains within Mountjoy Prison can be demonstrated in an exchange relating to the request, by a minister of the Jehovah Witness faith, that he be allowed to visit Mamie Cadden at her request. The Department of Justice were disinclined to allow the visit, and noted that the chaplain would also 'strongly object' to this visit. NAI, Department of Justice 18/3562. Letter, 13 March 1958.

65 NAI, Department of Justice 234/1744. Letter from John Fitzpatrick, Junior Roman Catholic chaplain, 6 November 1927.

66 NAI, Department of Justice 234/2016. Note of Canon McMahon, 2 February 1930.

67 NAI, Department of Justice 18/3110A. Letter, 14 November 1940.

68 NAI, Department of Justice 18/2737A. Letter from Cathal McCarthy, 9 July 1941.

69 NAI, Department of Justice 18/2770A. Memorandum, 20 August 1942.

70 Female convicts were otherwise required to report change of address to the nearest Garda station, while male convicts were required to report monthly. The licences were issued under the Penal Servitude Acts 1853 to 1891, and the remitting of reporting requirements was provided for by section 5 of the Prevention of Crime Act 1871.

71 See NAI, Department of Justice 234/2590 file on Deborah Sullivan. Minutes, 29 October 1929, for discussions on this.

72 NAI, Department of Justice 234/1744.

73 NAI, Department of Justice 18/2769A. Note, 6 October 1942.

74 NAI, Department of Justice 18/2769A. Report by P. Connolly, 27 July 1942.

75 Gloucester Street was first considered for Agnes McAdam, but she ultimately went to the Good Shepherd in Wexford, see NAI, Department of Justice 18/9074A.

76 NAI, Department of Justice 234/3118A.

77 Lindsey Earner-Byrne, 'Reinforcing the family: the role of gender, morality and sexuality in Irish welfare policy, 1922–1944', *History of the Family*, 13:4 (2008) 360–9, p. 364.

78 The 1907 Probation of Offenders Act established a more formal system, limited initially to Dublin, but the involvement of religious volunteers continued. Probation in Ireland remained small scale,

informal and supplemented by religious voluntary members until the 1970s. Gerry McNally, 'Probation in Ireland: a brief history of the early years', *Irish Probation Journal*, 4 (2007) 5–24.

79 NAI, Department of Justice 234/1744. Letter from Kathleen Sullivan to Department of Justice, 21 June 1930.

80 DDA of Archbishop John Charles McQuaid. AB8/b/XXVIII/983. Memorandum prepared by E. M. Carroll, probation officer at Dublin Metropolitan Courthouse, forwarded in a letter of 9 July 1941.

81 NAI, Department of Justice 234/1744. 12 March 1930.

82 NAI, Department of Justice 234/1744. Letter from Kathleen Sullivan, 21 June 1930.

83 NAI, JUS/18/11108 (Edward O'Connor), Justice Davitt to Mac Eoin, 28 October 1948, in David M. Doyle and Liam O'Callaghan, *Capital Punishment in Independent Ireland: A Social, Legal and Political History* (Liverpool: Liverpool University Press, 2019), p. 93.

84 DDA of Archbishop John Charles McQuaid. AB8/b/XXVIII/983. Memorandum prepared by E. M. Carroll, probation officer at Dublin Metropolitan Courthouse, forwarded in a letter of 9 July 1941.

85 The McAleese Report recorded that an estimated 8.8 per cent of women either died in a Magdalen laundry or died elsewhere and were buried there. The Report found 879 such cases.

86 NAI, Department of Justice 18/9074B. Letter, 15 February 1965.

87 O'Donnell, *Justice, Mercy, and Caprice.*

88 Such as: 'The convict should be informed that while she is liable to be detained in the Institution named, she may, if her conduct is satisfactory, be released in a few years, the period being largely dependent on her good behaviour.' NAI, Department of Justice 234/3118A. Letter, 26 September 1933.

89 NAI, Department of Justice 18/3540.

90 NAI, Department of Justice 234/1744.

91 NAI, Department of Justice 18/885A. Letter from Kathleen Edwards, 1 December 1938.

92 NAI, Department of Justice 18/2770A. Memorandum, 20 August 1942.

93 NAI, Department of Justice 18/9074A. Note from Catholic chaplain, 4 March 1949, and letter from Agnes's family, 15 March 1949.

94 NAI, Department of Justice 18/2769A. Garda report, 29 May 1942.

95 NAI, Department of Justice 18/2769A. Letter from Gerald Foley to Governor Sean Kavanagh, 19 February 1939. In the Garda report, 8 February 1939, Hannah's brother was recorded as being in the employment of a farmer named Gerald Foley.

96 NAI, Department of Justice 234/3118A. Garda report, 31 July 1933.

97 NAI, Department of Justice 234/3118A. Garda report, 31 July 1933.

98 NAI, Department of Justice 18/3540.

99 NAI, Department of Justice 18/2770A. Letter, 27 January 1939.

100 NAI, Department of Justice 234/2016. 15 January 1932.

101 NAI, Department of Justice 234/2016. 13 April 1932.

102 NAI, Department of Justice 18/3540. 14 June 1929.

103 NAI, Department of Justice 234/1744. Memorandum prepared by Stephen Roche, 15 April 1932.

104 NAI, Department of Justice 234/2016. Document, 13 April 1932.

105 NAI, Department of Justice 234/1744. Letter from Catholic chaplain, 8 November 1927.

106 On the file of Elizabeth and Rose Edwards, NAI, Department of Justice 18/885A.

107 On the file of Elizabeth and Rose Edwards, NAI, Department of Justice 18/885A.

108 NAI, Department of Justice 234/2590. Letter from probation officer Sullivan, 27 June 1932.

109 NAI, Department of Justice 18/6678A. Memorandum, 11 April 1949.

110 NAI, Department of Justice 18/6678A. Letter, 16 March 1949.

111 NAI, Department of Justice 18/6678B. Letter from Kate Owens, 14 September 1956.

112 NAI, Department of Justice 18/3110A.

113 NAI, Department of Justice 18/3110A. Letter, undated.

114 NAI, Department of Justice 18/3110A.

115 NAI, Department of Justice 18/885A. Report by chief wardress Watters, 14 September 1938.

116 NAI, Department of Justice 18/885A. Letter from chief wardress Watters, 17 July 1937, and from Reverend Mother, 24 August 1937.

117 NAI, Department of Justice 18/9074A. Letter from Superioress, 13 August 1949. Underlining in original.

118 NAI, Department of Justice 18/3540. Letter from probation officer Mary O'Brien, 7 May 1936.

119 McAleese Report, p. 3.

120 NAI, Department of Justice 234/3332. Letter from Stephen Roche to the Minister for Justice, 17 November 1933.

121 NAI, Department of Justice 18/885A. 3 December 1938.

122 NAI, Department of Justice 234/2016. Letter from probation officer Kathleen Sullivan to Minister for Justice, 27 June 1930.

123 NAI, Department of Justice 234/1744. Letter from probation officer Kathleen Sullivan, 10 February 1931.

124 NAI, Department of Justice 234/1744. Document prepared by Stephen Roche, 15 April 1932.
125 NAI, Department of Justice 18/2737A. Letter, 8 July 1941.
126 NAI, Department of Justice 18/3540. 20 May 1936.
127 NAI, Department of Justice 18/3540. Letter from Sacred Heart Home, Roscommon to probation officer O'Brien, 23 July 1936.
128 Anette Ballinger, 'Feminist research, state power and executed women: the case of Louie Calvert', in Stephen Farrall, Mike Hough, Shadd Maruna and Richard Sparks (eds), *Escape Routes: Contemporary Perspectives on Life after Punishment* (London: Routledge/Cavendish, 2011).
129 Elaine Farrell, '"The salvation of them": emigration to North America from the nineteenth-century Irish women's convict prison', *Women's History Review*, 25:4 (2016) 619–37.
130 O'Donnell, *Justice, Mercy, and Caprice*.

6

Motherhood and child-killing

Most women prosecuted for murder had been accused of killing a child, most commonly an infant. Of 292 women, 258 were charged with the murder of a child, in the great majority of instances their own (220 of the 258 women).[1] That most of the women who stood accused were the mother of the victim raises questions about the meanings of motherhood and strongly implicates the wider context of Irish society in these decades, particularly in cases of 'illegitimate motherhood'. This chapter explores the cases of women charged with child-killing, and elaborates on the distinctive cohort of women who were capitally convicted. The fact of a murder conviction for this handful of women is suggestive of cases exhibiting more heinous circumstances, yet their death sentences instead reflected a more punitive period. The chapter explores the ambiguities in attempting to define murder in the context of child-killing, both legally and socially. The chapter also investigates the women charged with the murder of children beyond their own family, a vanishingly small cohort of just two teenage girls whose cases necessitated a strikingly different narrative. The chapter finally considers how motherhood figured for the women appearing before the courts, both in mitigation of wrongdoing and in those cases in which women were separated from their children and in which we can occasionally glimpse the concerns of mothers who worried about the welfare of children in their absence.

Overwhelmingly, as research from other jurisdictions has also demonstrated,[2] child-killing in Ireland was bound up with 'illegitimacy'. Of the cases which involved child-killing within the family, the overwhelming majority involved cases of either illegitimacy or ambiguous legitimacy. The individualisation of responsibility in these cases, and the promotion of institutional responses to unmarried motherhood, can be devastatingly counterpointed by the levels of infant mortality in these institutions.[3] The 'solution' to illegitimacy, and indeed the preferred punishment for many women convicted of doing away with an unwanted infant, were those same institutions in which thousands of infants died.

Mothers accused

When the press reported on cases of child-killing by a mother, illegitimacy was often included as a newsworthy detail, suggesting an immediate frame of understanding. And in most cases, illegitimacy *was* a relevant consideration. For cases of married women who killed their children, explanation was harder to come by and, as discussed in Chapter 3, insanity was more readily found in such cases.[4] Of the cases under review, 220 mothers were accused of the murder of their child. The great majority of these victims were infants. Extensive research by other scholars has produced a stark and compelling view of illegitimacy and infant murder in Ireland through the nineteenth and twentieth centuries. Rattigan has noted the profile of these 'girl murderers', generally in their mid-twenties, from the lower socio-economic classes, typically from rural areas or small towns, and most often employed in domestic service or providing similar work within their own families without remuneration.[5] Beyond the 'girl murderer', others among the accused were married but separated, or widowed, and could not have hoped to pass the infant as the legitimate child of a husband. Illegitimacy, and the impetus to conceal, provided the immediate spur to act for a considerable proportion of women before the courts tried with murder.

Inevitably, considerable numbers concealed their pregnancies and gave birth alone.[6] Many women in this period, especially in rural Ireland, continued to give birth at home without medical assistance, often availing of untrained local midwives or 'handywomen'.[7] Efforts to conceal, compounded by evidence that no preparation had been made for the care of an infant, were often cited as evidence of motive. Mary McCreanor, who pleaded guilty to concealment in 1939, revealed that she had given birth alone in the early hours, on a Wicklow beach: 'Shortly afterwards the baby was born where I was on the sand. I cried a little. I was very weak. I tried to stand up with the baby in my arms but I staggered and it fell out of my arms into the sea.'[8] Home births could be traumatic experiences, as recounted by the father of Joan Carroll:

> She was throwing her hands and gnashing her teeth during all that period. The fits were accompanied by snoring and a little screaming. I am quite satisfied she was unconscious during all that period. I could not put her back in bed without the help of [her sister]. She appeared to be lifeless.[9]

Women who gave birth alone or without medical assistance were often recommended to mercy explicitly because of the difficult circumstances of childbirth. Conflicting accounts in the case of Catherine Ahearne, capitally convicted in 1929, demonstrated the desirability of a narrative of solo birth, which rendered the mother a more sympathetic figure while avoiding the suggestion of family complicity. Ahearne's evidence stated that she had given birth alone in a field.[10] However, her young brother's initial statement claimed that the infant had been born early on Sunday morning, and that he had seen his mother with the child in her arms after Easter Sunday mass.[11]

Many women continued in their employment as domestic servants until the birth, concealing their condition from employers who sometimes turned a very blind eye to what was happening. As both Farrell and Rattigan illustrated, pregnant women in domestic service risked being turned out of their employment.[12] Hannah O'Brien, who pleaded guilty to concealment in 1931, had given birth in the home of her employer, and when he found the soiled clothing he told Hannah to leave.[13] Mary Carty, who pleaded guilty to concealment in 1925, gave birth in an outhouse at the Galway docks after her dismissal from the Skeffington Arms Hotel, a fact condemned by the judge in the District Court (but denied by her employers).[14] Bridget O'Neill, who pleaded guilty to concealment in 1928, had been employed as a domestic for 14 months, and in the District Court the judge criticised her employer's failure to render assistance: 'And do you consider you are discharging your duty towards this poor girl in leaving her over there ... absolutely abandoned and without any legal assistance?'[15] Although a handful of employers were commended for their benevolence,[16] overwhelmingly unmarried pregnancy was cause for expulsion.

It was hardly surprising that many women gave birth in the network of institutions established in response to the deep societal taboo of illegitimacy. Of 245 children killed, 33 had been born in institutions, including hospitals, county homes, and private nursing homes. Others had left home with the purpose of giving birth away from their community, such as Mary Anne Madden who had taken a room at a hotel in Loughrea.[17] For those asked to account for the whereabouts of their newborn, enough was often known about the network of institutions to construct plausible accounts, such as the 1944 case of Catherine and Mary Teresa Walsh, who pleaded guilty to manslaughter and concealment respectively of Mary Teresa's infant. In her statement, Mary Teresa said that when informed by a doctor that she was going to have a baby, she had asked the doctor for a ticket to 'Roscrea' (the Sean Ross Abbey Mother and Baby Home operated at Roscrea). The sisters later informed the doctor that the infant had been sent to the 'Regina Hostel' in Dublin (the Regina Coeli Hostel had been founded by the Legion of Mary and accepted unmarried mothers and their infants).[18] Kathleen Dalton, found not guilty in 1936, had given birth on 13 September, and had admitted herself to the Central Hospital Kilkenny the following day. On 25 September she left the hospital with her child, and when she arrived home alone, she told her father it was with the Legion of Mary at Waterford.[19] The cases reveal how women used institutions as best they could and as needed. Eileen Ryan pleaded guilty to manslaughter in 1941. She had travelled to Dublin when she found out that she was pregnant and found employment in Jervis Street Hospital where she gave birth alone in her bedroom. She killed the infant immediately after giving birth, put the body in a case, and went to Henrietta Street:

> The nuns took me in but I didn't tell them I had a child. I was two nights in the Convent and paid 1/0 for the two nights. I was in this convent hostel on the nights before I returned to Limerick, Wednesday 30th April 1941.[20]

Many women sought to pass as married when they entered an institution. Mary Ellen Bohan travelled from Leitrim to Dublin in advance of the birth of her baby, taking a room in a hotel under the name 'Mrs Mary Mattimore' and gave birth in the Rotunda maternity hospital. She killed the infant prior to departing Dublin, travelling with the body in an attaché case that she intended to bury in her garden. Bohan was found guilty of manslaughter at her trial in 1935.[21] When Elizabeth Edwards, capitally convicted in 1935, entered Roscommon County Home, she gave her name as 'Mrs Mannion' and wore a wedding ring, but the ruse was unsuccessful and a nurse remarked that she 'did not know any Mrs Mannion in Fuerty'.[22] This was a necessary dissimulation in a society in which young unmarried women, especially those of the labouring and working classes, were subject to significant informal surveillance in their communities.[23] This was clear in the case of Christina Russell, capitally convicted in 1930. During her trial, a nurse in the South Dublin Union explained: 'You see this woman was supposed to be a married woman and we did not take as much notice of her as if she had been a single woman.'[24]

The case of Delia Lyons offers some insights into the financial arrangements that could be made for women seeking to conceal pregnancy. Charged initially with the murder of her infant in 1923, a *nolle prosequi* was entered on the case in 1924. Delia had given birth in Galway Central Hospital on 25 March 1923, and stood accused of the murder of her infant that same day.[25] In the District Court when she was charged, details of Delia's stay in the hospital were revealed by a nurse: 'The girl was some time a waiting patient for the maternity ward. I knew she was paying for her maintenance. It was to this girl's advantage to be in the hospital some time before the birth of the child.'[26] The secretary of the hospital confirmed that he had received a deposit receipt from Delia in the sum of £132, a receipt received by him from a nun who formerly worked at the hospital.[27]

Staff in institutions were aware that illegitimate infants were vulnerable. When discharged from Roscommon County Home, Elizabeth Edwards was instructed, with a reference that must have been comprehensible to her, 'not to do what Miss Hammil did with her baby'.[28] The suspicions of staff were often the first indication that a crime had been committed. In the case of the capitally convicted Elizabeth and Rose Edwards in 1935, the matron at Roscommon County Home had telephoned Roscommon Garda station to enquire whether Elizabeth still had the child to which she had given birth some weeks prior.[29]

Not only the infants but also their mothers were in a position of intense vulnerability; in the later stages of pregnancy many were destitute.[30] For some, release from an institution launched them into a state of precarity. When Mary Anne Keane, capitally convicted in 1929, was discharged from Roscommon County Home she was unable to return to her husband as he had turned her out of the house months before.[31] Keane wandered from place to place on foot and when met on the road 'appeared to be distressed, and was almost crying'.[32] Bridget Crowe, found not guilty in 1933, was reported to have been 'sent away from the County Home, Ennis, almost penniless with a weakly child'.[33] The jury in the case of Ellen O'Dwyer, found not guilty and discharged in 1930, expressed serious concerns about Ellen's claim that she would not have been admitted to the county home to give birth. They asked that inquiries be made on this: 'The foreman said the feeling of the jury was that the unfortunate girl had taken steps to have the child born properly, and was not able to do so.'[34]

Despite the serious issues with institutions designated as suitable for unmarried mothers, they were often suggested uncritically as the solution to the problem of infant murder. The defence counsel in Mary Ellen Bohan's case argued:

> If there had been a convalescent home to which girls in her sad portion could be sent for a few weeks after discharge from hospital so that their mental anguish might be eased, this tragedy might not have occurred.[35]

Justice Meredith, in the case of Mary Doolin, acquitted in 1933, commented on the frequency of infant murder and declared that, 'There were plenty of homes which took up cases of girls like this.'[36] However, the words of the nurse at Galway Central Hospital in the case of Delia Lyons suggested the narrow support that was offered to vulnerable women and children; on the matter of ensuring that the infant was provided for, the nurse stated: 'It was no part of my work to interfere in a matter of that sort.'[37]

While most mothers accused of the murder of their child involved cases of recently born infants, in some cases women were accused of the murder of older illegitimate children. These cases demonstrated the impossibility of illegitimate motherhood for many. In 1945, Mary Margaret Harvey pleaded guilty to the manslaughter of her two-year-old son Michael. Mary paid monthly towards Michael's fostering, and demands for money from the foster parent were cited by Mary as motivation to kill. She argued that 'I never intended to do away with my child'.[38] Disputing this, the foster parent stated that Mary had not paid the recent instalments, but that she had not demanded payment and had 'loved the child like one of my own'.[39] A further motivation to kill may have been Mary's hopes of marriage. Writing to the man she wished to marry, Mary asked him to 'forgive me and forget the past'.[40] In 1946, Eily Quaid pleaded guilty to the manslaughter of her two-year-old daughter, Mary Teresa. Again, Eily's daughter had been informally fostered out, an arrangement that had been paid in full up to September 1945. On 18 December 1945, after receiving no further payments from Eily, her daughter was returned to her. The body of the child was found by Eily's mother two days before Christmas.[41]

Frances Bright was acquitted of the murder of her nine-month-old daughter in 1949. Sheila Roycroft was born to Frances Roycroft in November 1948. When the infant was a week old, Frances authorised the Children's Fold, an agency of the Church of Ireland's Irish Church Missions, to undertake the care of her child.[42] However, although the organisation had arranged for the adoption of the infant in January 1949,[43] a minister with knowledge of the case learned that Frances had married, becoming Mrs Frances Bright, and consequently sought to return her daughter to her. He noted that Frances was unwilling to take Sheila but explained: 'Here you had a child whose father and mother were married. Their home was her home, so why bring the child up as an illegitimate?'[44] Frances herself stated that her husband had declared he would not marry her unless the child was given up. She further reported that she had been asked for payment for the child's maintenance, although she had not anticipated this when she authorised the adoption, and that she had been warned that she would be arrested if she did not take Sheila.[45] It was Frances's contention that Sheila had died by injuries sustained from an accident when she had let her fall to the floor. The jury took just five minutes to find Frances not guilty of murder.

Family denial and complicity

When charges were brought for child murder, family members of the accused mother often denied any knowledge that she had been pregnant. The younger brother of Ellen Keogh claimed no knowledge that Ellen was pregnant although they lived in the same house. Ellen testified that she would not have expected him to be observant because 'he is a quiet lad who comes in from his work and would never notice anything like that';[46] the judge meanwhile concluded that he 'must have been a simple and unobservant man'.[47] Kate Owens had experienced multiple previous pregnancies, and her mother's comment on the birth of an earlier stillborn infant revealed the prevailing attitude in the household: 'I never asked Katie anything more about it.'[48]

Cramped living conditions ensured that judges and prosecution counsel met claims to obliviousness with incredulity. Mary Lenihan, acquitted of the murder of her granddaughter's infant in 1929, lived in a labourer's cottage, whose occupancy ebbed and flowed through the year. When her granddaughter, Hannah, gave birth on New Year's Day 1928, Mary was there with her husband, children and grandchildren.[49] Prosecution counsel pursued this line of enquiry to suggest family complicity:

Prosecution: This is the first child you ever had?
Hannah: Yes.
Prosecution: It was painful?
Hannah: Yes.
Prosecution: You never uttered a cry; did you cry during the delivery of the child?
Hannah: No.
Prosecution: You lay on the floor, the child was delivered the most painful operation in the world and you never made a noise that your wakeful cousin Bridget, your grandfather, and your cousin Timothy might hear in this little labourer's cottage, is that so.
Hannah: [No answer].[50]

The role of the family was also evident in family members' complicity. Mary Kenny pleaded guilty to the manslaughter of her daughter Bridget's infant in 1926 in a case in which the entire family was first arrested. At the inquest, when it emerged that Bridget's brothers were in the kitchen when she had given birth, the coroner commented, 'They must be queer slug.'[51]

In cases such as that of Mary Lenihan or Mary Somerville, both older women accused of murdering their great-grandchild and grandchild respectively, the lived experience of illegitimacy may have motivated them to act. Mary Somerville had previously given birth to an illegitimate infant, while Hannah Lenihan was the illegitimate granddaughter of Mary Lenihan. In the Garda report on Somerville, the parentage of a number of her children was considered suspect and it was recorded that, 'In her extreme youth Mary Somerville, who was then employed as a domestic servant, gave birth to an illegitimate child.'[52] In her trial, the illegitimacy of Mary Lenihan's granddaughter Hannah was put to her: 'this girl was born before your daughter was married?'[53] Rattigan has argued that many women accused of infant murder were already marginalised within their own communities by the stain of family illegitimacy and poverty.[54]

Shame

Fischer has explored how shame was mobilised in the service of a new Irish identity after independence.[55] Shame necessitated the hiding away of sexually suspect women. This same shame also motivated women to kill, to destroy the children that were the manifestation of 'sin'. Shame operated as a disciplinary form of social control, but it was also intensely criminogenic. An editorial in the *Irish Times*, following the reprieve of Elizabeth and Rose Edwards in 1935, was critical of unflinching Irish attitudes towards 'moral lapses':

> We do not advocate leniency towards infanticide. We hold, however, that one of its chief causes is the cruel and often hypocritical attitude of Irish public opinion, especially in the rural areas and small towns – towards moral lapses, and we hold that such intolerance is the chief of all crimes.[56]

To an extent, there was recognition that society created the conditions in which infant murder occurred. Despite this, concerted state efforts to 'deal with' the unmarried mother only heightened the miasma of shame, and the links between illegitimacy and infant murder remain sobering. In her nineteenth-century sample, Farrell found that the infant victim was illegitimate in 84.7 per cent of cases.[57] Immorality and illegitimacy were viewed as a fundamental threat to the social order.[58] In 1944, when reform was being considered, a memorandum was circulated to cabinet which elaborated on the current practice: 'An unmarried mother who kills her child is guilty of murder and liable to capital punishment unless she establishes a defence on the ground of insanity.'[59] This document provides an officially recorded slip of the tongue in its reference to an 'unmarried mother'. Clearly the law made no distinction based on the marital status of the mother, and yet discussion of infant murder always spoke to the case of the unmarried mother.

The women before the courts clearly identified shame in their own motivations. Mary Kiernan, capitally convicted in 1926, petitioned that: 'I did not know what I was doing at the time with shame and disgrace, that it would turn out so serious, or I would not have done it at the time.'[60] Women were keenly aware of the intolerability of life as the mother of an illegitimate child. Rose Edwards, convicted of the murder of her sister's infant in 1935, asserted that the child 'was better off dead'.[61]

Notions of respectability and religious propriety recurred in the frequent claims made regarding the burial of infants, exposing the contrast between the exigencies of shame and the need to be seen to observe Catholic practices. In many cases, accused women first told guards that they had buried the body in local graveyards, with some noting that they had performed a 'lay' baptism.[62] Such claims generally proved untrue, such as in the case of Mary and Margaret McGrath, a mother and daughter who both pleaded guilty to concealment in 1928; although the body was first stated to have been buried in the grounds of the chapel it was found buried in the kitchen of the house.[63] Local wisdom about what happened to illegitimate infants who died was at odds with official concern. During the inquest in the 1926 case of Mary Kenny and Bridget McCabe, a mother and daughter charged with the murder of Bridget's infant,

Mary was asked if she knew it was illegal to bury the body in the garden, to which she responded: 'No. I always seen the children that didn't get baptism buried in the back of a ditch.' The coroner countered such a suggestion: 'You must have travelled a good deal for your rotten experience. I am sure no member of the court ever knew of such an occurrence.'[64]

The complicity, or wilful ignorance, of family members signalled the extent to which the shame of illegitimacy marred the reputation of the entire family. In a 1941 memorandum, a list of hereditary weaknesses was outlined as 'inebriety, insanity or immorality'.[65] As Earner-Byrne argued, an individual's shame had serious ramifications beyond the self:

> The issue of reputation was central to much of the social control exercised in Ireland. The fear of the loss of one's reputation was based largely on the understanding of the family as a unit: if one member disgraced themselves the rest of the family was tarnished by association.[66]

In some respects, as Brennan concluded, feelings of shame were a conventional response in accordance with respectability.[67] Shame was a motive that made sense, although judges forcibly countered such arguments by reiterating the sanctity of infant life. As Brennan writes, the criminal law individualises culpability, and the refusal to formally admit structural factors in cases of infant murder was not unique to such cases.[68] Without an incorporation of structural factors, which would have necessitated a more cold-eyed judgement of Irish society, the clemency extended to condemned women, and the lesser verdicts for other women accused of murder, had to be couched in acceptable discourses. Therefore, as Brennan observed, the leniency shown to women was always premised on the person in the dock and never wider society.[69]

Law reform

Although not a separate offence in Ireland until 1949, the murder of an infant was often referred to as 'infanticide'. In the decades prior to 1949, the deployment of discrete terminology for the murder of an infant suggested an offence that was 'different' from murder. However, despite legislative reform in Britain from the 1920s, there was little agitation for similar in Ireland.[70] Following the 1927 murder conviction of Elizabeth Hannon, the Religious Society of Friends wrote to the Minister enquiring whether legislation would be introduced which removed the necessity of sentencing such women to death. The Department responded that, 'The advisability of introducing legislation to deal with the crime of infanticide is at present under discussion between the Minister for Justice and the Attorney General.'[71] However, concerted attention was not diverted to reform until over a decade later. In April 1939, the Minister invited the Chief Justice to convene a committee to produce proposals for the reform of capital punishment. One suggestion was the downgrading of infant murder from its status as a capital offence. When the committee delivered their report in 1941, this formed one of its few recommendations. The conservative nature of the proposals disappointed Stephen Roche, the Secretary at the Department, who noted that the recommendation amounted to little more than 'the reconciliation of the law with commonsense'.[72] However, his remark that 'such women are never, in recent years, charged with murder'[73] would have been of little comfort to women such as Kate Owens, who was convicted of murder and sentenced to death in 1942, or those women tried on the capital charge through the 1940s. Further, despite Roche's dismissal of this reform as overly cautious, it was not to be enacted for a further eight years.

Roche was also dubious about the arbitrary limits of the proposal, recalling, as an example, the case of Rose Edwards, who would still have been liable on the murder charge as she had been convicted of the murder of her sister's infant. However, there was not universal acceptance that infant murder should be considered as a lesser offence. A response from Dr Conn Ward, Parliamentary Secretary at the Department of Local Government and Public Health, expressed unease:

> If the killing of a helpless baby is as serious a crime as is the killing of an adult, I do not think the baby slayer ought to be given any special consideration. In making this submission I am mindful of the fact that the mother of an unwanted baby is sometimes a hardened sinner

who appears to kill with full deliberation. It can, of course, always be argued that she had not fully recovered from the effect of giving birth to her child.[74]

That same year, and perhaps anticipating reform, Justice Conor Maguire remarked:

> I am sceptical ... of the defences put up in these cases, that unmarried mothers become of unbalanced mind, and that their action in murdering their newly born infants is the result of their insanity. It is strange that this insanity always take the same shape, and it is my experience that it is only in the case of unmarried mothers it takes this shape.[75]

The reform, when it came in the form of Infanticide Act 1949, followed the British Infanticide Act 1938 in almost all respects. The law held that a woman charged with the murder of her own child aged under 12 months could be charged with the lesser offence of infanticide in cases where 'the balance of her mind was disturbed by reason of her not having fully recovered from the effect of giving birth to the child or by reason of the effect of lactation consequent upon the birth of the child'.[76] The case could be heard in the Circuit Criminal Court, rather than the Central Criminal Court, and a wide discretion as to sentencing was available with a maximum penalty of life imprisonment. One departure from the British model was that infanticide could not be charged at first instance; a woman had to be indicted on the murder charge, and a district justice decided at preliminary hearing if this should be reduced to infanticide or whether the murder charge should continue to the Central Criminal Court.[77] Brennan has revealed the likely role of the Catholic Archbishop of Dublin, John Charles McQuaid, in the stipulation that a woman be first charged with murder.[78] Brennan identified at least 11 cases where the charge was not reduced, but noted that prosecution then generally accepted a plea of infanticide in the Central Criminal Court.[79]

In the trial of Margaret Ryan, who pleaded guilty to infanticide in the Central Criminal Court in 1949, Justice Maguire noted that there was some confusion in the public mind about the new law.[80] However, almost a decade after its enactment, a 1958 case demonstrated ongoing uncertainty as to the new procedures. Kathleen

Cawley was initially charged with murder and returned for trial to the Central Criminal Court. However, the Attorney General intervened, alleging that this was in error.[81] There were other cases which proceeded to the Central Criminal Court and did not result in a conviction for infanticide, such as Mary Ellen Smyth, who pleaded guilty to the manslaughter of her four-month-old infant in 1959.[82] The older age of her infant may have contributed to this outcome. It was generally the more atypical cases which continued to the Central Criminal Court on a murder charge.[83]

Women capitally convicted of child murder

Twelve women were convicted for the murder of an infant through these decades. Ten had murdered their own infant, and two women were convicted of killing an infant within their family. The death sentence may have been a fiction in infant murder cases, but its application in a minority of cases suggested that those cases were somehow 'different'. In fact, there was often little to differentiate these cases from the cases of women who were acquitted or convicted of lesser offences.

One aggravating feature was obviously marital status and the fact of illegitimacy. All but one of the infants were illegitimate, and the unplanned pregnancy of Catherine Ahearne had precipitated a hasty marriage to Laurence Ahearne before the birth of the child six weeks later.[84] However, the fact of illegitimacy was one shared by almost all cases of women who killed their children. On its own it was not a remarkable feature of the capital conviction cases. Women who were 'persistent offenders' were also judged more harshly.[85] Kate Owens had been convicted in April 1934 for concealment,[86] but the multiple bones found at her home suggested a series of illegitimate pregnancies. Persistent offenders need not have had previous criminal convictions, as the terminology of 'offence' was drawn widely. Elizabeth Hannon reported that she had twice before given birth to stillborn infants and could be branded as a 'persistent offender', morally if not legally.[87] Mary Kiernan had given birth to an infant in 1919 which died in infancy. This fact provoked consternation, and both Justice O'Byrne and the Department of

Justice believed she deserved a lengthier stay in prison as a result: 'It is against the prisoner to some extent that she had an illegitimate child in 1919. It cannot be argued that she was overcome by the overwhelming shame.'[88] Mary Kiernan was 22 when she was sentenced to death in 1926; she would have been just 15 when she gave birth in 1919. Again, however, there were others who received less punitive outcomes who were similarly placed. There were women such as Margaret Walsh or Delia Murphy who had been previously convicted of infanticide-related offences and were, strictly speaking, persistent offenders, while others had previous illegitimate children and were construed as 'persistent offenders' morally.

The age of the infant at death was relevant. Most of the infant victims were killed immediately following birth. Among those who were capitally convicted, it was more likely that their infants were older at death. Cases in which the infants were not killed immediately following birth were considered more serious, evident in the remarks of the judge following the conviction of Christina Russell that, 'This is not an ordinary case of infanticide, inasmuch as the murder did not take place until some 20 days after the birth of the child.'[89] In her case, the Secretary at the Department claimed the murder was committed 'in cold blood'.[90] In many cases of infants born in institutions, staff could confirm that the infant had been healthy. Institutional birth is over-represented among the death-sentenced women. The infant's age, and sometimes their baptism and naming, may have compounded the sense of wrongdoing.

Moral panic

What is clear is that the majority of the women death-sentenced for the murder of an infant were convicted in a period of 'moral panic'. As noted by McAvoy, from the late-1920s through the 1930s, a 'moral panic' permeated Irish society regarding infant mortality, illegitimacy and infant murder.[91] Prosecution counsel, addressing the jury at the close of Mary Gorman's 1927 trial, referenced 'the massacre of the innocents', advising that: 'One example of sternness would have more effect in suppressing the crime in this country than any amount of pious exhortation.'[92] From 1926 to 1929 slight year-on-year increases in the number of illegitimate births provoked alarm.[93] In 1920, Irish infant mortality rates stood at 83 per 1,000, considerably higher than other European countries.[94] The 1926 census showed that some inner-city areas of Dublin registered infant mortality rates as high as 170 per 1,000 and this figure was consistently worse for illegitimate infants; in 1930 it was 251 per 1,000.[95]

This period of heightened official concern was not unique to Ireland. It can be interpreted through the lens of independence and the desire to forge a new national identity. Jaffary, for instance, writes that post-colonial Mexico experienced a huge increase in the prosecution of abortion and infanticide, attributable, in part, to the post-colonial government's need to shape a new nation.[96] The Irish response to infant murder in this period exemplifies Gurevich's view of such criminal trials as, following Durkheim, 'symbolic, boundary-making' events.[97]

The case of Deborah Sullivan, in particular, can be interpreted in light of the specific political and social context in which her offence occurred.[98] Sullivan was sentenced to death before Justice O'Byrne on 13 June 1929, a harsh outcome in view of the circumstances. Sullivan, aged 21, had first experienced labour pains at home, and set out with the intention of making her way on foot to an infirmary. This path took her across mountainous terrain, in poor weather, and while outdoors she had given birth. In prison, Sullivan revealed that she had become pregnant from rape. Her trial was also considerably delayed due to illness, and there is evidence that Gardaí considered her sympathetically: 'I did all I could for accused. I called in the doctor to see her three times on my own responsibility.'[99]

The case presented an obvious opportunity for conviction on a lesser charge. The jury clearly struggled with arriving at a decision. During deliberations they returned to court, unable to reach a verdict, and Justice O'Byrne precluded them from returning a verdict of guilty but insane, stating that the defence had not established the requisite proof.[100] The jury returned a verdict of guilty with a strong recommendation to mercy having regard to the exceptional circumstances of the birth. The outcome suggested that the pervasive debates on infant life and morality were finding traction.

During this period of concern, judges took the opportunity to reinforce the symbolic function of the death penalty.[101] Justice O'Byrne presided over the capital conviction cases of Mary Anne Keane,[102] Deborah Sullivan,[103] Catherine Ahearne[104] and Christina Russell,[105] as well as the 1935 case of Elizabeth and Rose Edwards[106] and the later 1938 case of Mary Somerville.[107] Following the conviction of Catherine Ahearne, the headline of one article read 'Another Death Sentence',[108] in a summer in which a significant number of death sentences had been handed down to women. Throughout these cases, O'Byrne articulated his opinion that infant murder had reached epidemic levels, that the murder of an infant was no different to the murder of an adult and that the verdict was obliged to follow the evidence. At Sullivan's trial in June 1929, O'Byrne commented:

> it was regrettable that cases of this kind had become of such frequent occurrence. The prerogative of mercy did not lie with either the judge or the jury, for they were bound by their oaths to find according to the evidence.[109]

O'Byrne was not alone in making such exhortations from the bench; other judges too, as well as prosecution counsel, made similar pronouncements, such as Justice Haugh in the 1943 case of Mary Kate Murphy, who was ultimately found not guilty. Addressing the jury, Haugh stated:

> In what way then could such crime be prevented? The answer was by bringing the guilty person to the bar of that court. By punishing the guilty it would have the effect of preventing others similarly inclined from perpetrating this form of offence.[110]

In 1929, the Bishop of Ossory's Lenten Pastoral lambasted the 'easy treatment' infanticide cases received in courts, where 'It would seem as if the law did not value the life of the illegitimate child.'[111]

In his charge to the jury in the trial of Elizabeth and Rose Edwards, O'Byrne argued that:

> law cannot step in to save a life. The only protection it can give, is that which arises from a realisation of the fact that any person who interferes with or takes away human life, must answer to 12 of his fellow-countrymen for his action.[112]

Yet O'Byrne's comment that law could not 'step in to save a life' obscured the degree to which societal attitudes were hardened by a legal infrastructure which had created a 'maternity trap' for women. Law had actively 'stepped in' by creating legal realities out of the religious discourse on shame.

Reprieve

Of the 12 women sentenced to death for the murder of an infant, clemency had assumed the status of precedent,[113] evident in the case of Mary Kiernan in which it was held that 'The Department of Justice strongly recommend that the sentence should not be carried out and state that it would be against all our precedents to do so.'[114] The formal legal status of infant murder, as indistinct from murder, created tensions between its legal and social meanings. That this dichotomy was resolved through the default application of leniency to such cases was little comfort to those women ignorant of such matters. Mary Kiernan, convicted of the murder of her child in 1926, was quite deaf and had not heard the verdict as it was delivered. When counsel delivered this news to her in her cell, he reported that, 'She broke down somewhat and said she did not think they would hang her when it was the first time.'[115]

Further institutional norms gave more guidance on what should happen. A Department of Justice 'working rule' from the late 1920s set out procedures for women convicted of the murder of an infant:

> As a working rule in infanticide cases I think that the mother convicted should be kept in prison for a period of two years and then placed in a home. ... Each case therefore must be examined on the merits, in some cases the above mentioned period may have to be abridged in others extended. It applies only to average cases.[116]

While conviction on the murder charge was considered legally and morally just, it was also unthinkable that the sentence would be carried out. The judge could simultaneously view the guilty verdict in the trial of Elizabeth Hannon as 'very proper' while also endorsing the jury's recommendation to mercy.[117] These cases generally attracted considerable sympathy (and all 12 women were recommended to mercy by the jury) and reprieves were swift. The women sentenced to death for infant murder around this period, from the latter half of the 1920s into the early 1930s, experienced the shortest waiting period between conviction and reprieve.

Child-killing beyond the family

There were only a handful of cases in which women were charged with the murders of children beyond their own family. These relate to two cases of girls employed in domestic service who killed children under their care, and two cases in which women were charged with their involvement as nurses or 'handywomen' in cases resulting in the death of an infant.

In a trial which attracted intense publicity, Mary Cole was found guilty on 23 March 1928 of the murders of Philomena and Maureen Flynn. Because she was just 15, she was not sentenced to death. Instead, she was ordered to be detained in custody 'at the pleasure of the Governor General'. Cole worked for the Flynn family in County Laois. On 27 July 1927, the body of one-year-old Philomena Flynn was found drowned in a stream near her home. On 22 August, six-year-old Maureen Flynn died in similar circumstances. In December, in a 'sensational development', the *Irish Independent* reported that Mary Cole had been arrested.[118] The killings were motivated by a grudge Mary harboured against the Flynns following an incident which occurred a month before the first murder. In June, Mrs Flynn heard reports that Mary had spent a night with a man in the Flynn's motor car which was kept in their garage. When confronted, in the presence of the parish priest Father Walsh, Mary eventually admitted her infraction. Mrs Flynn duly asked Cole's mother to take her home 'and get her father to give her a good beating'.[119] Shortly after this rebuke, Mary returned to the Flynn household, and appeared to settle back into her work.

The prosecution narrative depicted Mary as intelligent but unnatural, with one newspaper report proclaiming her 'Powerful Intellect'.[120] State counsel Carrigan presented her as intent on taking her revenge for her humiliation:

> This phenomenal juvenile criminal, untaught, and without experi-
> ence presents to you the case of a girl who looks a woman in appear-
> ance, and has a mind more powerful, and more agile an imagination
> than any you could come across in the experience of a lifetime.[121]

Newspaper commentary made repeated reference to Cole looking
older than her 15 years, often in sexual terms, such as the comment
that she was 'looking overdeveloped for her 15 ½ years'.[122] In Mrs
Flynn's evidence, she recalled that Father Walsh had referred to
Mary as 'The poor Magdalene'.[123]

Motherhood animated the closing stages of the trial. Defence
counsel declared, somewhat surprisingly, that 'very little of my
sympathy goes out to Mrs Flynn'.[124] He noted the relative affluence
of the Flynns and contrasted the position of Mary as 'the absolute
slave in this household'.[125] Defence then weighed the sorrow of
the Flynns with that of the Cole family, concluding that 'the parting
of a mother with her convict daughter, her first-born child, was a
greater sorrow'.[126] Justice O'Byrne, in his summing up, took up the
theme of attacking Mrs Flynn, stating that:

> It was quite possible they [the jury] would come to the conclusion
> that in connection with this incident Mrs Flynn was not as kind or
> as sympathetic as she might have been towards this girl. Such a view
> seemed a reasonable one.[127]

The second case in which a woman was charged with the murder
of a child beyond her own family was that of Kathleen Harmon,
considered in more detail in Chapter 8. Like Cole, Harmon was
young, just 17, which would have nonetheless made her eligible for
a death sentence had she been convicted of murder. Kathleen was
instead found guilty of the manslaughter of four-year-old Penelope
Willoughby, and was sentenced to seven years penal servitude in
1950.[128] In Harmon's case, the blame for her crime was laid largely
at the door of her parents, particularly drawing on ideas of hereditary degeneracy which made much of the fact that her parents were
Irish Travellers.

These two cases, both involving teenage girls who killed children
in their care, were atypical, and offered a signally different profile
of child-killing compared to those cases in which mothers and other
family members killed illegitimate infants. Green has noted that

such cases in which children kill children have the power to act as signifiers of societal ill, and can become totemic in calls for punitive responses.[129] Yet the societal and criminal justice responses to such cases are not universal, and are informed by different political cultures across jurisdictions. While Cole and Harmon's cases attracted more newspaper coverage than most other cases of child-killing, they did not act as lightning rods for hand-wringing about the general state of Irish society.

Exploring motherhood

The concept of motherhood within the cases was an ambiguous one. The conflict between the symbolic importance of motherhood in Irish society and the abject position of the unmarried mother is evident throughout. As Luddy wrote:

> While the idealization of motherhood was a significant feature of the rhetoric of politicians in the new Irish State, the maternal body, particularly in its unmarried condition, became a central focus in the development of welfare policies of the state and the Catholic Church.[130]

The women capitally convicted for infant murder, by the very nature of their crime, failed to achieve true motherhood. Witnesses were often questioned about the extent to which accused women appeared to be 'attached' to their infants, a stunning failure to grasp the near impossibility of illegitimate motherhood. Milne, in her analysis of maternal filicide cases from 2010 to 2019 in England and Wales, found that the normalisation of pregnancy, and the expectation of good mothering, trumped consideration of the gendered harms and risks of pregnancy.[131]

There was, however, room for nuance, particularly in the minds of letter writers. In the case of Mary Somerville, motherhood emerged for some as an argument in mitigation. Somerville's actions in support of her unmarried daughter drew admiration and pity from some who framed the maternal role as one of sacrifice. The Society for the Abolition of the Death Penalty wrote that Somerville had acted 'to save her daughter from disgrace'.[132] In this light, her actions were wrong but understandable, and in service of her children. Mary Daly was interpreted by some members of the public as motivated to kill by the financial pressures of motherhood. A narrative emerged of a desperate mother, who killed a stranger in a church in a misguided and unplanned attempt to steal money for rent. This redeemed her in the eyes of some, one of whom noted: 'In her insanity of desperation torn between love for her baby and a father & husband & a home to shelter them from temporary insanity drove her to it.'[133] Daly's case represents an example of Jones' idea of populist leniency.[134] Seal drew on this concept to take a gendered, classed and historicised reading of it, noting one 1934 English case in particular in which a woman who killed her 30-year-old 'invalid' son was nonetheless viewed with compassion by the public, an example of someone considered 'guilty of but not blameworthy for [the] crime they have committed'.[135]

Many of those charged with infant murder were already mothers and were further judged on this. In the case of Maggie McGrory, a woman with two living children who pleaded guilty to the manslaughter of her infant in 1947, Justice Haugh noted that: 'You were quite a good mother to two of your children.'[136] As a mother to four older children, Ellen Keogh was judged for her domestic and maternal failings. A Garda report stated that her children:

> were very badly looked after by their mother who kept a dirty and very filthy house. It is doubtful if they were fully fed by the mother who did not seem to be keen on her household and maternal duties.[137]

The marginalisation and poverty of many women was clear. Margaret Somerville, who pleaded guilty to the manslaughter of her infant in 1944, already had eight children aged between seven and 13 and her husband worked in England. She painted a bleak picture of her life: 'I have no clothes not even a pair of shoes & do not go out at all except to [a neighbour's] where I visit during the day & listen to the wireless every night.'[138] When Mary and Margaret McGrath appeared in Maryborough District Court in 1928 on the charge of murdering Margaret's infant, one newspaper described them as follows: 'Both women were wretchedly clad and appeared to be very poor.'[139] Many of the cases reveal the scale of poverty, and the straitened conditions in which women raised their children, often without assistance.

If unmarried mothers who killed their infants could not be accommodated within rigid understandings of 'motherhood', it was unlikely that the concept of fatherhood would find traction, especially as 'The weight of social control fell on the woman as her pregnancy was visible, whereas the man's fatherhood was not.'[140] One of the key, and controversial, conclusions in the Mother and Baby Homes Commission of Investigation Final Report, was that:

> Women who gave birth outside marriage were subject to particularly harsh treatment. Responsibility for that harsh treatment rests mainly with the fathers of their children and their own immediate families.[141]

The cases of women charged with the murders of illegitimate infants in these decades turns up many clear incidences of fathers who were aware of the situation and did nothing to help. In a letter received by Elizabeth Edwards, we can hear the voice of the father of her child, in which he reiterated his refusal to return to Ireland from England: 'I would hang before I do that.' He appealed to her not to have the child, writing: 'What wood [sic] the people say, or have you anny [sic] sence [sic] at all. So if you don't like that you can please yourself.'[142] While the actions of individuals in such circumstances can be positioned as a further contributing factor in the deaths of illegitimate infants, it is implausible to position these men as ultimately responsible.[143] Many of the fathers were themselves young, and all of them were bound by the same forces which named illegitimacy as the greatest shame.

Occasional comment on the role of fathers was passed during infant murder trials. In the 1928 trial of Margaret Slattery,[144] against whom all charges were withdrawn, the prosecution counsel suggested that fathers should be criminalised. In this case, the father of the infant had also been charged with murder, and Carrigan referred to 'circumstances here … of an exceptional character, inasmuch as here it was the man, the origin of the wrong-doing, who was in the dock'.[145] However, Carrigan also admitted that 'legislation of a punitive character might possibly endanger innocent people'.[146] Unusually, in this case, the mother of the infant was discharged from court and the father, 24-year-old John Luby, was convicted of manslaughter and sentenced to three years' penal servitude. Nevertheless, Luby's defence had argued that in similar circumstances many men would have done less, and would certainly have denied the connection with Slattery.[147] The widening of notions of blame to encompass the fathers of infants was never seriously attempted, but in any case, such blame would still have been an individual's blame in the face of an intractable society. The idea that men should shoulder blame was also somewhat fantastical in a society which so invested the bodies of women with such national symbolism, and it remained the case that illegitimate infants were viewed as being 'of' their mother solely.

In some cases, we can glimpse the circumstances of women and their children at the point of arrest and trial. As Farrell noted with regard to convict women in the nineteenth century, 'incarceration dislocated the family, separated siblings or initiated institutional care that could break the familial bond permanently'.[148] While, as Johnston writes, 'imprisoned mothers used the little agency they had' to influence childcare arrangements, for many women imprisonment involved total disruption.[149]

When Ellen Gavan was arrested for the murder of her father in July 1925, her three children were reportedly sent to the Dublin Union.[150] In this case, their grandmother and their father, Ellen's husband, had also been arrested. The children's father was discharged at the direction of the judge in January 1926; it is unknown if his children were returned to him. In the 1927 case of Mary Downey, her husband undertook to look after the eldest boys, but two of the youngest children were sent to an industrial school in Kilkenny for a year.[151] In 1942, when Sarah and Nora Madigan were arrested for the murder of Sarah's husband Patrick Madigan, seven children aged between three and 12 were taken to Ennis (perhaps a reference to the girls' Industrial School in Ennis, operated by the Sisters of Mercy). Both women were discharged from court without conviction, and again it is unknown whether these children were then returned to their families. Under a binary understanding of gender roles, Farrell suggested that when mothers were incarcerated, fathers were often encouraged to give their children up to institutional care.[152] State intervention into their children's lives was inevitable for many women before the courts.[153]

There are instances throughout in which women seek assurances as to their children's welfare, such as Bridget Catherine Cleary, arrested in 1934 and ultimately found not guilty of the murder of her illegitimate infant after her conviction for manslaughter was quashed on appeal. Cleary was married and had six living children. In the District Court she asked, 'I want to know who are the children being taken care of by?' The district justice informed her that they were being cared for by a Miss Duffy, and when she further asked if she would get them back, he responded, 'I can't tell you that at present.'[154] When she was cautioned, in 1936, Elizabeth Doody said, 'I have nothing to say, except I hope I will be back to my two little children again to-night.'[155] Elizabeth, a widow with four children, ultimately pleaded guilty to manslaughter.

Mary Somerville, convicted of her illegitimate grandchild's murder in 1938, resisted the recommendations of a local clergyman that her children be sent into care while she was in prison. The local Protestant minister had arranged to send Mary's younger children to an institution but she 'would not consent to this course', and the children remained on the small family farm with Mary's eldest son.[156] Despite her initial protestations, Mary's three youngest children seem to have ultimately been sent to the Boys' Home in Dublin.[157] In a petition, Somerville undertook not to interfere with 'the education and upbringing' of these children if she were released from prison.[158]

In 1939, when Nora Sullivan appeared before the District Court, she did so very obviously as a mother. Nora had been charged along with her husband Patrick for the murder of Patrick's mother. Nora's appearance in the court was described thus: 'The female accused, who wore a black shawl, appeared in the dock beside her husband with a baby in her arms.'[159] Both Nora and her husband pleaded guilty to manslaughter. Two women charged with murder also gave birth in prison during this period. This was an inescapable fact of women's imprisonment. Farrell found that from 1854 to 1882, at least 98 infants were born in Dublin's convict prison.[160] Julia O'Neill, while on remand in Mountjoy Prison on a charge of murdering her neighbour, gave birth in May 1926.[161] O'Neill was ultimately convicted as an accessory. Her partner, James McHugh, the father of the infant, was executed for the crime. Nan Maher also appears to have given birth while in custody. At the end of June, the prison medical officer estimated that Nan was eight months pregnant and dubbed her fitness for trial as 'problematical'.[162] The trial was held fewer than two weeks after this, and Nan's pregnancy does not appear to have been remarked on in what little press coverage there was.

Conclusion

Irish society, bolstered by the policies and discourse of Church and state, lived under overwhelming taboos in relation to sex and sexuality in the decades post-independence. Within these limits, illegitimacy became an unthinkable prospect for many unmarried women who found themselves pregnant. The intensity of this shame moulded the profile of women's lethal violence, ensuring that the criminogenic powers of shame motivated women to destroy evidence of extramarital sex. Despite these clear patterns, and the example of Britain, there was no urgency in government to reform the law on infant murder. Instead, there was a clear symbolic function in retaining the legal condemnation for as long as it remained unchanged. This commitment to a symbolically punitive regime appears more perverse in light of the sobering rates of infant mortality within those institutions established for the confinement of unmarried pregnant women and their infants. Despite the structures of censure, the cases offer glimpses throughout of the experiences of motherhood in Ireland in these years, demonstrating the complexities of the meanings of maternity, and providing examples of offending women as mothers.

Notes

1 O'Donnell refers to the decline in the rates of child-killing from the nineteenth through the twentieth century as 'one of the most dramatic shifts in lethal violence'. Ian O'Donnell, 'Lethal violence in Ireland, 1841 to 2003: famine, celibacy and parental pacification', *British Journal of Criminology*, 45:5 (2005) 671–95, p. 686.

2 Anne-Marie Kilday, *A History of Infanticide in Britain, c. 1600 to the Present* (Basingstoke: Palgrave Macmillan, 2013); Mark Jackson, *New-born Child Murder: Women, Illegitimacy and the Courts in Eighteenth-Century England* (Manchester: Manchester University Press, 1996); Lionel Rose, *Massacre of the Innocents: Infanticide in Great Britain 1800–1939* (London: Routledge & Kegan Paul, 1986).

3 Mother and Baby Homes Commission of Investigation, 'Mother and Baby Homes, Commission of Investigation Final Report' (Dublin: Department of Children, Equality, Disability, Integration and Youth, 2021).

4 Also noted by Farrell in her nineteenth-century sample. Elaine Farrell, *'A Most Diabolical Deed': Infanticide and Irish Society, 1850–1900* (Manchester: Manchester University Press, 2013).

5 Clíona Rattigan, *'What Else Could I Do?': Single Mothers and Infanticide, Ireland 1900–1950* (Dublin: Irish Academic Press, 2012).

6 Many women subsequently required medical attention. Clíona Rattigan, '"I thought from her appearance that she was in the family way": detecting infanticide cases in Ireland, 1900–21', *Family and Community History*, 11:2 (2008) 135–52; Elaine Farrell, '"Infanticide of the ordinary character": an overview of the crime in Ireland, 1850–1900', *Irish Economic and Social History*, 39 (2012) 56–72.

7 Ciara Breathnach, 'Handywomen and birthing in rural Ireland, 1851–1955, *Gender & History*, 28:1 (2016) 34–56.

8 NAI, SBCCC, November 1933 to 22 April 1941; SFCCC, Wicklow 1939. Statement of Mary McCreanor, 29 September 1939.

9 NAI, SFCCC, Kerry 1944. Deposition of John Carroll.

10 NAI, SFCCC, Wexford 1929. Statement of Catherine Ahearne, 17 April 1929.

11 NAI, SFCCC, Wexford 1929. Statement of Davy Nolan, 19 April 1929.

12 Farrell, 'Infanticide of the ordinary character'; Rattigan, *'What Else Could I Do?'*.

13 'Child's Death', *Evening Echo* (17 July 1931), p. 1.

14 'Infanticide Charge', *Irish Independent* (23 July 1924), p. 5.

15 'Charge of Infanticide', *Kerry Reporter* (26 May 1928), p. 2.

16 In 1927, Mary Ellen O'Donnell's employer was commended for her 'kindly, Christian-like manner'. 'Central Criminal Court', *Irish Independent* (17 December 1927), p. 11.

17 'A Gruesome Loughrea Find', *Kerry News* (1 September 1926), p. 2.

18 NAI, SFCCC, Carlow 1944. Statement of Mary Teresa Walsh, 24 May 1944. On the Regina Coeli Hostel, see Lindsey Earner-Byrne,

Mother and Child: Maternity and Child Welfare in Dublin 1922–60 (Manchester: Manchester University Press, 2007).

19 'Infanticide Charge', *Irish Times* (19 November 1936), p. 2.
20 NAI, SFCCC, Limerick 1941. Statement of Eileen Ryan.
21 NAI, SBCCC, February 1928 to November; 'Charge of Murder of Child', *Irish Independent* (23 November 1933), p. 4.
22 NAI, CCA, 13/1935. Evidence of Margaret Campbell.
23 Louise Ryan, 'The press, the police and prosecution: perspectives on infanticide in the 1920s', in Diane Urquhart and Alan Hayes (eds), *Irish Women's History* (Dublin: Irish Academic Press, 2004); Rattigan, '*What Else Could I Do?*'.
24 NAI, CCA 24/1930. Evidence of Alice Kelly.
25 NAI, SFCCC, Dublin Commission, Galway 1923.
26 'In Her Mother's Arms', *Connacht Tribune* (5 May 1923), p. 9.
27 'In Her Mother's Arms', *Connacht Tribune* (5 May 1923), p. 9.
28 NAI, CCA 13/1935. Evidence of Sally O'Gorman.
29 'On the Trail: The Case of the Two Sisters', *Garda Review* (April 1947), 389–92.
30 Rattigan, '*What Else Could I Do?*'.
31 NAI, Department of Justice 18/3540. Memorandum.
32 NAI, SFCCC, Roscommon 1929. Deposition of Patrick McGowan.
33 'Alleged Infanticide', *Irish Independent* (1 July 1933), p. 5.
34 'An Infant's Death', *Longford Leader* (22 November 1930), p. 6.
35 'Child's Body in Her Case', *Irish Press* (2 December 1933), p. 4.
36 'Co. Wexford Girl Acquitted', *Irish Independent* (24 November 1933), p. 6.
37 'In Her Mother's Arms', *Connacht Tribune* (5 May 1923), p. 9.
38 NAI, SFCCC, Limerick 1945. Statement, 4 April 1945.
39 'Boy's Body in Lake', *Cork Examiner* (11 May 1945), p. 3.
40 NAI, SFCCC, Limerick 1945. Letter, 3 April 1945.
41 'Co. Limerick Girl Sent for Trial', *Cork Examiner* (29 January 1946), p. 3.
42 NAI, SFCCC, Sligo 1949.
43 This must have been an 'informal' adoption arrangement as the Adoption Act 1952 was the first provision for legal adoption in Ireland.
44 'Sligo Woman on Murder Charge', *Irish Press* (23 November 1949), p. 13.
45 'Child's Death Was Accidental Mother Says', *Irish Press* (24 November 1949), p. 7.
46 NAI, CCA 56/1944. Second statement of Ellen Keogh, 12 January 1944.

47 NAI, CCA 56/1944. Trial judge's charge to the jury.
48 NAI, SFCCC, Westmeath 1943. Deposition of Annie Owens, 15 June 1943.
49 NAI, SFCCC Cork 1929–31.
50 NAI, CCA 30/1928.
51 'Granard Infanticide Charge', *Longford Leader* (14 August 1926), pp. 1–2.
52 NAI, Department of An Taoiseach S.11040. Garda report, A. E. O'Reilly, 17 November 1938.
53 NAI, CCA 30/1928.
54 Rattigan, '*What Else Could I Do?*'.
55 Clara Fischer, 'Gender, nation and the politics of shame: Magdalen laundries and the institutionalization of feminine transgression in modern Ireland', *Signs*, 41:4 (2016) 821–43.
56 'Reprieve', *Irish Times* (20 May 1935), p. 6.
57 Farrell, 'Infanticide of the ordinary character'.
58 Lindsey Earner-Byrne, 'Reinforcing the family: the role of gender, morality and sexuality in Irish welfare policy, 1922–1944', *History of the Family*, 13:4 (2008) 360–369.
59 NAI, Department of An Taoiseach S.7788A. Memorandum, 4 January 1944.
60 NAI, Department of Justice 234/1491. Petition of Mary Kiernan, 31 January 1927.
61 NAI, CCA 13/1935. Statement of Elizabeth Edwards, 30 October 1934.
62 Jaffary notes similar practices in nineteenth-century Mexico. Nora E. Jaffary, 'Maternity and morality in Puebla's nineteenth-century infanticide trials', *Law and History Review*, 1–21, online first, 26 January 2021, https://doi.org/10.1017/S0738248020000292.
63 'Sensational Case at Ballacolla', *Nationalist and Leinster Times* (3 November 1928), p. 9.
64 'Granard Infanticide Charge', *Longford Leader* (14 August 1926), pp. 1–2.
65 DDA of Archbishop John Charles McQuaid. AB8/b/XXVIII/983. Memorandum prepared by E. M. Carroll, probation officer at Dublin Metropolitan Courthouse, forwarded in a letter 9 July 1941.
66 Earner-Byrne, 'Reinforcing the family', p. 363.
67 Karen Brennan, '"A fine mixture of pity and justice": the criminal justice response to infanticide in Ireland, 1922–1949', *Law and History Review*, 31:4 (2013) 793–841.

68 Karen Brennan, 'Murderous mothers and gentle judges: paternalism, patriarchy and infanticide', *Yale Journal of Law and Feminism*, 30:1 (2018) 139–95.

69 Karen Brennan, 'Punishing infanticide in the Irish Free State', *Irish Journal of Legal Studies*, 3:1 (2013) 1–35.

70 Although occasional comments can be found in newspaper coverage, such as Justice Johnston's remark in a 1927 case that a change in the law might be made 'so as to obviate a charge of wilful murder'. 'Great Wave of Infanticide', *Irish Times* (7 December 1927), p. 4.

71 NAI, Department of Justice 234/2016. Letter from Religious Society of Friends, 15 December 1927, and response, 21 December 1927.

72 NAI, Department of An Taoiseach S.7788A. 25 August 1941.

73 NAI, Department of An Taoiseach S.7788A. 25 August 1941.

74 NAI, Department of An Taoiseach S.7788A. Department of Local Government and Public Health memorandum relating to Insanity as a Defence in Criminal Cases and Infanticide, 2 February 1944.

75 'Charges against Three Women', *Irish Independent* (26 June 1944), p. 2.

76 The terminology was amended in the Criminal Law (Insanity) Act 2006 substituting reference to 'lactation' with 'mental disorder'.

77 Karen Brennan, 'Traditions of English liberal thought: a history of the enactment of an infanticide law in Ireland', *Irish Jurist*, 50 (2013) 100–37.

78 Brennan, 'Traditions of English liberal thought'. Brennan notes that a meeting between the Minister for Justice, the Attorney General and Archbishop McQuaid was scheduled, and finds memoranda on the proposed bill in McQuaid's papers written by advisor Monsignor Dargan. Dargan was critical that the death sentence was *always* reprieved in 'infanticide' cases, but noted that Ireland would be strongly condemned if such sentences were carried out.

79 Karen Brennan, 'Social norms and the law in responding to infanticide', *Legal Studies*, 38:3 (2018) 480–99.

80 'Infanticide Act Explained', *Irish Times* (18 February 1950), p. 9.

81 'Novel Development in Infanticide Case', *Donegal Democrat* (11 July 1958), p. 1.

82 NAI, SBCCC, Books (Counties) 1957 to 1961.

83 Brennan, 'Murderous mothers'.

84 NAI, Department of An Taoiseach S.5891. Memorandum.

85 The differential treatment was visited on her child as well; while children born to first-time mothers were often boarded out or informally

adopted, the children of 'persistent offenders' were more likely to end up in industrial schools. See Mary Raftery and Eoin O'Sullivan, *Suffer the Little Children: The Inside Story of Ireland's Industrial Schools* (Dublin: New Island, 1999).

86 Kate had been bound over to good behaviour for a period of five years on her father's bail to the sum of £25. NAI, Department of An Taoiseach DT S.13383A.

87 NAI, Department of An Taoiseach S.5571.

88 NAI, Department of Justice 234/1491. Handwritten notes, February 1927.

89 NAI, Department of An Taoiseach S.6096. Letter from Justice O'Byrne, 27 November 1930.

90 NAI, Department of Justice 234/3332. Letter from Stephen Roche, 17 November 1933.

91 Sandra McAvoy, 'The regulation of sexuality in the Irish Free State, 1929–1935', in Greta Jones and Elizabeth Malcolm (eds), *Medicine, Disease and the State in Ireland, 1650–1940* (Cork: Cork University Press, 1999).

92 'Great Wave of Infanticide', *Irish Times* (7 December 1927), p. 4. Despite this exhortation, Gorman was found guilty of concealment.

93 Maria Luddy, 'Moral rescue and unmarried mothers in Ireland in the 1920s', *Women's Studies*, 30:6 (2001) 797–817.

94 Breathnach, 'Handywomen and birthing'.

95 Finola Kennedy, *Cottage to Crèche: Family Change in Ireland* (Dublin: IPA, 2001).

96 Nora E. Jaffary, *Reproduction and Its Discontents in Mexico: Childbirth and Contraception from 1750 to 1905* (Chapel Hill: University of North Carolina Press, 2016).

97 Liena Gurevich, 'Parental child murder and child abuse in Anglo-American legal system', *Trauma, Violence & Abuse*, 11:1 (2010) 18–26, p. 19.

98 NAI, SFCCC, Kerry 1929; Department of An Taoiseach S.5886; Department of Justice 234/2590.

99 NAI, SFCCC, Kerry 1929. Deposition of Superintendent Quinn, 12 March 1929.

100 NAI, Department of An Taoiseach S.5886. Memorandum, 17 June 1929.

101 Deale wrote that 'the authority of the Judge's position, and of his personality if he is a strong Judge, together ensure that the jury will either totally accept the Judge's view of the case, or be seriously influenced by it.' Deale wrote that Justice O'Byrne was 'too strong minded'.

Kenneth E. L. Deale, *Beyond Any Reasonable Doubt? A Book of Murder Trials* (Dublin: Gill and Macmillan, 1971), p. 108.

102 Convicted 10 June 1929.

103 Convicted 13 June 1929.

104 Convicted 25 June 1929.

105 Convicted 27 November 1930.

106 Convicted 28 March 1935.

107 Convicted 15 November 1938.

108 'Another Death Sentence', *Leitrim Observer* (29 June 1929), p. 2.

109 'Infant in Bush', *Cork Examiner* (14 June 1929), p. 13.

110 'Woman Acquitted of Murder', *Connacht Sentinel* (30 November 1943), p. 1.

111 'The Infanticide Scandal', *Irish Independent* (11 February 1929), p. 9.

112 NAI, CCA 13/1935. Trial judge's charge to the jury.

113 Of 29 women sentenced to death for infanticide in the second half of the nineteenth century, all were reprieved. Farrell, 'Infanticide of the ordinary character'.

114 NAI, Department of An Taoiseach S.5195. Memorandum, 4 November 1926.

115 NAI, Department of An Taoiseach S.5195. Letter from Michael Lennon to Kevin O'Higgins, 18 March 1927.

116 This 'working rule' was found on various files within the archives, see NAI, Department of Justice 234/2016 (Elizabeth Hannon); Department of Justice 234/2603 (Catherine Ahearne); Department of Justice 234/3332 (Christina Russell).

117 'Woman Sentenced to Death in Dublin', *Irish Independent* (13 December 1927), p. 7; NAI, Department of An Taoiseach S.5571.

118 'Drowned Leix Children', *Irish Independent* (2 December 1927), p. 7.

119 'Remarkable Case', *Evening Echo* (10 December 1927), p. 1.

120 'Mary Cole in the Dock', *Evening Herald* (20 March 1928), p. 1.

121 'Girl Prisoner's Tears', *Evening Herald* (23 March 1928), p. 1.

122 'Girl Aged 15½', *Irish Independent* (24 March 1928), p. 7.

123 'Drowned Children', *Belfast Newsletter* (22 March 1928), p. 5.

124 'Girl Prisoner's Tears', *Evening Herald* (22 March 1928), p. 1.

125 'Girl Prisoner's Tears', *Evening Herald* (22 March 1928), p. 1.

126 'Girl Prisoner's Tears', *Evening Herald* (22 March 1928), p. 1.

127 'Girl Prisoner's Tears', *Evening Herald* (22 March 1928), p. 1.

128 NAI, SBCCC, February 1946 to 1952; SFCCC, Dublin 1950.

129 David A. Green, *When Children Kill Children: Penal Populism and Political Culture* (Oxford: Clarendon, 2008).

130 Luddy, 'Moral rescue', p. 798.
131 Emma Milne, *Criminal Justice Responses to Maternal Filicide: Judging the Failed Mother* (Bingley: Emerald Publishing, 2021).
132 NAI, Department of Justice 18/3110. Letter from the Society for the Abolition of the Death Penalty, signed by Rosamond Jacob, 13 December 1938.
133 NAI, Department of Justice 170/7622. Letter, 28 November 1948.
134 Richard Jones, 'Populist leniency, crime control and due process, *Theoretical Criminology*, 14:3 (2010) 331–47.
135 Lizzie Seal, 'She killed not from hate, but from love': motherhood, melodrama and mercy killing in the case of May Brownhill', *Women's History Review*, 27:5 (2018) 669–87, p. 670.
136 'Manslaughter of Infant Son', *Strabane Chronicle* (15 November 1947), p. 1.
137 NAI, Department of Justice 18/7448A. Garda report, 12 January 1944.
138 NAI, SFCCC, Louth 1944. Statement of Margaret Somerville.
139 'Sensational Case at Ballacolla', *Nationalist and Leinster Times* (3 November 1928), p. 9.
140 Kennedy, *Cottage to Crèche*, p. 143.
141 Mother and Baby Home Commission of Investigation Final Report, p. 1.
142 NAI, SFCCC, Roscommon 1935. Letter, 28 October 1934.
143 Not least because many of the fathers remained ignorant of the pregnancy.
144 NAI, SBCCC, November 1927 to June 1935.
145 'Sordid Story', *Evening Herald* (17 July 1928), p. 2.
146 'Sordid Story', *Evening Herald* (17 July 1928), p. 2.
147 'Judge's Comments', *Cork Examiner* (18 July 1928), p. 7.
148 Elaine Farrell, '"Poor prison flowers": convict mothers and their children in Ireland, 1853–1900', *Social History*, 41:2 (2016) 171–91, p. 174.
149 Helen Johnston, 'Imprisoned mothers in Victorian England, 1853–1900: motherhood, identity and the convict prison', *Criminology & Criminal Justice*, 19:2 (2019) 215–31, p. 216.
150 'Brutal Murder of a Tramp', *Irish Independent* (5 July 1925), p. 7.
151 'Portarlington District Court', *Nationalist and Leinster Times* (22 October 1927), p. 5.
152 Farrell, 'Poor prison flowers'.
153 Johnston, 'Imprisoned mothers in Victorian England'.
154 'Infanticide Charge', *Anglo-Celt* (7 April 1934), p. 1.
155 'Newcastlewest Woman', *Liberator* (3 March 1936), p. 2.

156 NAI, Department of An Taoiseach, S.11040. Garda report, 17 November 1938, prepared by A. E. O'Reilly.

157 NAI, SFCCC, Monaghan 1938; CCA 36/1938; Department of An Taoiseach S.11040; Department of Justice 18/3110A.

158 NAI, Department of Justice 18/3110A. Petition of Mary Somerville, 14 December 1940. Luddy describes this home as part of the 'philanthropic empire' of Ellen Smyly. Maria Luddy, *Women and Philanthropy in Nineteenth-Century Ireland* (Cambridge: Cambridge University Press, 1995), p. 82.

159 'Matricide Charge in Cork', *Evening Herald* (15 February 1939), p. 9.

160 Farrell, 'Poor prison flowers'.

161 'Harbouring Charge', *Cork Examiner* (28 October 1926), p. 8.

162 NAI, SFCCC, Tipperary 1949. Prison medical officer, 28 June 1949.

7

Marriage and sexuality

Nagy writes that 'contemporary normative gender ideals are still part of the legal narratives of women accused of murder'.[1] The cases of women brought to trial go some way to illuminating the normative gender expectations which shaped Irish society in these decades. Offending women navigated a complex web of merits and demerits according to their performance of womanhood.[2] This chapter discusses the ways in which women prosecuted for murder were understood within this schema. As noted in Chapter 2, rationales of mercy premised on gender were dominant throughout this period. These arguments were evident in assumptions about a woman's role, and particularly her private, passive domesticity. In the 1925 case of Hannah O'Leary, these discourses contributed to the differential punishments experienced by Hannah and her brother Con O'Leary. Although both were death-sentenced for the murder of their brother, Hannah was reprieved and Con was executed. In his charge to the jury, the judge shared his suspicions of their respective roles:

> There are certain aspects of this case which may suggest themselves to you as being matters in which women may be more likely to be concerned than men. ... It was not light work to decapitate the man and carve up his body; it was not a job of the easiest also to dispose of them. It took some time to do it and you may remember the marks of the washing upon the wood work on the top of the bed. That may be a woman's job.[3]

Imbricated within notions of womanhood was a host of assumptions related to how women should conduct themselves. In particular, these expectations clustered around headline items like marriage and sexuality. Consideration of how they adhered to such expectations informed criminal justice responses. Worrall, for instance, proposed a 'gender contract' by which women benefited from the social dividends of femininity when they held up their end of the bargain. This chapter explores the nuanced, often surprising, criminal justice responses to women who were failing to reach the lofty heights of appropriate womanhood.

The poisoner

The figure of the poisoner has traditionally been gendered female, representing an absolute betrayal of domesticity. Through the nineteenth century, an androcentric fear of the poisoner was allied to concerns of the hidden house devil.[4] Burney has noted the 'poisoning mania' which gripped the English public at this time,[5] while Ballinger, writing on the twentieth century, found that 'Women poisoners were never reprieved.'[6] The twentieth-century Irish cases are a counterpoint to this. The two women, Agnes McAdam and Frances Cox, who were convicted of murder by poisoning and sentenced to death were reprieved. A further eight women brought to trial for the murder of an adult by poisoning walked free from court.[7]

The censure that could be expected for female poisoners was entirely absent in the case of Agnes McAdam. On Friday 28 September 1945, Agnes delivered two cakes to the nearby Finnegan family. The cakes were intended for a church social, but a substantial portion of one was eaten by James Finnegan who died later that day. Agnes was sentenced to death for his murder when strychnine was found in the cakes. The lack of motive suggested a pathological explanation, which insulated Agnes from representation as 'evil'. This was reinforced by a view of her as 'weak-minded'. The only suggested motive was that Agnes harboured a grudge at being excluded from the organisation of the church social, described in a memorandum as 'a failure which many women of her type would regard as a serious social slight on their social standing'.[8] Finnegan's death was viewed as a tragic accident: the fault of a pitiful woman who harboured no true intent to harm.

Frances Cox, in contrast, was understood as cold and callous. Frances was sentenced to death for the murder of her brother, Richard Cox, who died on 29 May 1949 after four agonising days. When concerns over the manner of his death were raised, the funeral was halted and strychnine was found in his organs. In an article for the *Garda Review* written just three years after her conviction, Superintendent George Lawlor relied heavily on mythical notions of female poisoners, writing that 'invariably, when a woman decides to kill she resorts to its use'.[9] The censure expressed towards Frances was evident in the description of the killing by the prosecution as 'a particularly malevolent, malicious, and utterly callous murder'.[10] Lawlor articulated this when he wrote: 'It is hard to conceive that a sister could continuously administer strychnine to a brother and look placidly on his suffering. It is difficult in words to describe such utter callousness.'[11] Neither judge nor jury recommended mercy.[12]

The cases of Agnes McAdam and Frances Cox, while both involved murder by poisoning of adult men, offer two very different narratives. Agnes McAdam was portrayed as a sympathetic figure while Frances Cox was constructed as deliberate and cunning. This distinction may have related to the simultaneous construction of Frances as dominant and agentic, and therefore as masculine. Although both women were reprieved, there *was* evidence of particular condemnation for poisoners in this period. In a 1951 Dáil Debate on capital punishment, poisoners were singled out as deserving of the most serious punishment, being described as: 'the crafty deliberate poisoner who poisons quietly and secretly over a period for the purpose of amassing wealth or the property of a particular person'.[13] The cases discussed below, though, in which women walked free from court, suggest a less punitive approach. The striking profile of those acquitted was that most stood accused of poisoning their husbands (Nora Madigan had been accused jointly with her mother of her father's murder, while Kathleen Clogher was accused of killing her brother). The cases represented, as one prosecuting counsel lamented, 'a sad climax to a married life'.[14]

Elizabeth Reilly's husband Edward died in March 1925. Despite her account of a happy life together, the evidence told of a fractious marriage marred by physical fights. Elizabeth was also having an affair with a local man.[15] Elizabeth herself, unusually, defended this extramarital relationship, stating that she was doing nothing wrong in light of her husband's behaviour.[16] The eccentricities of the victim were made much of through the trial.[17] Despite medical evidence that Edward had died by strychnine poisoning, the circumstantial case presented by the state floundered on a number of points: the lack of strychnine in the house and the failure to show Elizabeth had purchased any, as well as the implications of the victim's mental instability which raised the possibility that he had taken the poison himself (or suggested to the jury that she could hardly be held responsible if she *had* poisoned him).

Six years later, Bridget Walsh also walked free after being tried for the murder of her husband. Michael Walsh died mysteriously in May 1931.[18] Traces of strychnine were found in a glass used by Michael, as well as in the defendant's coat, and the local chemist testified that Bridget had purchased strychnine the day before her husband's death under a false name. In her statement, Bridget told of her unhappy marriage, while letters sent to another man suggested her affections lay elsewhere. This was unsurprising: Michael Walsh had deserted his wife seven years earlier, only returning in the months before his death.[19] The jury, after 90 minutes' absence, found Bridget Walsh not guilty of her husband's murder in a case which had seemed to present ample evidence of intentional killing.

In 1933, Kate Shanley was likewise tried for her husband's murder and found not guilty.[20] James Shanley died shortly after returning from Kinnegad fair on 9 May 1932. After suspicions began to build in the local area, in October the body was exhumed and strychnine found in the deceased's organs. Although one witness gave evidence that Kate had confessed to giving her husband the poison in a bottle of stout, medical evidence also showed that the 71-year-old James had a weak heart.[21] It seemed likely that this weakness had been the cause of death, although exacerbated by poison. It took the jury just 30 minutes to reach a verdict of not guilty, a verdict 'received with an outburst of applause' in the court.[22]

Soon after, Anne Hanley was found not guilty of her husband Phelim's murder in 1934.[23] Anne and Phelim had married in February 1933; by July he was dead. The prosecution narrative presented a financially independent woman, who had lived in America for a decade, and who now bitterly regretted her marriage.[24] A witness recalled Phelim's words to his wife during one argument: 'You call me thick and ignorant. It is you who are thick and ignorant, and you have broken every vow you made at our marriage.'[25] Numerous witnesses gave evidence of marital strife and it was suggested that Anne wished to extract herself from this union to marry another man. During the trial, one witness recounted that some days before her arrest, Anne had cried 'why did I do it?'[26] The jury, after deliberating for an hour, found her not guilty. Justice Hanna, perhaps unimpressed by the verdict, replied: 'Very well. Discharge the prisoner.'[27]

Similar circumstances were again evident in Elizabeth Conway's acquittal that same year. Elizabeth's husband Martin had died on 24 May 1934. The deceased had suffered from rheumatic arthritis and gastritis for which he regularly took salts.[28] There was again a suspicion that Elizabeth had been having an affair with a man named Rahilly.[29] There was no evidence Elizabeth had purchased strychnine, although evidence was given that Rahilly had recently purchased some. The poison seemed to have been administered in the salts Martin had taken on the day of his death, which Elizabeth had prepared.[30] After an hour, the jury found her not guilty.

Sarah and Nora Madigan, mother and daughter, were also tried for murder by poisoning. Patrick Madigan was the husband of Sarah and the father of Nora. He had died in September 1941, and the following February both were brought to trial. Sarah was ultimately found not guilty, while the charge against 18-year-old Nora was dropped. In this case, the judge had nudged the jury in Sarah's acquittal. Again, there was the suggestion of infidelity, and evidence that Sarah had purchased strychnine before Patrick's death. Echoing other of the cases too, the deceased's behaviour was characterised as difficult, and physical violence in the marriage was alleged. One further issue of expert opinion arose, a disagreement as to the cause of death between the state pathologist and another expert.[31] There was considerable sympathy for the prisoners and, in charging the jury, the judge expressed his view that there was 'not a shred of evidence' as to improper relations and that 'It would be terrible if an innocent woman was convicted.'[32] After 55 minutes, the jury found Sarah not guilty, a verdict the judge was inclined to agree with: 'You can tell your friends and neighbours that the Judge entirely agrees with the verdict of the Jury.'[33]

The discovery that the family dogs were dead, in the case of Kathleen Clogher, caused sufficient concern that the funeral of her brother was stopped and the body sent for examination.[34] Kathleen was the last woman tried for murder by poisoning before the threat of a capital sentence was removed. The state alleged that Kathleen had killed her brother George in December 1962 by adding strychnine to his food.[35] Early in the investigation, Kathleen had confessed to mistakenly sprinkling poison on his meal, revealing to one guard: 'I could have put a little Enheptin in the fish, but if I did it was only a little bit and the fish was flavoured anyway.'[36] In court, she claimed that these admissions had been made under pressure during questioning and were not truthful. After 90 minutes, the jury found her not guilty.[37]

These cases suggest an unwillingness to condemn women suspected of killing by poison in cases which presented sympathetic circumstances. This appears to be in contrast to patterns in the nineteenth century, for which Vaughan found that 'Men who poisoned their wives, and wives who poisoned their husbands, were hanged.'[38] Particularly damning, Robb noted, was when infidelity was alleged. Perhaps, as admitted by the state in Elizabeth Conway's case, it was simply a difficult matter to bring home to a jury that poisoning had taken place.[39] Robb identified four elements that were important in securing conviction: poison as the proven cause of death, evidence the suspect had acquired poison, evidence the suspect had administered the poison and a motive.[40] In many of the cases, these elements were present, yet the defendants were acquitted. Through the cases, there were both 'moral' arguments against conviction alongside evidentiary issues; the moral arguments included the difficult or volatile temperaments of the victims, which inspired sympathy in juries. However, in many of the cases the verdict could be viewed as perverse.

Concerns about female poisoners in the mid-nineteenth century have been interpreted as a response to the threat of women's campaigning for greater legal status.[41] Irish juries and judges through the decades post-independence, in contrast, viewed many of the suspect women with compassion. This may have been an attempt to ameliorate the harsh realities of marriage for many Irish women of the labouring classes. The acquittals may represent humane, albeit individualised, acknowledgements of desperate circumstances. Although marriage would seem not to have been an institution under threat in these years, its indissolubility achieved constitutional status in 1937, in a period which saw concern about the decline of the traditional Irish family, particularly the rural family.[42] The cases then appear as a negotiated form of community response to marriage gone wrong. In 1847, one Irish newspaper had noted the near impossibility of obtaining a divorce in Ireland, joking that 'Toxicology supplies the deficiency of the legislation.'[43] A century later, there may have been some remnant of this thinking.

Marriage and murder

It is pertinent here to consider the wider category of cases in which women were tried for the murder of husbands. Thirteen women were tried for the murder of their husbands, of which two were found guilty: Annie Walsh (1925) and Annie Walsh (1929). Another woman, Mary Power, was found guilty of the manslaughter of her husband and sentenced to six months' imprisonment.[44] Meanwhile, Elizabeth Reilly, Bridget Walsh, Kate Shanley, Anne Hanley, Elizabeth Conway, Sarah Madigan and Delia Laffey were found not guilty and discharged. All but Delia Laffey had been accused of killing by poison. Meanwhile Anne McGorry, Kate Duffy and Bridget Daly were found unfit to plead.[45] As the poisoning cases demonstrated, women brought before the courts for the murder of a husband were unlikely to be convicted. Somewhat against the literature, these cases do suggest a certain inclination towards leniency when the circumstances warranted.

For unhappily married women in Ireland, there was no legal way out. Had there been, it is unlikely that poor rural women would have availed of such an option in great numbers. As it was, Ireland was 'marked by its lack of divorce provision for much of the twentieth century'.[46] Parliamentary divorce had been available pre-1922, ensuring it was a recourse for only the most affluent. In the 1937 Constitution, it was entirely prohibited.[47] Nonetheless, Fitzpatrick writes that 'if divorce was scarcely known in Ireland separation in many guises was ubiquitous'.[48] In census returns through the 1800s, Fitzpatrick found tens of thousands of married women living apart from husbands; separation offered 'an essential safety-valve'.[49] The cases throughout this book demonstrate that many married couples lived apart and navigated marital breakdown in the ways available to them.

The 1931 poisoning case of Bridget Walsh presented an example of prolonged separation. Giving evidence, Bridget said that seven years prior to his death, her husband had left her and their child, forcing her to go out to work.[50] In these years, Bridget formed a bond with another man but was debarred from marriage due to the unknown status of her husband. In December 1930, Elizabeth placed an advertisement with the hope of ascertaining the whereabouts of her errant husband. Michael Walsh duly answered, and they were reunited in January. As prosecuting counsel pointed out, after a period of seven years Bridget likely hoped to have her husband declared dead.[51] In the end, her path to marital freedom was to be more tortuous.

The separation of husband and wife seemed to offer motivation in many cases of alleged infant murder too. Norah Brown pleaded guilty to the manslaughter of her illegitimate infant in 1944. She had married some years previously and had two children with her husband. However, her mother complained that her husband 'never provided a home for his wife',[52] and he soon abandoned her entirely. Kathleen Ogal's case was similar: she had pleaded guilty to the manslaughter of her infant in 1942. Kathleen's husband had left her almost two years prior to the killing. In her statement she said: 'I would not have done this only through my husband's fault. He drove me to it. He would not make a home for me. I wrote to him to make a home. No one wanted me when I had the baby.'[53] Annie Murphy pleaded guilty to infanticide in 1953. She had three living children, but had been separated from her husband for a year. She said in her statement: 'I was tormented. I did not know what I was doing, because my husband denied he was the father of my child.'[54]

Couples were also separated, whether as a temporary matter of necessity or otherwise, by the need to find work. There are many examples of wives remaining in Ireland while their husbands worked abroad. Christina McCarthy pleaded guilty to infanticide in 1955; she had killed her infant just days after her husband left for England stating that she could not cope without him.[55] For other women, pregnancy during their husband's absence created significant problems. Mary Downey, found guilty of concealment of birth in 1927, had become pregnant while her husband was in America; she was accused of killing this infant when he announced his plan to return.[56] Catherine Forde, found not guilty of infant murder in 1933, had experienced a similar quandary. After six years abroad, her husband had returned in August and an infant was born the following January. A doctor recalled Catherine saying: 'If I don't do away with this child, I will have no life with him.'[57] Alice Jones, found not guilty of murdering her infant in 1938, had been living separately from her husband, who had worked as a tailor in America for 12 years. She had married in 1920 and had three children with her husband before his departure in 1925.[58] As the prosecution argued, the motive to kill a newborn infant in such circumstances was clear.[59]

Such evidence of extramarital sexuality was condemned. For example, in the case of Ellen Keogh, who was convicted of manslaughter in 1944, the judge remarked:

> I should imagine that you do agree that it is a shocking thing that this woman should betray her husband ... I am sure you feel that whatever party was responsible for bringing about that association that both of them should feel sorrow and shame.[60]

The judge did not consider Ellen's separation from her husband, who had worked in England for some years, as worthy of mitigation. These cases demonstrate the potentially devastating consequences of separation, and the particular difficulties faced by women who were sexually active under such an arrangement. While separation was common as both an informal response to marriage breakdown and as an economic necessity, these cases also revealed the stagnation of women's lives which could result, and the precarious position many found themselves in when they attempted to live beyond the limits of the stalled status of 'wife'.

Sexuality

Appropriate womanhood was typically construed as sexually passive. This was evident in cases of infant murder, in which unmarried women were presented as 'weak-minded' victims of male persuasion and their own deficiencies. As noted in Chapters 4 and 5, such passivity bolstered arguments for women's institutionalisation. Mary Moynihan's case, meanwhile, offered an example of how female sexuality could be rendered passive to mitigate culpability. Although it was accepted that Mary Moynihan and Jeremiah Horgan, the victim's husband, had been engaged in a sexual relationship,[61] efforts were made to reframe Mary as the victim of a dominant man.[62] Mary encouraged these efforts when she spoke out from the dock following conviction, alleging that Jeremiah 'tempted me with murder'.[63] Despite the illicit relationship, Mary was reclaimed as a sympathetic figure, which ensured that the blame was laid with Horgan. The chaplain of Mountjoy Prison, petitioning on Mary's behalf, wrote that she had fallen under the influence of a married man, 'who was unscrupulous enough to make love to her'.[64]

Where possible then, the sexual appetite of women was not countenanced. In cases in which female sexuality was not neutralised, more insidious interpretations were deployed. As an alternative to passivity, Ellen Keogh and Frances Cox were constructed as possessing dangerous and pathological sexuality. The Garda report speculated that Ellen Keogh's first child was not her husband's and another report surmised that Ellen 'is believed to be sexually inclined'.[65] Ellen was elsewhere condemned as 'addicted to sexuality', presenting female sexuality as a pathologised weakness.[66]

Frances Cox was similarly understood. Although Cox had been sentenced to death for her brother's murder, she had killed her illegitimate infant shortly before the killing of her brother. The motivation for her brother's murder emphasised Frances's engagement to a local Catholic farmer; this clandestine engagement and Frances's admission that she had an earlier pregnancy presented her as sexually agentic. The local Protestant clergyman, appealing for mercy on behalf of Frances, confided that Frances was 'a sex maniac'.[67] Even in the cases of Ellen Keogh and Frances Cox, deliberate engagements in sexual relationships were denied under the guise of compulsion.

Despite the notion of women as sexually passive, there was evidence throughout of quotidian sexual practices which offer a less dogmatic picture of Irish life, and which Delay argues present an argument against Inglis' position of Irish sexual exceptionalism.[68] The seeming sympathy for many married women who stood accused of the murder of their husbands itself offered a corrective to an idea of uncritical condemnation for illicit sexuality. As McLoughlin argued, while marriage was officially represented as the only appropriate site of sexuality, Irish people did not simply stop having premarital or extramarital sex after the Famine.[69] Numerous cases among the accused women demonstrated this. Teresa Conlon, who pleaded guilty to concealment in 1934, named the father of her infant, before confessing 'I can't be positive.'[70] Mary Geraghty, who pleaded guilty to the manslaughter of her infant in 1943, stated: 'I have kept the company of different boys since I was 18 years of age, about four or five different boys had connection with me during the past four years.'[71] In the Garda report on Elizabeth and Rose Edwards, condemned to death in 1935, it was stated with disapproval that their 'main interest has been the seeking of amusement in the form of dances, and the company of men'. The report concluded: 'It had come to be regarded here as the normal thing for looseness on the part of women to be, if not what was expected of them, then something one need not feel astonished at.'[72] The existence of such relationships between unmarried persons is also evident in the case of Mary Kiernan, convicted of murder in 1926, in defence counsel's summary of her lifestyle:

> Her story was that she had been 'company-keeping', – a phrase which sessions has taught me means, among the rural – i.e. most of my countrymen – habitual immorality with someone who had left her when she had become pregnant.[73]

While women were officially constructed as sexually passive, the cases betrayed the prevalence of sexual relationships outside marriage. The rigid template of Catholic morality was not the entirety of experience.[74] As Earner-Byrne noted, despite hopes to the contrary, Ireland 'was not a country devoid of sex or sexuality'.[75]

In one respect, the cases from Ireland do exhibit a notable absence, namely, the media sexualisation of women who kill. The particular context of the sexual mores operating in these decades sits uneasily with a glamourised depiction of violent women.[76] In these years, to focus on fashion and glamour was distinctly un-Irish.[77] Beyond the limits of acceptable representations of Irish womanhood, the reticence to glamourise the women before the courts can be located in the class and social position of the suspect women, the 'roughness' of rural farming life and the unsuitability of discourses of glamour in these cases. Unique among the cases, the press reporting of Mamie Cadden offered an example of a woman who was glamourised by the press, with reports variously describing outfits, such as: 'Miss Cadden wore a beaver lamb coat, fur cap and pink scarf. She had cluster earrings with a matching cluster on the collar of her coat.'[78]

Reputation

Many of the cases demonstrated networks of local knowledge, and the tangible effects of rumour. In 1926, state counsel in the case of Elizabeth Reilly referenced the difficulty of conducting extramarital affairs in rural areas, noting that 'She was carrying on an intrigue with a man in Granard, as if she were living in some great city.'[79] There was a clear presumption that while cities offered anonymity for deviant sexuality, rural Ireland left such activity exposed to prying eyes. Women who were understood by their local community as sexually deviant held a devalued reputation. Women such as Annie Walsh (1929) and Jane O'Brien were depicted in this light. The extramarital relationship between Walsh and Martin Joyce, both condemned to death for the murder of Annie's husband, was the subject of local rumours. One witness gave evidence that he had remarked to Joyce that 'he would get it very hard on account of the fact that everybody in the country knew he was going with the woman'.[80] Indeed, the judge stated that it would be 'almost impossible' to think that an 'intrigue' had not taken place.[81] Walsh's devalued reputation infused Garda reports on her character, evident in a memorandum which reported:

> Mrs Walsh, if the police are to be believed, is far from being the patient and suffering angel. ... She certainly lived in sin with Joyce and the police say that she actually offered him her own young daughter for his amusement in order to keep him hanging about the house.[82]

Another memorandum alleged serious previous wrongdoing: 'Mrs Walsh is a wicked criminal, it is also alleged she dispensed of her first husband in America.'[83]

The construction of Jane O'Brien as sexually deviant compounded the already unflattering portrait of her as dominant and masculine. Again, these allegations were unearthed by Gardaí from a reservoir of 'local knowledge'. One Garda report noted that Jane 'bears a very bad repute – she is said to have lived a very immoral life'.[84] She was also the subject of informal allegations of previous, serious wrongdoing; it was noted that her brother had died 'rather mysteriously and the local people suspect that he was poisoned and that Jane O'Brien who was described to me as the Devil would be responsible for committing the act.'[85]

The deviant sexuality of certain women was linked to views of them as masculine, dominant and therefore unnatural.[86] Some of the women who were most vilified demonstrated a dominant sexuality, as evidenced in the exceptional fate of Annie Walsh (1925). That sexual immorality could have tangible criminal justice repercussions was demonstrated by the English case of Edith Thompson, executed along with her lover in 1923 for the murder of her husband. As noted by many commentators, Thompson's execution was justified as much by reference to her infidelity as to her crime.[87]

In contrast to these patterns, the case of Elizabeth Reilly represented a stunning counter-example of the active resistance to the rumours which swirled in her local town of Granard. As noted, Elizabeth had been acquitted of the murder of her husband in 1926. Elizabeth's husband had been a difficult man, possessed of a devalued reputation due to this eccentric behaviour. In light of this, under cross-examination Elizabeth expressed herself as 'sincere in her devotions, and did not consider that she was doing wrong' in having an affair.[88] In a robust defence, her barrister lambasted both the people of Granard as well as Carrigan, who was acting as prosecuting counsel.[89] Of her community, defence counsel criticised 'the mob down in Granard … howling for her head!' In particular, he singled out 'those Puritans and Evangelists of Granard'. Acknowledging her extramarital affair of some years, Reilly's counsel noted the incredibly difficult circumstances of her life, and the cruelties of her marriage to 'a demented maniac'.[90]

Abortion

On the morning of 18 April 1956, the body of a woman was found outside 15 Hume Street in Dublin. The post-mortem revealed that the woman, identified as 33-year-old Helen O'Reilly, had died as a result of an embolism which caused heart failure. O'Reilly had been five months pregnant, and died while undergoing an abortion. Mamie Cadden lived in a one-bedroom flat at 17 Hume Street and immediately became the chief suspect. On 1 November, she was convicted of murder, and on 4 January 1957, Cadden's sentence was commuted to penal servitude for life.

As discussed in Chapter 2, efforts were made to convict Cadden on the capital charge, notably the doctrine of constructive malice, which 'constructed' the necessary *mens rea* for the offence of murder from the lesser abortion offence. Influencing appeal arguments, the British 1953 Royal Commission on Capital Punishment had recommended the doctrine's abolition and their Director of Public Prosecutions had recommended that a charge of manslaughter rather than murder should be brought in abortion deaths.[91] On appeal, such arguments were dismissed in relation to the procedure in Ireland.

Two cases from the 1940s offer comparators to Cadden's experience.[92] In 1940, John Daly and Ellen Anthony were indicted for murder following the death of 26-year-old Bridie Kirk. In this case, the judge permitted the charge of manslaughter to go to the jury, and John Daly, who was the victim's partner, was convicted on this charge, while nurse Ellen Anthony was acquitted. Bridie Kirk and the married John Daly began a relationship in 1938. In 1939, Bridie had become pregnant and, under the pretence that they were attending the Galway races, Daly checked Bridie into a hotel in Cork and arranged for an abortion. The state case was that Ellen had, along with Daly, administered abortifacient drugs, which caused Kirk's death. John Daly had previously been convicted at the Liverpool City Sessions in 1936, for supplying a noxious drug with intent to procure an abortion. Ellen Anthony, meanwhile, bore a good reputation, evidenced in the statement of a doctor who gave evidence that he had known her for some years and 'found her efficient, conscientious and extremely good in a difficult case'.[93]

In 1948, Kathleen Gilbourne was indicted on multiple counts of attempting to procure a miscarriage and two counts of murder: that of Wilhelmina Birney in 1948 and the unnamed infant of Julia Dunne in 1945.[94] Gilbourne ultimately pleaded guilty to eight counts of procuring a miscarriage and one count of manslaughter relating to the death of the infant, and was sentenced to two sentences of seven years penal servitude to run concurrently.[95] The murder charges were not pursued and all charges relating to the death of Wilhelmina Birney were dropped. Gilbourne, a widow in her forties, was known locally to provide such services, and her expertise was regularly sought out by young unmarried women, often with the support of their family, or married women who wished to limit their family size. Very high rates of marital fertility produced clear strains on maternal health and wellbeing.[96] As Justice Maguire commented, she undertook this work 'systematically' for a number of years.[97] For Gilbourne's services, she received small sums of money, and at trial her counsel argued that she was driven to perform such services because of destitution.[98] The woman whose murder she was charged with, Wilhelmina Birney, wished to end her pregnancy as a result of poor health.[99] Some days after the procedure, she died due to toxaemia and haemorrhage.

Exploring the response to Cadden, McAvoy questioned whether a 'respectable' midwife would have faced such a harsh response.[100] The cases of Ellen Anthony, Kathleen Gilbourne and Mamie Cadden offer three very different profiles of female abortionists: that of a respectable maternity nurse in private practice; an older and financially precarious 'handywoman'; and Cadden,[101] the disgraced former midwife, who had become 'the face of "backstreet" abortion' in Ireland.[102] The case of Gilbourne, in particular, demonstrated the 'domestic' nature of abortion in these years (in contrast to the urban image of the backstreet abortionist).[103] As Breathnach noted, the figure of the handywoman has inevitably become steeped in the literature of deviancy, as a character who colluded in the destruction of infants, but this must be read against a backdrop in which home birth with only the assistance of untrained midwives was still common.[104]

Abortion cases which found their way to court were typically those cases in which the worst had happened (although Kathleen Gilbourne's case offers the voices of women who had benefited from her help without incident). These cases do not capture the experiences of women who attempted to deal with unwanted pregnancies and whose efforts went undetected. Mary Creane, for instance, had pleaded guilty to the manslaughter of her infant in 1941, and revealed that the man she had been seeing had given her a bottle of syrup he said would cause a miscarriage. The case demonstrated an escalating response to illegitimate pregnancy which had ended in the killing of the infant.[105]

These practices continued a tradition of asserting control of bodily autonomy, especially when faced with a desperate situation. Despite an official cultural revulsion for the practice of abortion, the necessities of day-to-day life ensured it persisted as an option for many.[106] These women troubled the Irish cult of domesticity, although this was not their intention.[107] Delay notes Bonnie Shepard's use of 'double discourse' in this regard, in which women profess commitment to stated public policy while subverting this in their everyday lives.[108] Relatedly, McCormick's research on abortion in Belfast outlines how the authorities struggled to bring home to women that they were engaged in wrongdoing when attempting to induce miscarriages.[109]

The condemnation for women who availed of such options, though, was clear from the following remark from probation officer E. M. Carroll:

> We have also to consider that the women charged with such offences as infanticide are far less guilty than the larger numbers in the more exalted walks of life who have recourse to the use of contraceptives and abortifacients and who never appear charged with such crimes.[110]

Relatedly, ambivalence around discussions of abortion was noted throughout such cases. Certain terms were perpetually couched euphemistically, with the term 'illegal operation' typically used, while the term 'abortion' itself was seldom used prior to the 1980s.[111] Further, despite voluminous reportage on Cadden's case, there was squeamishness on the details, evident in Justice McLoughlin's summary of the pathologist's evidence: 'the details of it are not very savoury and I don't want to discuss it if I can avoid it'.[112] The barring of women from unsavoury topics was a recurring theme. In 1927, the Minister for Justice had restricted the rights of women to serve on juries and to take employment as court stenographers.[113] Such views were also evident throughout the physical archives, in the exclusion of female civil servants when typed copies of certain notes were required. Two case files involving detailed discussion of sex, birth and infant murder were marked for a 'male typist'.[114]

Sexual and domestic violence

There was impressive form in these decades when it came to suppressing unpalatable details of a sexual nature, such as the suppression of the 1931 Carrigan Report and its revelations on the prevalence of sexual violence.[115] The government was skilled in 'ideologically driven news management' when it came to questions of sexual deviance.[116] The coded nature of reporting on abortion was matched by the limited and oblique nature of reporting on sexual violence.[117] As Finnane concluded, in the early years of independence there was an obsession with visible manifestations of sex which 'avoided a more considered attention to the contexts and harm of serious sexual offending'.[118] As a result, it is rare to hear first-hand accounts from victims of sexual violence.[119] When such experiences were revealed, victimhood was extended to certain women only, and 'for a woman to establish her victimhood when raped, she needed to prove her moral character and physical resistance to assault'.[120] As Maguire argued, in many cases of sexual violence, there was a general suspicion that the victim had been as much to blame as the perpetrator.[121]

Deborah Sullivan was sentenced to death for the murder of her infant in 1929. In a statement made after her arrest, Deborah disclosed that she had been raped: 'he forced his family affair into my private part and I wanted to get him off me all the time but he would not get off, he was a long time lying down on me and he had his family affair all the time in my private part'.[122] An investigating Garda deposed, 'I believe the accused was telling the truth'.[123] Following conviction, her solicitor made reference to these 'strong extenuating circumstances', writing that: 'It is shown that the said Deborah O'Sullivan [sic] ... was raped and as a result gave birth to a child she was found guilty of murdering.'[124] Despite evident sympathy, the jury found her guilty of murder. Although Gardaí were aware of Deborah's allegation of rape, there was no record of criminal proceedings being taken against her attacker.

Meanwhile, there was direct censure for Margaret Dillon, who pleaded guilty to the manslaughter of her infant in 1940. Defence counsel revealed that Margaret had been 'criminally assaulted' but had not reported this to Gardaí. Justice Maguire admonished Margaret, stating that 'She neglected a very serious duty to the public',[125] and sentenced her to four years' penal servitude, an atypically severe sentence.

In 1942, Julia Wilmot pleaded guilty to the manslaughter of her infant. Wilmot's husband lived in England, and she alleged that she had been raped while her husband was away: 'He caught a hold of me and had a connection with me forcibly and against my will. I did not scream or shout as I did not know what he was going to do to me.'[126] Julia had not confided in her husband on his return as 'I thought there was nothing wrong with me and I did not want to be worrying him'.[127] Julia's sister, however, confirmed that she had heard this allegation at an earlier date.[128] Julia's husband Daniel, whether believing the story or not, was not inclined to support her, and communicated that he wished leniency for his wife, so that he could 'start life anew in some other country'.[129] Mary Considine, who pleaded guilty to the manslaughter of her infant in 1946, revealed in her statement that: 'I shouted at him to stop it but he did not stop. ... I struggled with him but he knocked me down on the floor of the shed.'[130]

A number of cases explicitly dealt with incest, while others implied as much. Due to the hidden nature of the crime, few cases came to light, and many were only detected when the victim became pregnant.[131] Margaret Moore, brought to trial for the murder of her illegitimate infant in 1938, had become pregnant following a sexual relationship with her uncle, with whom she had gone to live to escape her drunken and volatile father.[132] Rattigan notes that Garda questioning often betrayed their suspicions of incest, such as in the case of Delia Murphy in 1935, in which both Delia and her father John were indicted for infant murder.[133] Delia had been previously convicted of concealment in 1929, and had been delivered of a stillborn infant in 1931. When investigating the 1935 death, Gardaí made enquiries as to sleeping arrangements, particularly whether Delia slept in the same room as her father. At trial, Delia pleaded guilty to manslaughter, and her father pleaded guilty to concealment. Sentencing him to two months' imprisonment, the judge said he had received a custodial sentence because it was not the first time this had happened.[134] The judge's comments may have referred to the suspicion of incest, as, despite Delia's previous conviction, John Murphy had no criminal record.

In the case of Nora Cronin, found guilty of two counts of concealment, the coroner's comments seemed to allude to something, possibly incest: 'It would seem to be very undesirable that the poor girl should be left in her present surroundings. … It was certainly a very shocking state of affairs.'[135] In the 1931 case of Nora Hannigan, in which she pleaded guilty to concealment, Nora herself claimed that her father was the father of the infant victim.[136] The *Evening Herald* reported this allegation in an unsympathetic manner, noting that it had been denied by her father under oath: 'She made a very abominable charge as to the paternity of the child, and suggested that her father had an interest in its destruction quite apart from the shame that would fall on him as her father.'[137]

In these cases, the women were living with their fathers, and in some cases brothers, after their mothers' deaths. Both Cronin and Hannigan had given birth to multiple illegitimate infants over a number of years. The Punishment of Incest Act 1908 specifically criminalised incest but did not offer protections, an inadequate legal framework which governed responses until the 1990s. Not only were incest offences incredibly difficult to detect and prosecute, but Buckley writes that victims also acquired the taint of immorality, and were treated in the same way as prostitutes, unmarried mothers and women who committed adultery.[138] The motivation to suppress the Carrigan Report was, in large part, due to its specific findings on the scale of child sexual abuse and incest, and a desire to avoid adverse publicity.[139]

As the poisoning cases above revealed, there were accounts of domestic violence throughout the cases. In these particular examples, there was evident sympathy for women who had lived with violent men. In the case of Delia Laffey too, tried for the murder of her husband in 1962 and found not guilty, she also alleged an unhappy marriage with the suggestion of violence.[140] One newspaper reported: 'The evidence was that the deceased was hard-working and industrious but when he took drink he changed completely and became truculent.'[141] However, violent victimisation within the family was generally not considered 'criminal' in these decades.[142] It is likely that much of the violent victimisation experienced by women never made it into evidence. Those women who alleged that they had been raped revealed this information because it was specifically relevant to the offence with which they were charged. In cases of incest, little was alleged, although suspicions were evident. Experiences of domestic violence emerged in a number of cases of women charged with husband-murder, again in cases where such facts were relevant to the charge. Beyond the cases in which victimisation could be persuasive in eventual outcome, it is unlikely that defendant women would have disclosed sexual or domestic victimisation. As Urquhart writes, the incredibly classed and gendered assumptions about domestic violence, combined with the unavailability of divorce, 'left many women open to very serious abuse'.[143] Violence perpetrated by husbands and fathers was not necessarily considered a threat to the family, the community or the new nation.[144]

Conclusion

Women accused of murder were understood according to normative womanhood. The insistence on passive sexuality was mandated by the dominant moralist discourses. Yet, appropriate womanhood was an idea mediated by place and time, and for most of the women before the courts they were understood within a cipher of identity that revolved around rurality, poverty and their position as members of the 'labouring classes'. Inevitably, gender discourses were refracted through this situatedness. While there were very clear views, then, on the most privileged ways of being a woman, there was considerable nuance within this, according to circumstance. For instance, the cases of wives accused of husband-murder by poisoning suggest that accommodations were made when it was evident that women were labouring in a marriage to a 'bad' husband. The disapproval towards extramarital sexuality was not a blanket condemnation. While unmarried women were generally subject to punitive surveillance and treatment, there was more leeway for married women. The poisoning cases in particular disrupt ideas of 'double deviance'.

Notes

1 Victoria Nagy, 'Narratives in the courtroom: female poisoners in mid-nineteenth century England', *European Journal of Criminology*, 11:2 (2014) 213–27, p. 225.
2 Anne Worrall, *Offending Women: Female Lawbreakers and the Criminal Justice System* (London: Routledge, 1990).
3 NAI, CCA, 18/1925. Judge's charge to the jury.
4 Anette Ballinger, *Dead Woman Walking: Executed Women in England and Wales* (Dartmouth: Ashgate, 2000). The numbers were always small: only 40 women and 20 men were tried for spousal murder by poisoning through the century. George Robb, 'Circe in crinoline: domestic poisonings in Victorian England', *Journal of Family History*, 22:2 (1997) 176–90.
5 Ian A. Burney, 'A poisoning of no substance: the trials of medico-legal proof in mid-Victorian England', *Journal of British Studies*, 38:1 (1999) 59–92.
6 Ballinger, *Dead Woman Walking*, p. 28.
7 In 1937, Kate Reilly pleaded guilty to the manslaughter of her two-year-old child. Kate had poisoned the child by strychnine. She was considered to be mentally disturbed. NAI, SBCCC, November 1933 to 22 April 1941.

8 NAI, Department of An Taoiseach S.13804. Extract from local district officer.

9 Superintendent George Lawlor, 'Green Street: The Cox Poisoning Case', *Garda Review*, October 1952, p. 847. Lawlor was head of the Garda Technical Bureau at the time and had investigated the case.

10 'Woman Accused of Poisoning Brother', *Irish Press* (16 November 1949), p. 5.

11 Lawlor, 'Green Street', p. 860.

12 'Woman Condemned to Death', *Anglo-Celt* (26 November 1949), p. 11.

13 Dáil Debate, 5 December 1951, Vol. 128, Number 3.

14 'Clare Woman Charged', *Evening Herald* (23 February 1942), p. 4.

15 'Alleged Poisoning', *Irish Times* (19 March 1926), p. 5.

16 'Story of Double Life in Granard Poison Drama', *Longford Leader* (27 March 1926), p. 2.

17 'Longford Poisoning Case', *Irish Times* (20 March 1926), p. 8.

18 NAI, SBCCC, November 1927 to June 1935.

19 'County Cork Murder Charge', *Irish Times* (17 June 1931), p. 8.

20 NAI, SBCCC, November 1927 to June 1935.

21 'Woman Charged with Murder', *Sunday Independent* (12 February 1933), p. 9.

22 'Failure of Meath Murder Case', *Irish Press* (23 March 1933), p. 7.

23 NAI, SBCCC, November 1933 to 22 April 1941.

24 'Charge of Murder', *Offaly Independent* (30 June 1934), p. 6.

25 'Charge of Murder', *Offaly Independent* (30 June 1934), p. 6.

26 'Charge of Murder', *Offaly Independent* (30 June 1934), p. 6.

27 'Widow Found Not Guilty', *Weekly Irish Times* (7 July 1934), p. 17.

28 'Kerry Murder Charge', *Irish Times* (23 July 1934), p. 8.

29 'Kerry Murder Charge', *Irish Times* (23 July 1934), p. 8.

30 'Kerry Murder Charge', *Irish Times* (23 July 1934), p. 8.

31 In cases with conflicting expert testimony, a humane jury often acquitted. Burney, 'A poisoning of no substance'.

32 'Co. Clare Widow Acquitted', *Irish Independent* (5 March 1942), p. 2.

33 'Co. Clare Widow Acquitted', *Irish Independent* (5 March 1942), p. 2.

34 'Woman Said to Have Put Strychnine on Fish Tea', *Irish Press* (7 May 1963), p. 4.

35 'Woman Said to Have Put Strychnine on Fish Tea', *Irish Press* (7 May 1963), p. 4.

36 'Woman Said to Have Put Strychnine on Fish Tea', *Irish Press* (7 May 1963), p. 4.

37 NAI, SBCCC, 1962 to July 1964.

38 W. E. Vaughan, *Murder Trials in Ireland, 1836–1914* (Dublin: Four Courts Press, 2009), p. 320.

39 'Castleisland Woman', *Kerry Reporter* (24 November 1934), p. 1.

40 Robb, 'Circe in crinoline'.

41 Robb, 'Circe in Crinoline'.

42 Mary E. Daly, *The Slow Failure: Population Decline and Independent Ireland, 1920–1973* (Madison: University of Wisconsin Press, 2005); see also Lindsey Earner-Byrne, 'The family in Ireland, 1880–2015', in Thomas Bartlett (ed.), *The Cambridge History of Ireland*, Vol. 4 (Cambridge: Cambridge University Press, 2018).

43 *Freeman's Journal* (5 September 1847), cited in Diane Urquhart, 'Ireland and the Divorce and Matrimonial Causes Act of 1857', *Journal of Family History*, 38:3 (2013) 301–20, p. 302.

44 This case is examined further in Chapter 8. See NAI, SBCCC (change of venue cases for all counties) June 1925 to December 1926.

45 These cases are discussed in Chapter 3.

46 Urquhart, 'Ireland and the Divorce and Matrimonial Causes Act of 1857', p. 301.

47 David Fitzpatrick, 'Divorce and separation in modern Irish history', *Past & Present*, 114 (1987) 172–96.

48 Fitzpatrick, 'Divorce and separation', p. 174.

49 Fitzpatrick, 'Divorce and separation', p. 185.

50 'County Cork Murder Charge', *Irish Times* (17 June 1931), p. 8.

51 'Verdict of "Not Guilty" in Cork Murder Trial', *Irish Times* (18 June 1931), p. 10.

52 NAI, SFCCC, Carlow 1944. Deposition of Nora Dwyer.

53 NAI, SFCCC, Tipperary 1942. Statement of Kathleen Ogal, 14 August 1942.

54 NAI, SFCCC, Carlow 1953. Statement of Annie Murphy, 3 November 1952.

55 'Insane When She Killed Child', *Evening Echo* (28 February 1955), p. 1.

56 'Alleged Murder of Child', *Offaly Independent* (22 October 1927), p. 5.

57 'Alleged Murder of Infant', *Evening Herald* (23 March 1933), p. 10.

58 'Returned for Trial', *Nenagh Guardian* (13 November 1937), p. 5.

59 'Woman on Trial for Murder', *Evening Herald* (5 May 1938), p. 10.

60 NAI, CCA 56/1944. Judge's charge to the jury.

61 A Garda report referenced local knowledge that Moynihan had previously given birth to a child which was rumoured to be Jeremiah Horgan's. NAI, Department of Justice 234/1744. Garda report, 5 November 1923.

62 An investigation by the Department of Justice following Moynihan's conviction concluded that Horgan 'may or may not have instigated the murder. That is a matter of mere conjecture.' The report found that there was no evidence on which to proceed against him. NAI, Department of Justice 234/1744. Report by T. A. Finlay, 24 March 1925.

63 NAI, SFCCC, 1924 Cork.

64 NAI, Department of Justice 234/1744. Letter from John Fitzpatrick, Junior Roman Catholic Chaplain, 6 November 1927.

65 NAI, Department of Justice 18/7448A. Garda report, 25 October 1944.

66 NAI, Department of Justice 18/7448A. Garda report, 12 January 1944.

67 NAI, Department of Justice 18/11757A. Note, 21 December 1949.

68 Cara Delay, 'Kitchens and kettles: domestic spaces, ordinary things, and female networks in Irish abortion history', *Journal of Women's History*, 30:4 (2018) 11–34, p. 12; Tom Inglis, 'Origins and legacies of Irish prudery: sexuality and control in modern Ireland', *Éire-Ireland*, 40:3/4 (2015) 9–37, p. 10.

69 Dymphna McLoughlin, 'Women and sexuality in nineteenth-century Ireland', in Alan Hayes and Diane Urquhart (eds), *The Irish Women's History Reader* (London: Routledge, 2001).

70 NAI, SFCCC, Clare 1944. Statement of Teresa Conlon, 7 November 1934.

71 NAI, SFCCC, Meath 1943. Statement of Mary Geraghty, 17 August 1943.

72 NAI, Department of Justice 18/885. Garda report, 2 April 1935.

73 NAI, Department of Justice 234/1491. Letter from Michael Lennon, 18 March 1927.

74 Sandra McAvoy, 'The regulation of sexuality in the Irish Free State, 1929–1935', in Greta Jones and Elizabeth Malcolm (eds), *Medicine, Disease and the State in Ireland, 1650–1940* (Cork: Cork University Press, 1999).

75 Lindsey Earner-Byrne, 'Reinforcing the family: the role of gender, morality and sexuality in Irish welfare policy, 1922–1944', *History of the Family*, 13:4 (2008) 360–9, p. 364.

76 Tom Inglis and Carol MacKeogh, 'The double bind: women, honour and sexuality in contemporary Ireland', *Media, Culture and Society*, 34:1 (2012) 68–82.

77 Cara Delay and Annika Liger, 'Bad mothers and dirty lousers: representing abortionists in postindependence Ireland', *Journal of Social History*, 54:1 (2020) 286–305.

78 'Nurse Sent for Trial on Threat Charge', *Irish Times* (9 May 1956), p. 8.

79 'Alleged Poisoning', *Irish Times* (19 March 1926), p. 5.

80 NAI, CCA, 16/1929. Evidence of Thomas Canavan.

81 NAI, Department of An Taoiseach S.5904. Judge's charge to the jury.

82 NAI, Department of Justice 234/2599. Memorandum, 30 June 1932.

83 NAI, Department of Justice 234/2599. Memorandum, 4 July 1929.

84 NAI, Department of Justice 18/2737. Garda report from McCarthy, from his recollections, undated.

85 NAI, Department of Justice 18/2737. Garda report by C. O'Halloran, from his recollections, 11 June 1932.

86 Worrall argued that offending women could be 'neutralised' by labelling them as 'not criminal' or 'not woman'. Worrall, *Offending Women*. Ballinger argued that women who were viewed as rational risked masculinisation and a harsher criminal justice response. Ballinger, *Dead Woman Walking*.

87 Ballinger, *Dead Woman Walking*.

88 'Longford Poisoning Case', *Irish Times* (20 March 1926), p. 8.

89 'Longford Poisoning Case', *Irish Times* (20 March 1926), p. 8.

90 'Longford Poisoning Case', *Irish Times* (20 March 1926), p. 8.

91 *Report of the Royal Commission on Capital Punishment, 1949–53* (London: HMSO, 1953). The doctrine of constructive malice was abolished in Britain in the Homicide Act 1957.

92 *Attorney General v Daly*, unreported, 1940 (CCC).

93 'Maternity Nurse on Trial', *Irish Times* (29 May 1940), p. 3.

94 Sandra McAvoy, 'Before Cadden: abortion in mid-twentieth-century Ireland', in Dermot Keogh, Finbarr O'Shea and Carmel Quinlan (eds), *Ireland in the 1950s: The Lost Decade* (Cork: Mercier Press, 2004).

95 NAI, SBCCC, February 1946 to 1952; SFCCC, Laois 1948.

96 Daly, *The Slow Failure*; Mary E. Daly, 'Marriage, fertility and women's lives in twentieth-century Ireland (c.1900–c.1970)', *Women's History Review*, 15:4 (2006) 571–85.

97 'Woman Sentenced to Seven Years', *Irish Times* (12 June 1948), p. 9.

98 McCormick noted that the defence typically downplayed financial motive and concentrated on the desire to help desperate women.

Leanne McCormick, '"No sense of wrongdoing": abortion in Belfast 1917–1967', *Journal of Social History*, 49:1 (2015) 125–48.

99 NAI, SFCCC, Laois 1948. Statement of Robert Birney.

100 McAvoy, 'Before Cadden'.

101 Although, in these years, the formerly upwardly mobile Cadden was also a financially precarious older woman.

102 Delay and Liger, 'Bad mothers', p. 1.

103 Delay, 'Kitchens and kettles'.

104 Ciara Breathnach, 'Handywomen and birthing in rural Ireland, 1851–1955', *Gender & History*, 28:1 (2016) 34–56.

105 NAI, SFCCC, Meath 1941. Statement of Mary Creane, 25 April 1941; 'Meath Infanticide Charge', *Drogheda Independent* (28 June 1941), p. 2. Creane also revealed that he had given her the address of the Bethany Home.

106 Delay notes that there were 33 abortion trials from 1900 to 1950 (outside of the six counties that would become Northern Ireland). Cara Delay, 'Pills, potions and purgatives: women and abortion methods in Ireland, 1900–1950', *Women's History Review*, 28:3 (2019) 479–99.

107 Delay, 'Kitchens and kettles'.

108 Bonnie Shepard, 'The "double discourse" on sexual and reproductive rights in Latin America: the chasm between public policy and private actions', *Health and Human Rights*, 4:2 (2000) 110–43; Delay, 'Pills, potions and purgatives'.

109 McCormick, 'No sense of wrongdoing'.

110 Dublin Diocesan Archives, AB8/b/XXVIII/983. Memorandum prepared by E. M. Carroll, probation officer at Dublin Metropolitan Courthouse, and forwarded by the County Registrar of the Circuit Court to Archbishop McQuaid, enclosed in a letter, 9 July 1941.

111 Finola Kennedy, *Cottage to Crèche: Family Change in Ireland* (Dublin: IPA, 2001), p. 38.

112 NAI, Department of An Taoiseach Files, S16116. Charge to the Jury, para. 114.

113 Thomas Mohr, 'The rights of women under the constitution of the Irish Free State', *Irish Jurist*, 41 (2006) 20–59.

114 NAI, CCA 30/1928. Letter from Green Street Circuit Court office (Mary Lenihan) and CCA 36/1938 (Mary Somerville).

115 Mark Finnane, 'The Carrigan Committee of 1930–31 and the "moral condition of the Saorstát"', *Irish Historical Studies*, 32:128 (2001) 519–36.

116 Anthony Keating, 'Sexual crime in the Irish Free State 1922–33: its nature, extent and reporting', *Irish Studies Review*, 20:2 (2012) 135–55, p. 135.

117 Keating, 'Sexual crime in the Irish Free State'.

118 Finnane, 'The Carrigan Committee of 1930–31', p. 530.

119 Lindsey Earner-Byrne, 'The rape of Mary M.: a microhistory of sexual violence and moral redemption in 1920s Ireland', *Journal of the History of Sexuality*, 24:1 (2015) 75–98.

120 Earner-Byrne, 'The rape of Mary M.', p. 86.

121 Moira J. Maguire, 'The Carrigan Committee and child sexual abuse in twentieth-century Ireland', *New Hibernia Review*, 11:2 (2007) 79–100.

122 NAI, SFCCC, Kerry 1929. Statement of Deborah Sullivan, 20 February 1929.

123 NAI, SFCCC, Kerry 1929. Deposition of Superintendent Quinn, 12 March 1929.

124 NAI, Department of Justice 234/2590.

125 'Child's Death', *Cork Examiner* (4 December 1940), p. 3.

126 NAI, SFCCC, Kerry 1942. Statement of Julia Wilmot, 18 January 1943.

127 NAI, SFCCC, Kerry 1942. Statement of Julia Wilmot, 18 January 1943.

128 NAI, SFCCC, Kerry 1942. Deposition of Bridget Enright, 6 February 1943.

129 NAI, SFCCC, Kerry 1942. Letter from Daniel Wilmot, received 17 February 1943.

130 NAI, SFCCC, Dublin 1946. Statement of Mary Considine, 17 July 1946.

131 Sarah-Anne Buckley, 'Family and power: incest in Ireland, 1800–1950', in Anthony McElligott, Liam Chambers, Ciara Breathnach and Catherine Lawless (eds), *Power in History: From Medieval Ireland to the post-Modern World*, Historical Studies XXVII (Dublin: Irish Academic Press, 2011).

132 NAI, SFCCC, Dublin 1938.

133 NAI, SBCCC, November 1933 to 22 April 1941. See discussion in Clíona Rattigan, *'What Else Could I Do?': Single Mothers and Infanticide, Ireland 1900–1950* (Dublin: Irish Academic Press, 2012), pp. 103–4.

134 'County Mayo Case', *Cork Examiner* (3 April 1935), p. 2.

135 'Infant's Body', *Cork Examiner* (1 March 1929), p. 9.

136 NAI, SBCCC, November 1927 to June 1935.

137 'Concealment of Birth', *Evening Herald* (18 June 1931), p. 5.
138 Buckley, 'Family and power'.
139 Maguire, 'The Carrigan Committee'.
140 NAI, SBCCC, 1962 to July 1964.
141 'Not Proposed to Call Accused in Murder Trial', *Irish Independent* (8 November 1962), p. 13.
142 Earner-Byrne, 'The family in Ireland'.
143 Diane Urquhart, 'Irish divorce and domestic violence, 1857–1922', *Women's History Review*, 22:5 (2013) 820–37, p. 828.
144 Cara Delay, '"Uncharitable tongues": women and abusive language in early twentieth-century Ireland', *Feminist Studies*, 39:3 (2013) 628–53.

8

Rural lives and class

Overwhelmingly, the women prosecuted for murder were rural women of the labouring classes. They came from families without land of their own, who were hired to work in the houses or on the land of others, or families who worked their own modest holdings. Most of the women were economically and socially marginalised. This identity not only shaped the contours of their lives, it also played a role in the killings for which they stood accused, and in the criminal justice responses they faced. In this chapter, I explore some of the issues identified by McAuliffe as in need of further untangling in the research on Irish women's history.[1] In particular, I explore the contradictions between rural and urban Ireland, what belonging to the 'labouring classes' meant for Irish women and Irish womanhood, and the treatment of Irish speakers and Travellers. The cases suggest the ambiguous status of many rural-dwellers before the courts, simultaneously representing ideal Irishness as well as perverting notions of national identity. A mythologised Ireland held considerable cultural purchase. Yet in the crucible of the trial, the mores of a rural society crashed into those of a Dublin urban elite, troubling these romanticised ideas.

The 'West' and the rest

Rural Ireland represented a culture distinct from Dublin, as was clear in the courtroom when a professional elite came face-to-face with their country brethren. Many cases subverted romantic notions of rural Ireland, an ideology stoked by narratives of Irish nationalism and bound up with the Gaelic Revival. This movement of the late nineteenth and early twentieth century envisioned the 'true' Ireland to be rural Ireland, especially the 'West' of Ireland, in which land was possessed of huge symbolic importance and was worked by a simple rural peasantry.[2] In this clash of cultures, the 'rural' was contrasted with the 'urban', which signified alien influence. O'Sullivan and O'Donnell suggested that: 'In Ireland, the term "rural" is invested with a range of symbolic meanings which are routinely invoked to articulate particular belief systems and to stress the importance and, often, presumed superiority of rural over urban life.'[3] As prosecution counsel in the 1925 case of Sarah Keane asserted, gainsaying any talk of poverty:

> They were all Connemara peasants. They lived on the shores of Galway Bay and they had a comfortable existence from the sea and the land. There was full and plenty despite the talk of distress in the West, which was sometimes used for political and other purposes.[4]

Yet the presumed moral superiority of rural Ireland was troubled by the occurrence of murders within this pastoral idyll. Disdain was evident in many of the comments made by the Dublin legal professionals. Defence counsel in the trial of Hannah Flynn referenced the John Millington Synge play *The Playboy of the Western World* when he wrote that: 'The only comment to be made on the case is that Synge erred considerably when he published "The Playboy" years ago, instead of keeping it till the present day.'[5] The play portrays a bravura young man, Christy Mahon, who is valorised by a County Mayo community when he tells them that he is on the run after brutally slaying his father.[6] It represents a rural culture enthusiastic in its embrace of violence.

Against notions of supremacy, the cases also betray the view of rural Ireland as backward and unsophisticated, shown in the judge's charge to the jury in the 1946 case of Agnes McAdam:

> you will, of course, remember that considerable allowance must be made for country witnesses in a very strange atmosphere, where they may feel ill at ease, especially with Learned Counsel talking to them sometimes in unaccustomed language.[7]

Such thinking was also evident in the 1934 case of Elizabeth Conway, one report of which paraphrased Conway's defence barrister: 'Counsel didn't think it part of his duty to put an ignorant Kerry peasant in the witness box, who might be badgered into an ill-considered answer to a half-understood question.'[8] Within this assumption of the 'backwardness' of rural Ireland, we can again find the judgements of 'weak-mindedness' which were routinely made about women appearing before the courts. These were deeply gendered *and* classed preconceptions, rooted also in ideas about the nature of the country beyond the capital.

Notwithstanding assumptions of backwardness, there were occasional disputes in court, often between defence counsel and Gardaí, with regard to the perceived intelligence of various women. This was clear in the 1944 trial of Ellen Keogh, convicted of the manslaughter of her infant. When asked to agree that Ellen was an 'ignorant type of woman', a detective responded, 'I say she is fairly well educated and I definitely say that she is a clever little lady'.[9] Assumptions of simplicity sometimes competed with allegations of cunning. Similar suspicion was evident in the case of Frances Cox during the cross-examination of Superintendent George Lawlor at her trial for the murder of her brother in 1949:

Defence: You are head of the Technical Bureau here and you were dealing with an ignorant country girl?
Lawlor: I would not agree to that.
Defence: A simple country girl?
Lawlor: Not even that.
Defence: Well, a country girl?
Lawlor: Yes.[10]

In contrast to assumed rural ignorance, some barristers made favourable allusions to the perspicacity of Dublin juries which drew on an accepted view of sophisticated Dublin against an uncivilised rural hinterland. In the 1926 case of Elizabeth Reilly, who was acquitted of the murder of her husband,[11] her counsel made sure to praise the jury: 'I know my Dublin jurymen, and I am not afraid to leave the decision in your hands. You are men of the world and you will not be influenced by the howls of the Granard mob.'[12] Likewise, in the 1931 case of Bridget Moylette, in which she pleaded guilty to concealment, her solicitor implored in the District Court that, surely, 'no Dublin jury could convict' if she was sent to the Central Criminal Court.[13] At the close of Agnes McAdam's trial, Justice Gavan Duffy also greatly esteemed the jury:

> Gentlemen, it is a comfort for a Judge in a criminal trial to have with him a Dublin Jury, because he knows they have experience and tradition, and he feels that they realise the gravity of their duty, and that he can trust their common sense.[14]

The gulf between the urban and rural was more than intellectual and cultural; for many, the physical distances were also too vast to overcome, as observed in the 1924 case of Annie Moore and Margaret Hillis, from Monaghan, in which it was noted that, although it was common for character witnesses to give evidence in court, 'owing to the fact that the woman came from the country witnesses were not there personally'.[15]

In a 1941 memorandum on infant murder, probation officer E. M. Carroll outlined the class gradations of women appearing before the courts, noting that many were 'from isolated places in the West', and that, 'As a class the majority spring from the ordinary labouring family some from the decent small farmer, a few from the riff-raff of the small town back street population.'[16] While rural and small-town Ireland was distinct from the Dublin elite, there were also significant distinctions to be made within and between the country beyond Dublin. Many of the cases alluded to these class differences, which were located on a spectrum between respectability and depravity. In his 1929 Lenten Pastoral, the Bishop of Ossory took aim at the 'humbler classes', claiming that they had 'less regard for purity and morality than in the past' and exhorting masters and mistresses 'to keep a more stringent control over these poor people, often the victims of their own ignorance or want of religion or the shelter of a home'.[17]

The 1925 case of Sarah Keane saw a harsh judgement passed on a remote island community off the Galway coast, condemned as one ruined by poteen. Sarah was charged with murder, along with her son Patrick, for the killing of a neighbour Matthew Connolly. The *Evening Herald* noted state counsel's words: 'You will find ... they are a highly intelligent people, living comfortably, according to their own habits, but that they, too are the slaver and victims of the vice of drunkenness and the debauchery that follows it.'[18] Carrigan remarked on 'the finest peasantry in the world being ruined and kept in poverty and deprived of the superior civilisation to which they might attain, if this vice was abolished from amongst them'.[19]

This case recalls the typical profile of violence in post-Famine Ireland as rural, of an idiosyncratic quality and characterised by 'recreational' brawling, often as a result of drinking.[20] Reflecting the nature of Irish society until the later twentieth century, the overriding feature of crime, and homicide particularly, was its rural character.[21]

Motivations to kill

The rural nature of Irish society is evident in the motivations to kill in the cases of women charged with murder. As McCullagh observed, 'It is hardly surprising that, in a situation of deprivation, a major source of conflict should be over the one resource that had the potential to relieve, or at least alleviate, the deprivation.'[22] The Famine of the 1840s devastated a predominantly rural and agricultural population. In the aftermath, land achieved even greater importance. Opening his work on the land question in Ireland, Dooley writes that, 'It is often difficult to appreciate or sympathise with the Irish psyche that attaches an almost obsessive importance to the ownership of land.'[23] Delayed industrialisation meant that many were dependent on agriculture throughout the nineteenth century and for much of the twentieth. Hannan and Commins argued that these forces resulted in a rural fundamentalist economy, in which the importance of family farms was paramount and rural society became a barometer for the health of a nation.[24] O'Donnell and O'Sullivan analyse the repercussions of this rural fundamentalism in Ireland, suggesting a rural society characterised by conservatism and ruled by economic imperatives.[25] The post-Famine Irish rural landscape was characterised by the structure of the stem family. This system provided for impartible inheritance by one offspring, typically the eldest son.[26] In this context, the elemental importance of land was apparent in motivations to violence and this provided the bedrock for much unrest, both at a societal level as well as offering individual reasons to kill in the satisfaction of feuds and grudges. Under the stem system, inevitably many family members were dispossessed, as it produced and reinforced 'lines of resentment within families'.[27] Agrarian violence in Ireland greatly contributed to Ireland's characterisation as a restless country in the nineteenth century.[28] The perceived threat to social stability that this violence posed meant that offences involving land disputes were punished severely.[29] Nevertheless, family conflict related to the division of labour, land and inheritance was a primary motivation for homicides in the late nineteenth and early twentieth centuries.[30]

The importance of land is evident in many of the cases of women prosecuted for murder, expressed as a stake in the family farm, in the cases of Hannah O'Leary and Frances Cox, or in the retention of the family home, as evidenced in Jane O'Brien's case. O'Sullivan and O'Donnell argued that patterns of ownership and inheritance left 'surplus' family members vulnerable, which contributed to the high numbers coercively confined post-1922.[31] These patterns carried consequences for women, and, as the cases demonstrate, a number of women took drastic action when facing such bleak prospects.

Hannah O'Leary's case illustrated many of the prevailing patterns of rural family life and inheritance. O'Leary was convicted of murder and sentenced to death on 30 June 1925. She had been convicted jointly with her brother Con for the murder of their older brother Patrick.[32] On 7 March 1924, a sack containing the head of a man was found under bushes in a field in rural County Cork; a search revealed other sacks close by, containing further body parts. When Con was questioned about the whereabouts of his brother Patrick, he told Gardaí that Patrick had travelled to Bandon fair ten days prior and had not yet returned. When asked to identify the remains, Con first confirmed that they were those of his brother, before expressing himself uncertain. When the remains were taken to a public house, 37-year-old Hannah O'Leary likewise refused to identify the remains, relenting only when her sister confirmed that the deceased was in fact their brother. The prosecution case was that Patrick had been killed in his bed by hatchet blows to the head and his body dismembered post-mortem. The alleged motive was a family dispute motivated by money, inheritance and resentment towards Patrick. The O'Learys lived on the family farm, a holding of 40 acres worth between £800 and £1,000, and which had been willed to Patrick by his father in 1921.[33] Hannah and Con were to be given lodging and maintenance for the duration of their life, and their sister Mary Anne would additionally receive £350, an amount, in the words of the solicitor who had drawn up the will, for 'a marriageable girl'; however, the farm would pass to Patrick following the death of their mother.[34] Patrick's temperament had made this an intolerable situation for Con in particular, who gave evidence at the inquest that: 'I was not on speaking terms with my brother for the past four or five years. My father is dead about three years, and it was before then that we commenced to disagree. The cause of the disagreement was that I would not stop at home and work.'[35] Con worked as a labourer to a local man, something which greatly vexed Patrick, who believed Con should apply his labour to the family land. However, as Con received no wage for labouring at home, and was not in a position to inherit, he preferred to work for himself.[36]

The local priest gave evidence that he had been asked to intervene in disputes caused by Patrick's refusal to hand over money to his mother earned from the sale of livestock. The family rupture was reflected in the sleeping arrangements, and it was Patrick's custom to sleep away from the house, in the barn. The family's failure to report the disappearance of Patrick was viewed with suspicion. Crucially, the solicitor who had made the will in 1921 gave evidence that Con had visited him on 7 March 1924 and asked again to hear the contents of the will.[37] On foot of this, the entire O'Leary family had been arrested, although a *nolle prosequi* was entered for Hannah's mother, due to her advanced age, and Mary Anne died in prison while awaiting trial. The case demonstrated the often desperate position of non-inheriting siblings who were expected to work on family farms for little benefit, and the simmering family tensions this could provoke.[38]

Frances Cox's murder of her brother Richard on 29 May 1949 can be viewed as the act of one who feared disinheritance because of her indiscretions. Frances was convicted of the murder of her brother on 21 November 1949. The Coxes were a County

Laois farming family; Richard Cox Senior had died in 1939 and Frances and her brother Richard lived on the farm with their mother, Jemima. The family owned a substantial farm comprising approximately 127 acres, land worked by Frances and Richard. On Richard's death, suspicion fell heavily on Frances because of her recent prosecution for the manslaughter of her illegitimate infant. On the same day on which Frances was convicted of manslaughter, she was arrested for her brother's murder.[39] This fact seemed to provide the motivation to kill Richard, despite all the evidence suggesting that brother and sister had been close. In her evidence, Jemima Cox remarked of brother and sister, that 'He was more in love with Francey than I, to tell you the truth.'[40]

At some point in 1948, Frances had arranged to marry a man named William Weston. Weston was a neighbouring farmer, a Catholic who lived with his mother on a small farm of six acres. This secret engagement would comprise a substantial prong of the prosecution case. The case presented the narrative that Frances wished to marry a man of whom her family would not approve, and had killed her brother to avoid possible disinheritance. On Frances' intention to marry Weston, prosecution counsel stated:

> One cannot say what Richard felt about this matter. ... It would seem that there was an obvious reason for the accused to want to get rid of her brother. Putting it no further than this – there was a farm of 126 acres which may well have attracted attention.[41]

The 'tap of the religious drum' was presented by the state as another obvious motive.[42] The Cox family were Church of Ireland, while the Westons were Catholic. In his evidence, Weston stated that he could not have married Frances unless she converted to Catholicism. The defence argued that it was a nonsense that religious prejudice could be a motive: 'In 1949, in this State, it had been alleged and pressed that a reasonable Irish jury should come to the conclusion that that was a motive they should consider.'[43] However, Frances's mother Jemima gave evidence which countered this, and when asked during the trial if she knew of any arrangements to get married, she responded: 'I did not; and I would not allow her. I want to get my own equals',[44] also expressly claiming that she wanted Frances to marry a Protestant.[45] Both Weston's religion and his lesser social status were important. In her own evidence, Frances was asked why she did not tell her family that she had arranged to marry Weston: 'I don't know; I suppose they would not be pleased.'[46] It was suggested by state counsel that the consequences of marriage to Weston would be material as well as spiritual, something which 'carried implications which were not likely to be ignored by anyone with experience of rural communities, and might or might not prove to be the key to this crime'.[47]

For Jane O'Brien, it was her nephew's impending marriage that risked unsettling her position.[48] On 8 June 1932, Jane was convicted of the murder of her nephew John Cousins, who had died following a fatal shotgun wound which he received as he walked home on the night of 26 March 1932. Jane O'Brien, and her son John, had lived in the Cousins' family home for 12 years. They had moved in 1920 at the request of Jane's brother William, following the death of his wife. Jane had sold her own property and invested the proceeds of the sale into their new home. Jane's brother had died in December 1931, leaving Jane's nephew, John Cousins, as the presumptive heir. Prosecution counsel sought to demonstrate that following her brother's death, Jane viewed her position in the household as precarious, especially as her nephew was engaged to be married. This fact was put forward as motivation for the murder; O'Brien had, they argued, murdered her nephew because she feared she would become homeless on his marriage, and as much was suggested by Jane in a letter to her sister in which she said: 'I told him I would not leave without being compensated.'[49]

The Irish family, and particularly the rural Irish family, has often been considered exceptional.[50] Following the Famine, it was characterised by falling rates of marriage, older ages at marriage (especially for men) and high rates of marital fertility. These trends ensured that the 'countryside was populated by lonely bachelors and spinsters'[51] until the 1950s.[52] The economic imperatives of the later nineteenth century contributed to these altered patterns, which also conspired to establish a rigid sexual propriety.[53] With fewer people marrying, and marrying later, prolonged periods or indeed a lifetime of celibacy was the expectation. These demographic trends provoked fears that rural Ireland was dying. The speculation internationally (many countries experienced similar population fears in the first half of the twentieth century) was that modernisation, education and the changing status of women were to blame for falling birth rates. Daly suggests that for those in government tasked with responding to this problem, 'The only way to maintain Irish fertility at its existing level was to keep the population poor, ignorant and away from cities.'[54]

The marriage patterns meant that families were large, and as many siblings would never marry, they would continue to live in the family home until old age. There are many women throughout the cases whose lives reflected this reality. Agnes McAdam was 53, living on the family farm with her brother and his wife, and contributing significantly to the domestic and farming work.[55] Mary Kate Doherty, described as 'a middle-aged woman',[56] lived with her brother Patrick whom she was accused of killing.[57] Kathleen Clogher, aged 57, lived with her brother George, of whose murder she stood accused.[58] Mary O'Brien, aged 38, lived with her brother, his wife and their children, and was found unfit to plead in the murder of her nephew.[59] Women had less chance of inheriting property, except widows who inherited their husband's land on his death, and who would, in turn, pass this on to their children. Throughout, there were frequent references to the use of the labour of 'surplus' female family members who lived in the family home, without significant prospect of inheritance or marriage. The structure of society, evident in the organisation of rural life around family farms, denied many women the opportunity to have their own home and family.[60]

The importance of children to the survival of family farms was a feature throughout much of the twentieth century. This was chiefly through the labour of sons and daughters on the farm or by the hiring-out of children through 'hiring fairs'. Mary Moynihan, who had worked as a domestic servant in the Horgan household for five years, had been hired out by her father and did not know what wage he received for her labour.[61] High rates of marital fertility provided a pool of free labour, although daughters had a lower status and Kennedy quotes the 1964 Limerick Rural Survey that girls were 'favoured by neither father nor mother and accepted only on sufferance'.[62] This disfavour was compounded by an expectation that one daughter at least would receive a dowry. For the non-inheriting and non-marrying siblings, beyond the possibility of remaining and contributing to the family home, even if it did become the home of a brother and his family, there were always the options of emigration (to Dublin or abroad) or joining a religious order.[63] As O'Sullivan and O'Donnell noted: 'It was those who remained on land that they could not own and women who gave birth outside of marriage who created obstacles to the preservation of the stem family.'[64]

Rural Irish womanhood

The nature of womanhood in such a society was antithetical to many of the supposed traits of an idealised femininity. As Delay writes, 'The low-voiced, gentle wife and mother played a limited role in the working-class and rural communities of the west. Here, women worked, often both inside and outside of the home.'[65] Notions of female vulnerability were inappropriate in this context. Instead, the employment histories of women and appraisals of them as 'hard-working' were always evidence in their favour. In contrast, Roscommon sisters Elizabeth and Rose Edwards were condemned in a Garda report for their 'shiftlessness': 'The two condemned girls have never been in remunerative employment … they appear to have drifted along without thought or concern for their future.'[66]

There were low numbers of women in remunerative employment in these decades, and Mahon has labelled Ireland as a private patriarchy for much of the period post-independence.[67] The majority of women worked within the domestic sphere, in occupations which related to traditional female roles. Many worked outside the home as domestic servants or within the family home performing similar functions. In the 1936 census, 86,102 women were recorded as domestic servants and a quarter of all adults were listed as homemakers, of which 552,176 were women and 1,301 were men.[68]

The migration of rural women to urban areas and overseas was a longstanding consequence of the limited prospects for Irish women,[69] and throughout the cases there are examples of women who returned to Ireland after a period living in England or the United States.[70] Bessie Dunleavy, who pleaded guilty to concealment in 1926, reported that she had returned from the US to find her sister pregnant, whose infant she had been accused of murdering.[71] Annie Walsh (1929) had emigrated to the US before the First World War, where she married an Irishman who died in the flu epidemic, leaving her 'with three children and some money'. The account of Catherine Philpot Curran Lennon, wife of the Church of Ireland rector of Aran, recorded that after Annie was widowed, her father-in-law had written asking her to return home to her husband's family at Aran. This move had left Annie in a miserable position, 'going from house to house, the country in awful turmoil'.[72] Some months after her return to Ireland, Annie Walsh married again, this time to Sonny Dan Walsh, the husband she would later be convicted of murdering. Mrs Lennon revealed that Annie herself had confessed: 'I'd rather throw myself in the sea, there is a house with nothing in it, there is land with nothing on it and a business were it twice as good he could drink every penny of.'[73]

As well as domestic work, there were also women whose occupation was characterised primarily as farmer or farm labourer. Of the death-sentenced women, for instance, Mary Somerville worked a farm of approximately 20 acres previously owned by her late husband,[74] Frances Cox worked a considerable family farm[75] and Elizabeth Doran worked as a farm labourer.[76] Due to later marriage, widows often inherited and ran family farms; the 1926 census recorded 135,000 widows, over 40 per cent of whom were employed and the largest proportion employed within farming.[77] Kennedy has argued that although many women were engaged in agricultural labour, it was typically valued less than the agricultural labour performed by men.[78] There is also evidence of the masculinisation of these women through the cases. In a Department of Justice memorandum, Frances Cox was described as 'the dominant member of the family'.[79] Frances's dominance was demonstrated through her ability to perform agricultural work, evident in her mother's comment that she was 'as good as any man on the farm'.[80]

While vulnerability has been cited as one of the rationales for chivalrous or paternalistic treatment,[81] it had little role in the lives of the women under investigation. Vulnerability must be interpreted through the prism of class and, as so many of the women accused of murder were women of the labouring classes, vulnerability was an inappropriate quality for many. The case of Mary Moynihan illustrated this positionality. Moynihan claimed that her employer, Nora Horgan, had been killed by a male intruder who had also struck Moynihan unconscious. When neighbours gathered in the house on the day of the killing, they were dismissive of her claims to victimhood and one asked 'how it was that herself and the Misses [*sic*] were not better able for the man?'[82] The 'toughness' expected of Moynihan was antithetical to notions of vulnerability.

Irish speakers

At various stages throughout the trials there were moments of translation. From 'country' to 'city', as in the trial of Frances Cox when a guard explained that, 'Behind the fire is a common expression in the country. When they say behind the fire they mean into the fire.'[83] However, the act of translation was literal in cases involving the Irish language. Certainly, as argued by Phelan, despite the primacy of the Irish language to the Gaelic Revival, Irish speakers before the courts were at a disadvantage.[84] The cause celebre case on this theme was that of Myles Joyce, posthumously pardoned in 2018; Joyce, a monoglot Irish speaker, was convicted and executed for his part in the 1882 Maamtrasna murders following a trial he could not comprehend.[85]

Various cases, such as that of Annie Walsh (1929), in which the witnesses in the trial were almost all Irish speakers, demonstrated the difficulties of such persons before the courts. Walsh, capitally convicted for the murder of her husband Sonny Dan, along with her co-accused Martin Joyce, lived in rural County Galway in an Irish-speaking area in the West of Ireland.[86] The case notes of Detective George Lawlor, published in 1991 in edited form, described the locale:

> Its inherent character had changed little, emigration was a feature of growing up, and there was little prospect of a job in the area. Farmers scratched a livelihood out of poor ground in harsh conditions. All the farms were small, their holdings rarely stretching beyond a ten-acre horizon. Living conditions for most people were poor, and life had changed little in the past hundreds of years.[87]

The unintelligibility of life in this Irish-speaking region was evident throughout the trial, which revealed the paradoxical position of Irish-speaking regions as 'the cultural heartland of the country'[88] *and* an uncivilised backwater. As Kelleher notes, in relation to the 1882 Maamtrasna murders, newspaper reporting was often particularly unflattering in its description of the living conditions in these Irish-speaking Gaeltacht areas.[89]

There are clear points of contention in relation to the Irish language in Walsh's case. In cross-examination, Cecil Lavery, QC, presented her as difficult due to her insistence on giving evidence in Irish despite her ability to speak English. He first suggested to her: 'You are perfectly familiar with the English language', and a follow-up exchange between Lavery and Walsh expanded this theme:

> Lavery: Though you would rather speak in Irish you have no difficult in following the English?
> Walsh: I am not able to follow the English as well as the Irish.
> Lavery: You follow it quite well?
> Walsh: I am not able to follow it very well. I would rather the Gaelic and the English.
> Lavery: Was it English you spoke the time you were in America?
> Walsh: Yes.[90]

Legal professionals were suspicious that Irish speakers feigned ignorance of English for their own benefit.[91] As Kelleher writes, not only were Irish speakers often accused of deliberately subverting trials with feigned ignorance, but Irish was so culturally devalued by the late nineteenth century that many Irish speakers denied even having competence in Irish.[92] English had become the language of commerce as well as the language of emigration.

Contrasting with the attempts to flatter Dublin juries, in this case a Dublin jury was considered unqualified to understand life in the West of Ireland. In a petition, it was claimed that the jury was 'out of touch with the realities of life along the Western sea-board and therefore, with the best intentions, very liable to error in their deductions; unfamiliar with the Irish language and probably irritated by the delay incident to its translation'.[93]

Issues relating to the Irish language informed the grounds for appeal when it was revealed that the stenographer, selected for the

case because of his proficiency in the Irish language, had not tran-
scribed the original Irish as spoken by nine of the witnesses, including both accused. The defence argued that this 'gravely prejudiced'
Walsh and Joyce and amounted to a breach of the constitutional
right to a fair trial and to give evidence in the 'National Language'.
Also included in these grounds of appeal was a claim that Walsh's
decision to give evidence in Irish had been used to reproach her.[94]
Addressing these matters in the Court of Criminal Appeal, Chief
Justice Kennedy argued that while Walsh was bilingual (unlike her
co-convicted Joyce who was a monoglot Irish speaker), persons
possessed a 'double right' to give evidence in Irish, being a right
under the Constitution and under natural justice. However, he also
cited the ability of counsel and Walsh herself to call attention to
inaccuracies in the translation. Dismissing the appeal, Chief Justice
Kennedy described the Irish language challenge as 'pure after-
thought and wholly unreal, factitious and untenable'.[95] The lack of
Irish language proficiency among members of the legal profession
was, however, acknowledged:

> We may infer and take judicial notice of the fact that many of the
> persons concerned in the administration of justice at present are
> not competent to conduct the business of the Courts in the Irish
> language – a state of affairs which is established, if proof were
> required, by the fact that the Oireachtas has found it necessary to
> enact a law imposing such competence as an obligation upon legal
> practitioners.[96]

Sarah Keane, whose 1925 case had seen her community condemned
as one ruined by the evils of poteen, was also an Irish speaker. The
case concerned the killing of Matthew Connolly, to which Sarah's
son Patrick pleaded guilty to manslaughter, while a *nolle prosequi*
was entered for Sarah. The killing occurred during a fight which
erupted from bad feeling between the two families. In the assault
that caused his death, Connolly had been struck on the head with
a stone by Patrick, before Sarah joined the fray.[97] When the case
came to Dublin, the *Evening Herald* described its principal pro-
tagonists as 'typical Western peasants'.[98] As reported, 'proceedings were conducted in the Irish language; none of the Connemara
witnesses present being able to speak English'.[99] In Dublin for the

trial was the official interpreter to Galway Circuit Court, Seumas Molloy. This interpreter was asked to translate proceedings for the jury. When the question of an expert stenographer arose, Justice Hanna was reported as saying: 'He knew there were expert stenographers who could take notes in Irish, but he did not think in this case it was absolutely necessary. Mr Molloy's translation was what the jury would have to go on.'[100] Both prosecution and defence counsel also confirmed that they had enlisted the assistance of junior counsel with knowledge of Irish. The case demonstrated that, while there were accommodations for Irish speakers, ensuring that these were of sufficient quality was not a priority. Indeed, the fact of Irish speaking came in for some humour on the part of the prosecution counsel and judge:

> Mr Carrigan [prosecution] created laughter by remarking that Mr Comyn [defence] had only a political knowledge of Irish. His lordship said he used to know some Academic Irish, but he did not know how far it would go amongst the peasants of the Western Islands.[101]

The language barrier had also precluded legal counsel from ascertaining the full context of the case until shortly before the trial started, as alluded to by Carrigan when he said that 'it was only last evening that he (counsel) and his friends had the advantage of getting the local colour and facts which did help one to form a true estimate of a case like this', and which 'local colour' had seen the charge reduced from murder to manslaughter.[102]

Keane's case was ongoing at the same time as the Coimisiún na Gaeltachta, established in 1925 to define Irish-speaking districts and devise recommendations for the support of the language.[103] The criminal trial was reported in newspapers which also carried updates from this commission. Often, the two matters overlapped in theme, such as the evidence to the commission of Professor Liam O'Briain, who recommended that the District Courts in Gaeltacht areas should conduct their business in Irish, before admitting that the legal profession was hardly proficient enough in the language to do so.[104]

Although it is impossible to tell from the extant archives, the language barrier may also have contributed to the verdict that Annie Connolly was unfit to plead on a charge of murdering of her infant in 1930. As noted in Chapter 3, her case seemed to bear the hallmarks of many other unmarried women in desperate circumstances who resorted to infant murder, and it is difficult to discern what marked her out as unfit to plead.[105] In a later case of Irish-speaking women before the courts on a murder charge, Máire and Cáit Ní Chéidigh, sisters from the coastal townland of Aille in County Galway, were prosecuted for the murder of Mary's illegitimate infant in 1941.[106] Mary pleaded guilty to manslaughter while a *nolle prosequi* was entered for Kate. In this case, there was evidence that greater efforts were made to support Irish speakers, for example in the provision of typed copies of translated depositions, in the use of Irish in legal documentation and in the Irish spelling of their names on many documents.

What the 1920s cases of Sarah Keane and Annie Walsh (1929), in particular, demonstrate, is the extent to which bilingualism continued into the twentieth century, particularly in the west of the country. Kelleher, exploring 'language shift' through the nineteenth century, has emphasised the extent to which Irish survived alongside English. The number of witnesses who were monoglot Irish speakers, or who spoke English but favoured Irish, illustrate that this spectrum of bilingualism persisted after independence. The cases further demonstrate that suspicion of Irish speakers persisted among legal professionals, something made clear in the insinuations levelled at Annie Walsh following her decision to give her evidence in Irish.

Irish Travellers

In considering the position of women before the courts, the labelling of some women as members of the Travelling community offers a brief glimpse into perceptions of Irish Travellers in these decades. Appearing at the end of the period under review, the 1963 Report of the Commission on Itinerancy positioned nomadic peoples as a 'problem', evident in its terms of reference 'to enquire into the problem arising from the presence in the country of itinerants in considerable numbers'.[107] The report recommended a policy of 'absorption' into the settled community. As Fanning outlined, the slow modernisation of Ireland from the 1950s led to the 'gradual economic and social closure' of settled society to Irish Travellers.[108]

Mary Power and Ellen Gavan were found guilty of manslaughter on 27 January 1926.[109] They had been convicted of killing William Power, the husband of Mary and the father of Ellen. The jury took approximately 50 minutes to find them guilty of manslaughter rather than murder, and both received strong recommendations to mercy. Mary was sentenced to six months' imprisonment and Ellen three years' penal servitude. Sixty-five-year-old William had been found dead in a field on the outskirts of Dublin.[110] It was known that he had been in dispute with his family prior to his death, and his wife and daughter had lately been seen in the area in which his body was found. When arrested, his daughter Ellen gave a statement which confirmed that an altercation with her father had taken place, in which he had hit her mother with an ash-plant loaded with lead. Ellen stated that she and her mother, and her two children, had shortly after left the encampment and had not seen her father since. One newspaper, paraphrasing state counsel, reported of the family that: 'They belonged to the tinker class and led a nomadic life, wandering around the country, living mostly in the open and making their living by collecting and selling, bottles, rags, etc.'[111] All were variously described in newspapers as 'itinerant' and a 'tramp',[112] as 'tinkers'[113] and 'of the tinker class',[114] and 'tinker travelling class'.[115]

In 1950, 17-year-old Kathleen Harmon was found guilty of the manslaughter of four-year-old Penelope Willoughby.[116] Kathleen worked as a domestic in a Dublin suburb, and on the day of Penelope's disappearance she had been looking after the little girl, who was a child of the next-door neighbour. Giving evidence, Kathleen said she had placed her hands around the girl's throat and shook her because she would not stop playing on the stairs. She was sentenced to seven years' penal servitude,[117] with Justice Davitt stating that 'the crime was one which had seriously shocked public feeling'.[118] During the trial, a number of witnesses gave evidence of Kathleen's 'sordid surroundings' and 'the brutality from which this girl sprang', and revealed that she was 'the child of parents who were almost itinerants'.[119] It was also stated that Kathleen had spent some years in an industrial school, an experience branded by her counsel as deeply damaging. Dr Thomas Murphy, medical officer of Mountjoy Prison, pointed to her 'heredity and upbringing', stating: 'We get a fair number of her type of people in Mountjoy. ... She was of the tinker class, and there are a number of that class there at present, all manifesting the same poker-faced appearance.'[120] Justice Davitt cited Kathleen's difficult background as a mitigating factor in sentencing. It was clear that there was a presumed degree of hereditary temperament exhibited by members of the Travelling community. As MacLaughlin argues, the increasing racialisation of Travellers was premised on ideas of evolutionary theory, in the ascendancy from the nineteenth century, as well as on 'an Irish variant of "common sense" social Darwinism'.[121] Racism through the mid-century tended to portray Travellers as a racialised and deviant underclass that represented a threat to the settled community.[122]

The case of Mary Flynn offered evidence of the explicit 'Othering' of Irish Travellers and the hostile reception many could expect. In January 1962, Mary Flynn was found guilty of the manslaughter of Maurice Ryan, receiving a sentence of 18 months' imprisonment.[123] Mary, aged 51, was described throughout as an 'itinerant'.[124] The victim, 39-year-old Maurice Ryan, had been assaulted on 23 July 1961 and died of his injuries some weeks later. The killing occurred near St Mullin's in County Carlow, in what, according to prosecuting counsel, 'almost amounted to a pitched battle between a group of itinerants and a number of local persons and a Garda'.[125] The state case was that a number of people had gathered in a St Mullin's public house,[126] and when the only Guard stationed in the area, Garda Foley, attempted to disperse this group at closing time, he had been struck by Mary Flynn's son.[127] Flynn and her family then left in a cart, but were pursued in cars by Garda Foley and local men, Maurice Ryan among them. The men caught up with the Flynn family at a crossroads, where a fracas developed in which Garda Foley and Ryan were injured. Ryan walked with the aid of a stick, and when he had arrived at the scene Mary Flynn had wrenched his stick from him and attacked him with it.[128]

The case clearly demonstrated the strength of hostility felt by some members of the local community towards the Flynns. It seemed unlikely that this animus was directed against the Flynn family in particular as Garda Foley admitted he did not know them;[129] rather it was a general animus against Travellers. It was suggested to Garda Foley by the defence that 'it was a very foolish thing to bring these carloads of farmers and farm labourers with you to chase the Flynns'. Foley, however, disagreed with this, and also with the suggestion made by the defence: 'would you blame the Flynns for thinking they were going to be murdered?'[130] He claimed instead: 'Our mission was not an aggressive one.'[131] Nevertheless, defence counsel characterised the group from the village as 'vigilantes'.[132] It is hard to argue with this conclusion, and Bhreatnach identifies such 'localised extra-legal action against Travellers' as a common occurrence through the period.[133]

Nevertheless, these cases do not straightforwardly suggest a harsher criminal justice response for women who were Travellers. The strong recommendations to mercy in the case of Gavan and Power, the consideration of background as mitigation in Harmon's case and the treatment of Flynn suggest greater nuance. Bhreatnach, in her research on homicide and Travellers through the mid-century, likewise found that killings committed by Travellers did not appear to be punished more severely than those committed by the settled community.[134] She noted one key difference between these communities as the role of Traveller women in deaths resulting from public fights (as is characterised by the case of Mary Flynn). But even this, arguably more masculine characterisation of defendant women, did not produce more punitive outcomes, and such women 'were not excessively penalised'.[135]

Conclusion

Overwhelmingly, the women before the courts were drawn from rural or small-town Ireland, a demographic fact which entailed some stark consequences for women in these decades. In the years of nation-building post-independence, notions of rural Ireland, and especially the 'West', enjoyed a vaunted status as an emblem of the 'real' Ireland. As Kennedy stated, 'Land, family and Church form a trinity which dominated much of Irish life at least until the 1960s.'[136] These ideals crumpled on impact with the Dublin legal sphere as notions of ignorance and depravity infused debate on the women's crimes. These assumptions laid bare the moral judgements which were targeted at members of the labouring classes. Crucially, minorities such as Irish speakers and Travellers were often doubly suspect, and were 'Othered' before the courts. Such positionality not only shaped criminal justice responses; the imperatives of Irish rural life could also shape the motivations to kill for some women before the courts.

Notes

1 Mary McAuliffe, 'Irish histories: gender, women and sexualities', in Katherine O'Donnell and Mary McAuliffe (eds), *Palgrave Advances in Irish History* (Basingstoke: Palgrave Macmillan, 2009).

2 Mary E. Daly, *The Slow Failure: Population Decline and Independent Ireland, 1920–1973* (Madison: University of Wisconsin Press, 2005).

3 Eoin O'Sullivan and Ian O'Donnell, *Coercive Confinement in Ireland: Patients, Prisoners, and Penitents* (Manchester: Manchester University Press, 2012), p. 269.

4 'Slain with a Stone', *Evening Herald* (17 June 1925), p. 1.

5 NAI, Department of Justice 18/2769A. Memorandum, 1 March 1924.

6 The play itself was said to be based on real-life cases, see Piers Beirne and Ian O'Donnell, 'Gallous stories of dirty deeds: representing parricide in J.M. Synge's "The Playboy of the Western World"', *Crime Media Culture*, 6:1 (2010) 27–48.

7 NAI, CCA, 16/1946. Trial judge's charge to the jury.

8 'Castleisland Woman', *Kerry Reporter* (24 November 1934), p. 1.

9 NAI, CCA 56/1944. Evidence of Detective Sergeant Thomas Delany.

10 NAI, CCA 72/1949. 18 November 1949.

11 See Chapter 7.

12 'Story of Double Life in Granard Poison Drama', *Longford Leader* (27 March 1926), p. 2.

13 'Castlebar Girl Returned to Trial', *Connaught Telegraph* (14 November 1931), p. 6.

14 NAI, CCA/16/1946. Judge's charge to the jury.

15 'Aged Woman's Trial', *Evening Herald* (24 October 1924), p. 1.

16 DDA of Archbishop John Charles McQuaid. AB8/b/XXVIII/983. Memorandum prepared by E. M. Carroll, probation officer at Dublin Metropolitan Courthouse, forwarded in a letter 9 July 1941.

17 'The Infanticide Scandal', *Irish Independent* (11 February 1929), p. 9.

18 'Slain with a Stone', *Evening Herald* (17 June 1925), p. 1.

19 'Slain with a Stone', *Evening Herald* (17 June 1925), p. 1.

20 Carolyn Conley, *Melancholy Accidents: The Meaning of Violence in post-Famine Ireland* (Lanham, MD: Lexington Books, 1999); John D. Brewer, Bill Lockhart and Paula Rogers, *Crime in Ireland, 1945–95: 'Here Be Dragons'* (Oxford: Clarendon, 1997).

21 Brewer et al., *Crime in Ireland, 1945–95*.

22 Ciaran McCullagh, 'A tie that blinds: family and ideology in Ireland, *Economic and Social Review*, 22:3 (1991) 199–211, p. 203.

23 Terence Dooley, *'The Land for the People': The Land Question in Independent Ireland* (Dublin: University College Dublin Press, 2004), p. 1.

24 Damian F. Hannan and Patrick Commins, 'The significance of small-scale landholders in Ireland's socio-economic transformation', in J. H. Goldthorpe and C. T. Whelan (eds), *The Development of Industrial Society in Ireland* (Oxford: Oxford University Press for the British Academy, 1992).

25 O'Sullivan and O'Donnell, *Coercive Confinement in Ireland*.

26 O'Sullivan and O'Donnell, *Coercive Confinement in Ireland*; Conrad M. Arensberg and Solon T. Kimball, *Family and Community in Ireland*, 3rd edition (Ennis: CLASP Press, 2001).

27 McCullagh, 'A tie that blinds', p. 205.

28 Ian O'Donnell, 'Lethal violence in Ireland, 1841 to 2003: famine, celibacy and parental pacification', *British Journal of Criminology*, 45:5 (2005) 671–95; Niamh Howlin, 'Controlling jury composition in nineteenth-century Ireland', *Journal of Legal History*, 30:3 (2009) 227–61.

29 Carolyn A. Conley, *Certain Other Countries: Homicide, Gender and National Identity in Late Nineteenth Century England, Ireland, Scotland and Wales* (Columbus: Ohio State University Press, 2007); W. E. Vaughan, *Murder Trials in Ireland, 1836–1914* (Dublin: Four Courts Press, 2009).

30 McCullagh, 'A tie that blinds'; O'Donnell, 'Killing in Ireland at the turn of the centuries'.

31 O'Sullivan and O'Donnell, *Coercive Confinement in Ireland*.

32 NAI, SFCCC, Cork 1925; CCA 18/1925; Department of Justice 18/2770A and 18/2770B.

33 NAI, CCA 18/1925.

34 NAI, SFCCC Cork, 1925. Copy of Will of Patrick O'Leary, 28 February 1921.

35 NAI, SFCCC, Cork 1925. Deposition of Coroner, 7 May 1924.
36 NAI, CCA 18/1925.
37 NAI, CCA 18/1925.
38 In contrast, in the 1934 case of Elizabeth Cahill, who was acquitted of the murder of her infant, Justice Hanna admonished her brother for turning her out of the house that she shared with her aunt and two brothers, stating that 'she had as good a right to reside there as he had'. 'Woman Acquitted', *Irish Press* (19 June 1934), p. 9.
39 NAI, SFCCC, Dublin 1949; CCA 72/1949; Department of An Taoiseach S.14689; Department of Justice 18/11757.
40 NAI, CCA 72/1949.
41 'Woman Accused of Poisoning Brother', *Irish Press* (16 November 1949), p. 5.
42 'Laois Murder Appeal', *Irish Press* (17 December 1949), p. 7.
43 'Frances Cox Appeal', *Irish Independent* (17 December 1949), p. 3.
44 NAI, CCA 72/1949.
45 NAI, CCA 72/1949.
46 NAI, CCA 72/1949.
47 'Frances Cox Found Guilty of Murder', *Irish Times* (22 November 1949), p. 1.
48 NAI, SFCCC, Wexford 1932; CCA 9/1932; Department of An Taoiseach S.8653.
49 NAI, CCA 9/1932. Copy of letter written by Jane O'Brien, 28 March 1932.
50 Daly, *The Slow Failure*.
51 O'Donnell, 'Lethal violence in Ireland', p. 687.
52 Lindsey Earner-Byrne, 'The family in Ireland, 1880–2015', in Thomas Bartlett (ed.) *The Cambridge History of Ireland*, Vol. 4 (Cambridge: Cambridge University Press, 2018); Daly, *The Slow Failure*.
53 Garrett argued that the long-running battles on issues such as illegitimacy, social welfare provision and legal adoption could all be traced back to the two fundamental concerns which emerged post-Famine and persisted in the post-1922 period: patriarchy and land ownership. Paul Michael Garrett, 'The abnormal flight: the migration and repatriation of Irish unmarried mothers', *Social History*, 25:3 (2000) 330–43.
54 Daly, *The Slow Failure*, p. 106.
55 NAI, PRES/1/P2735 Agnes McAdam Death Sentence 1946; SFCCC, Monaghan 1946; CCA 16/1946.
56 'Woman on Trial for Murder', *Evening Echo* (4 December 1934), p. 1.

57 NAI, SBCCC, November 1933 to 22 April 1941.

58 NAI, SBCCC, 1962 to July 1964.

59 NAI, SBCCC (change of venue cases for all counties) June 1925 to December 1926. See Chapter 3.

60 Finola Kennedy, *Cottage to Crèche: Family Change in Ireland* (Dublin: IPA, 2001).

61 NAI, CCA 17/1924. Evidence of Superintendent Peter Fahy.

62 P. McNabb, 'Social structure', in J. Newman (ed.), *The Limerick Rural Survey, 1958–1964* (Muintir na Tíre Tipperary, 1964), cited in Kennedy, *Cottage to Crèche*, p. 126.

63 Earner-Byrne, 'The family in Ireland'.

64 O'Sullivan and O'Donnell, *Coercive Confinement in Ireland*, p. 273.

65 Cara Delay, '"Uncharitable tongues": women and abusive language in early twentieth-century Ireland', *Feminist Studies*, 39:3 (2013) 628–53, p. 637.

66 NAI, Department of Justice 18/885A. Garda report, 2 April 1935.

67 Evelyn Mahon, 'Ireland: a private patriarchy?', *Environment and Planning A*, 26:8 (1994) 1277–96. Walby defined private patriarchy as 'a man in his position as husband or father who is the direct oppressor and beneficiary, individually and directly, of the subordination of women'. Sylvia Walby, *Theorizing Patriarchy* (Oxford: Basil Blackwell, 1990), p. 178.

68 Kennedy, *Cottage to Crèche*.

69 Jennifer Redmond, *Moving Histories: Irish Women's Emigration to Britain from Independence to Republic* (Liverpool: Liverpool University Press, 2018).

70 As noted in Chapter 7, many women were also separated from their husbands for lengthy periods of time because these men worked abroad.

71 'Charge of Child Murder', *Donegal Democrat* (31 July 1926), p. 3.

72 NAI, Department of Justice 234/2599. Letter from Mrs Lennon, July 25 1929; 'Galway Murder Trial', *Irish Times* (20 June 1929), p. 5.

73 NAI, Department of Justice 234/2599. Letter from Mrs Lennon, 25 July 1929.

74 NAI, CCA 36/1938.

75 NAI, SFCCC, Dublin 1949; CCA 72/1949; Department of An Taoiseach S.14689; Department of Justice 18/11757.

76 NAI, SFCCC, Wicklow 1926; Department of Justice 234/1297.

77 Kennedy, *Cottage to Crèche*.

78 Kennedy, *Cottage to Crèche*.

79 NAI, Department of An Taoiseach S.14689B. Memorandum, 4 March 1957.

80 NAI, CCA 72/1949. 16 November 1949.
81 Elizabeth F. Moulds, 'Chivalry and paternalism: disparities of treat-ment in the criminal justice system', *Western Political Quarterly*, 31:3 (1978) 416–30.
82 NAI, SFCCC, 1924 Cork. Evidence of Ellen Clifford.
83 NAI, CCA 72/1949.
84 Mary Phelan, *Irish Speakers, Interpreters and the Courts, 1754–1921* (Dublin: Four Courts Press/Irish Legal History Society, 2019).
85 Margaret Kelleher, *The Maamtrasna Murders: Language, Life and Death in Nineteenth-Century Ireland* (Dublin: University College Dublin Press, 2018). In 2018, Joyce received a posthumous pardon. Niamh Howlin, 'Report on the Trial of Myles Joyce, November 1882' (Dublin: Department of Justice, 2017).
86 NAI, SFCCC, Galway 1929–31; CCA 16/1929; Department of An Taoiseach S.5904; Department of Justice 234/2599.
87 Tom Reddy, *The Murder File: An Irish Detective's Casebook* (Dublin: Gill and Macmillan, 1991) p. 18.
88 Nuala C. Johnson, 'Building a nation: an examination of the Irish Gaeltacht Commission Report of 1926', *Journal of Historical Geography*, 19:2 (1993) 157–68, p. 157.
89 Kelleher, *The Maamtrasna Murders*.
90 NAI, CCA 16/1929.
91 Phelan, *Irish Speakers, Interpreters and the Courts*.
92 Kelleher, *The Maamtrasna Murders*.
93 NAI, Department of An Taoiseach, S.5904.
94 NAI, CCA 16/1929. Additional Grounds of Appeal.
95 NAI, CCA 16/1929. Chief Justice Kennedy.
96 NAI, CCA 16/1929. Chief Justice Kennedy. The reference is to the Legal Practitioners (Qualification) Act 1929 which stipulated proce-dures by which future members of the legal profession would have competent knowledge of the Irish language.
97 'An Ex-officer's Death', *Irish Times* (16 September 1924), p. 6.
98 'Slain with a Stone', *Evening Herald* (17 June 1925), p. 1.
99 'An Ex-officer's Death', *Irish Times* (16 September 1924), p. 6.
100 'Slain with a Stone', *Evening Herald* (17 June 1925), p. 1.
101 'Slain with a Stone', *Evening Herald* (17 June 1925), p. 1.
102 'Slain with a Stone', *Evening Herald* (17 June 1925), p. 1.
103 Johnson, 'Building a nation'.
104 'Native Irish Speakers', *Irish Times* (25 June 1925), p. 5.
105 NAI, SBCCC, November 1927 to June 1935. 'Child's Death', *Connacht Tribune* (7 June 1930), p. 7.

106 NAI, SBCCC, November 1933 to 22 April 1941; SFCCC, Galway 1941.
107 Commission on Itinerancy, 'Report of the Commission on Itinerancy' (Dublin: Stationery Office, 1963) p. 11.
108 Bryan Fanning, *Racism and Social Change in the Republic of Ireland* (Manchester: Manchester University Press, 2002), p. 153.
109 NAI, SBCCC (Change of venue cases for all counties) June 1925 to December 1926.
110 'Brutal Murder of a Tramp', *Irish Independent* (5 July 1925), p. 7.
111 'Found in Field', *Evening Echo* (27 January 1926), p. 1.
112 'Brutal Murder of a Tramp', *Irish Independent* (5 July 1925), p. 7.
113 'Roadside Murder', *Irish Independent* (17 July 1925), p. 2.
114 'Murdered Tramp', *Evening Herald* (27 July 1925), p. 3.
115 'Found in Field', *Evening Echo* (27 January 1926), p. 1.
116 Press reports from 1948 suggested that at the age of 15, Kathleen had gone missing for a period from her home in Bray. 'Missing Girl', *Evening Herald* (29 June 1948), p. 7.
117 NAI, SBCCC, February 1946 to 1952; SFCCC, Dublin 1950.
118 'Sentence for Manslaughter of Child', *Evening Echo* (8 May 1950), p. 1.
119 'Alleged Murder of Child', *Evening Echo* (5 May 1950), p. 1.
120 'Sentence for Manslaughter of Child', *Evening Echo* (8 May 1950), p. 1.
121 Jim MacLaughlin, 'The political geography of anti-Traveller racism in Ireland: the politics of exclusion and the geography of closure', *Political Geography*, 17:4 (1998) 417–35, p. 423.
122 Fanning, *Racism and Social Change in the Republic of Ireland*, p. 145.
123 NAI, SBCCC, 1962 to July 1964.
124 Mary's husband Daniel and her son Patrick both received suspended sentences for assault, and another son, Daniel Junior, received a 12-month sentence for the offence of wounding. 'Suspended Sentence for Assault', *Nationalist and Leinster Times* (14 July 1962), p. 6.
125 'Itinerant Woman Charged with Murder of a Man', *Evening Herald* (5 February 1962), p. 3.
126 Hostility to Travellers drinking in 'settled community' public houses often led to habits of drinking in different establishments. Aoife Bhreatnach, 'Policing the community: homicide and violence in Traveller and settled society', *Irish Economic and Social History*, 34 (2007) 47–64.
127 It was suggested that Garda Foley had shoved Mary Flynn's son, who had responded in kind.

128 'Itinerant Woman Charged with Murder of a Man', *Evening Herald* (5 February 1962), p. 3.
129 'Man's Death in Crossroad Clash', *Irish Press* (6 February 1962), p. 5.
130 'Woman Charged with Murder of Carlow Man', *Irish Independent* (6 February 1962), p. 10.
131 'Man's Death in Crossroads Clash', *Irish Press* (6 February 1962), p. 5.
132 'Woman Accused of Murder', *Evening Herald* (7 February 1962), p. 5.
133 Bhreatnach, 'Policing the community', p. 56.
134 She argues that the 'public' nature of many of the killings committed by Travellers made it more likely these would be considered as manslaughter rather than murder. Bhreatnach, 'Policing the community'.
135 Bhreatnach, 'Policing the community', p. 64.
136 Kennedy, *Cottage to Crèche*, p. 6.

Conclusion:
Women's lethal violence in Ireland

Analysis of women prosecuted for murder in Ireland in the decades post-independence offers a glimpse of aberrant womanhood within a national context that held very definite aspirations for women's behaviour. The impression of women, murder and the death penalty which emerges is one starkly demarcated by the profile of killings, with divergence between the cases of women prosecuted for infant and adult murder. Yet within this dichotomy there remain compelling commonalities which reveal much about the prevailing gender regimes and elaborate the segregated punishment landscape for women in post-colonial Ireland. Exploration of the offences for which women stood accused, and the official, press and public responses to them, exposes many of the fault lines in Irish society in these decades. This book has offered the first consideration of the spectrum of women's lethal violence in Ireland, finding peculiarities within the national context which contributes new perspectives to the literature on women who kill and gender and punishment. Seal, in her work on twentieth-century British cases of women who kill, joins examination of the 'regulatory discourses of womanhood to an exploration of the wider, cultural meanings that these discourses generate'.[1] This final chapter seeks to draw out wider conclusions about women, murder and the death penalty in the Irish context.

Earner-Byrne writes that:

> The degree to which national values shape the policy-making process is virtually impossible to quantify and can only be surmised through crude measurements such as the probable impact of religion, social perceptions of gender, and the cultural ideology of the family.[2]

However, as she goes on to note, close reading of the actions of individuals can uncover a sense of these values. Exploration of the decision-making occurring at both the more mundane, day-to-day scale, alongside loftier debates on policy, can illuminate the national context. The preceding chapters have offered in some detail the cases of women accused of murder; within each of these discrete moments of personal tragedy, the actions of persons such as judges, barristers and juries, of government and of the women themselves, can suggest much about the meanings of women's lethal violence in post-independence Ireland.

Women prosecuted for murder

Considering the cases of women prosecuted for murder, the overwhelming picture is of a seemingly arbitrary fate. Despite murder prosecutions being taken against 292 women, just 22 found themselves convicted for this offence. A murder conviction, and the ensuing death sentence, was a very rare fate for women prosecuted for this crime. Much of this apparent capriciousness related to the particular profile of offences appearing before the courts and the preponderance of infant murder. Of 253 infant murder prosecutions, only 12 ended in murder convictions. As Chapter 6 demonstrates, the cases of women facing capital trial revealed a pitiful calendar of capital prosecutions, brought against some of the most vulnerable members of Irish society. Hundreds of impoverished and desperate women appeared before the Central Criminal Court. In itself, the survival of the law on infant murder until 1949, alongside decisions to bring murder charges in many cases, suggested punitive treatment. Trial discussions and debate within government exposed a tortured view of these women, illuminating conflict between, on the one hand, notions of pity and leniency premised on individual weakness, and on the other hand, a hysterical need to be seen to punish 'moral' wrongdoing. Outraged condemnation was often uttered by judges, counsel and civil servants. Yet this generally gave way to amelioration, through jury verdicts or the negotiation of lesser charges, or in the proce-dures devised to divert convicted women from death, or indeed from prison. Notwithstanding these accommodations, the legal framework which persisted until the Infanticide Act 1949 ensured a bloated number of infant murder prosecutions. Government's failure to reform this law significantly shaped the profile of capital prosecutions in Ireland in these decades.

Considerably more women were convicted when coming to court on charges of adult murder. Of 34 women charged with the murder of an adult, ten were convicted on this count and death-sentenced. As shown in Chapter 1, this cohort was characterised by a distinct profile compared to those before the courts on infant murder charges. Women facing trial for killing an adult were more likely to be older and were more likely to be married. Of women prosecuted for adult murder for whom marital status was known, only 10 of 32 women were never married. Despite the greater likelihood of adult murder prosecutions resulting in a murder conviction, the Irish application of judicial death post-1922 ensured that only one, or 10 per cent, of these women was ultimately executed (one woman in 22 if all death sentences are considered). If, throughout the 292 cases, the chance of being convicted of murder were mercurial, the chance of being executed was outlandishly remote.

The Irish case clearly demonstrates the extent to which the national context contributed to the meanings attached to offending behaviour, the shaping of criminal justice responses and the arsenal of punishments considered appropriate. As explored in Chapter 8, the intensely classed and situated understandings of women emerged as they were positioned within their membership of the labouring classes and as rural-dwellers. These markers of identity carried implications for Irish womanhood, characterised by expectations of hardness and capability. Correspondingly, however, such women were also viewed as generally of 'low mentality'. Myriad prejudices conspired to inform debate: adverse assumptions about women and the vulnerabilities of female biology joined with the presumption that persons from rural communities were uncivilised and ignorant. While, as Chapter 3 suggested, prosecuted women were subject to parsimonious pathologising, with only a handful found unfit to plead or guilty but insane, they were nevertheless interpreted by reference to assumptions of weak-mindedness structured around gender and class.

Violent women, double deviance and chivalry

In England and Wales from 1900 to 1955, 91 per cent of condemned women were reprieved.[3] This figure is remarkably similar to Ireland, where 90 per cent of women condemned to death for the murder of an adult were reprieved. One difference lies in the numbers in each jurisdiction: while 9 per cent of condemned women in England and Wales amounted to 15 women, in Ireland, 10 per cent represented the sole case of Annie Walsh, executed in 1925. Ballinger observed the Royal Commission's acceptance, during its mid-century consideration of capital punishment in Britain, that there was a 'natural reluctance' to execute women.[4] However, in Ireland, this sentiment extended further than mere reluctance.[5] There was absolute acceptance of gender as an appropriate rationale against execution. Throughout the negotiation of reprieves, no apologies were made for the proffering of 'sex' as an argument against judicial death. This reinforced the explicit 'Othering' of women in Ireland within a societal context which sought to displace women as 'public' citizens and relegate them to the domestic. While in many contexts, more severe criminal justice responses to offending behaviour works to 'Other' and marginalise, the Irish case offers an unusual example in which perceived 'leniency' accomplished the same ends. Kaufman writes of the 'punitive citizenship' in which juries in US death penalty trials engage by virtue of their role in the penalty phase of trial.[6] In Ireland, due to the nature of the mandatory death sentence for murder in these years, jury decisions on guilt or innocence could likewise herald condemnation. However, the unyielding mandatory nature of the sanction paradoxically meant that these moments became discretionary and negotiated points of decision-making. For women, the period is remarkable as one in which there was little to no expectation that condemned women would be hanged. The starkness of this near blanket exemption from death can be teased out from the 22 cases of condemned women explored in Chapter 2. While Annie Walsh's (1925) case offered a cautionary tale, one which informed later petitioning for clemency, both those involved in the administration of justice *and* the public seemed to subsequently decide that no further women should be hanged in

Ireland after this anomalous outcome. In a country that manifested little concerted abolitionist zeal,[7] this implied commitment to the ending of the execution of women stands as a noteworthy societal marker. As Heberle argued, the state-sanctioned killing of women has not been normalised.[8] Instead, she suggested that judicial legal control was secondary to more informal systems of control. In Ireland, this was very explicit, in the view that it was inappropriate to execute women, and in the preferred use of more informal religious detention over state-administered imprisonment.

Key within feminist debates on violent women is the question of agency, and the extent to which this is diminished by the dominant discourses surrounding these women. Weare defined agency as 'the ability of an individual to choose to act or behave in a particular way'.[9] Rowe noted that it is the capacity to act even when choices are constrained.[10] The stripping of agency implies less intention and dilutes culpability: 'the greater the intentionality of a criminal act and/or the greater the transgression against femininity, the greater the condemnation is likely to be'.[11] Morrissey is particularly critical of the feminist scholarship on violent women for its contributory role in denying agency for such women.[12] The clemency, and 'lenient' sentencing that was a feature of responses to Irish women's lethal violence, would at first glance seem to suggest that agency had been stripped from such women.

In the Irish context, the structural conditions demand critique, particularly with regard to infant murder prosecutions. The profile of these capital prosecutions reflected a symbolic need to condemn, while policy, legislative and societal barriers contributed to the offence. As Brennan noted, infant murder could be viewed as entirely rational in the desperate circumstances many women faced.[13] Glimpses of this are visible in some of the cases, such as in the women's own words that their illegitimate infants would be better off dead. In some ways, women reclaimed their own agency in these acts, even while acting with constrained choices, but the trial processes and the adjudication of blameworthiness ensured that most were then subject to, and actively used, narratives of vulnerability and pathology. In this way, the notion of agency is not something that can so easily be stripped from violent women, who made use of assumptions of helplessness when it was appropriate to do so. As Chapter 2 demonstrated, the operation of chivalry and paternalism within criminal justice can work for the benefit of individual women while perpetuating harmful gender stereotypes.[14] But agency cannot be understood as a binary, and Comack and Brickey argue that 'women do make choices, though certainly not under optimal conditions'.[15] However, within Irish criminal justice responses, it is apparent that there was frequent refusal to acknowledge the circumstances under which women acted and to attribute rationality to women. The twin prejudices of female biology and women's class position, discussed in Chapters 2 and 8, conspired to ensure that most faced assumptions of 'weak-mindedness' at some stage of the proceedings.

Reviewing the state of feminist criminology, Heidensohn noted that by the turn of the century one of the flourishing issues was the interplay of double deviance and chivalry in women's experiences before the courts and penal treatment.[16] Broadly speaking, these ideas suggest that some offending women are doubly damned while others benefit from mild treatment; some women are treated more harshly *because they are women* while others are treated more leniently *because they are women*. The literature has proposed that certain women place themselves beyond the protections of chivalry, becoming 'bad women', when interpreted as too far removed from the trappings of acceptable womanhood.

However, this is not a neat formula, and as noted in the Introduction, these gender discourses obscure the complexity of how gender interacts with other considerations. Ballinger, for instance, suggested that attributing greater agency to violent women does not inevitably presage more severe treatment.[17] The Irish example offers a pertinent counter to the notion of 'double deviance'. For one, the reticence to make the weight of the law felt against women convicted of murder, including in cases which presented objectively 'heinous' facts, speaks to an alternative way of responding to deviance. Moreover, the professed desire throughout to favour what was viewed as 'lenient' sentencing for women, notably the preference for religious detention over imprisonment, offers a more complicated way of thinking about what 'deviance' looks like, and how punitive 'Othering' responses can be couched in language which obscures severity.

Much of the literature on women who kill, in particular, recounts the danger for women of exhibiting sexual deviance. The truism is that such women are likely to be parsed as 'bad women'. The Irish poisoning cases, explored in Chapter 7, represented an example counter to this. These cases involved women known to be engaged in extramarital affairs, who were tried for the murder by poisoning of their husbands. This group of cases was remarkable by their acquittals. While, as Chapter 6 outlined, unmarried women in these years were often subject to ongoing suspicious surveillance, for married women there was considerably more leeway, especially when they were living in difficult circumstances with 'bad' husbands. Instead, the acquittals in these cases speak to mediated responses to difficult lives and a certain sympathy for such women. Seal's analysis of Mary Wilson, too, demonstrates the complexity of public opinion on punishment in poisoning cases, cautioning that we cannot assume universal condemnation.[18] Others, too, have observed the beginnings of a more sympathetic response towards women who kill their partners from the beginning of the twentieth century in cases where the victim could be shown to be 'villainous'.[19]

Allied with responses to female deviance, and the literature on double deviance and the 'bad woman', is the sensationalist press reporting which often accompanied such cases. The rarity of women's violence has ensured particular interest when women do kill. Within the media coverage, many accounts carry 'ideological baggage', especially when relying on gender stereotypes.[20] Their 'enduring status as cultural icons speak to our cultural anxiety around dangerous femininities'.[21] Again, in the Irish case, such findings cannot be straightforwardly applied. Sensationalised reporting was remarkably muted in the decades under review. The signally different media landscape in Ireland, shaped as it was by heightened considerations of propriety and censorship, ensured that sexualised coverage of cases was largely proscribed. Keating, for instance, has argued that the censorship provisions enacted in the 1920s had a chilling effect that was deeply influential on the Irish press for decades to come, resulting in a risk-avoidant media culture.[22] In the Irish context too, press reporting which overtly sexualised women before the courts would have been deeply incongruous considering the class and profile of these women. As mentioned in Chapter 7, just one woman within the research was constructed in media reporting in a way which could be considered 'glamorous'. The 1956 case of Mamie Cadden offered a rare example of reporting which was comparable to its counterpart in Britain or the United States, through its focus on her fashionable clothing and outré lifestyle.

Punishing women who kill

The use of religious institutions as sites of confinement for convicted women presents a striking response to women's offending. As seen in Chapter 4, of 209 women convicted of non-capital offences, 86 were sentenced to spend time in a religious home. Chapter 5 outlined that of the 21 reprieved women sentenced to penal servitude for life, 11 were conditionally transferred from prison to a religious home. The use of these religious institutions contributed to the significant numbers of Irish persons experiencing some form of institutional detention post-independence.[23] As O'Donnell and O'Sullivan argued, the institutions which 'served as repositories for the difficult, the deviant and the disengaged'[24] were not particular to Ireland, but the intensity of their use post-independence was exceptional.[25] For instance, there were over 300 Magdalen institutions in England alone by 1898.[26] As the utility of such sites waned elsewhere, however, their use in Ireland increased. 'Coercive confinement' extended across institutions such as industrial and reformatory schools, psychiatric hospitals, county homes, prisons and religious homes for women.

In explaining this phenomenon, O'Sullivan and O'Donnell present an integrative framework which incorporates changes in the Irish rural economy and speaks to the role of Church, state and family.[27] The state maintained healthier balance sheets by outsourcing services to Catholic Church organisations, while the Church secured institutional power through the provision of key services such as education and welfare. Meanwhile, families used institutions strategically to rid themselves of troublesome family members. As McCullagh argued, such sites were important in

preserving existing inheritance patterns.[28] The coming to dominance of stem family inheritance, under which one son (typically)
would inherit, meant most siblings had no hopes of inheritance. With little other industry to occupy them, many faced very
limited prospects. To 'manage' the problems inherent in these
family forms, including the high numbers of celibate or unmarried persons and the need for the certainties of legitimate birth in
a system of impartible inheritance, Catholic teaching on sexual
prudery offered a useful model for informal social control. For
O'Donnell and O'Sullivan, coercive confinement represented the
consequences of the need for self-discipline and the 'shedding' of
unprovided-for family members under the dominant mode of the
rural economy, a process in which Church, state and family all played
their parts.

This integrated framework has considerable persuasive force.
Yet within each discrete institution type, further compelling elements shaped their particular usage. Religious homes as sites of
punishment for women are essential to understanding Ireland's
penal landscape post-1922 and the deeply gendered forms this
took. Contrary to the literature on gender and crime, which
shows that men comprise the majority of those caught within the
criminal justice system, women formed the majority of those coercively confined in Ireland in this period. One of the characteristics
of the network of religious homes for women was that despite their
use for convicted women, as detailed in this book, these institutions
primarily held women who had committed no offences and were
instead confined by the actions of persons such as family members
or priests, or by their own volition, or following their release from
institutions such as industrial schools. This book has elaborated
on the religious homes used by the courts, including Our Lady's
Home in Dublin, Magdalen laundries, mother and baby homes and
Legion of Mary hostels – a range of discrete institutional types all
deemed appropriate by the courts as sites of punishment for convicted women.

Our Lady's Home was run by the Sisters of Charity of
St Vincent de Paul. Following the enactment of the Criminal Justice
Act 1960, this was one of two institutions designated as a remand
home for girls aged 16 to 21. Throughout its life, it was used for

myriad criminal justice purposes, including as a place for sentenced women and those on remand, as well as for women and girls post-release from prison. As Smith outlines, because Our Lady's Home had accepted state funding for its work in this regard from the late 1800s it was subject to inspection, unlike Magdalen laundries.[29] Magdalen laundries in Ireland already had a long history by 1922. They were initially established as Protestant lay refuges for women working in prostitution and Ireland's first opened in Dublin in 1765. Through the nineteenth century, the Catholic Church's growing institutional power saw Catholic orders assume management of existing refuges while new laundries were established.[30] Their use was not primarily carceral through the first century and more of their existence,[31] but this shifted post-1922 as they became 'long-term, punitive institutions, driven by a quest for retribution and repentance'.[32] In these years they were also increasingly used as a disposal in sentencing.[33] Post-1922, the McAleese Report found that the criminal justice system accounted for 8.1 per cent of entries to Magdalen laundries.[34] In these decades, such institutions became part of an acknowledged network for the confinement of 'deviant' women. Contributing to this, mother and baby homes were a post-1922 policy innovation. As with the laundries, personal testimony offers an insight into the punitive experiences of these sites.[35] Luddy has described how mother and baby homes were one node in a system which included laundries and other institutions such as county homes, all established to respond to illegitimate motherhood.[36] In this schema, mother and baby homes were envisaged for those pregnant for the first time, while the laundries were considered more appropriate for women experiencing a second 'fall'. A number of women were also ordered to spend time in a Legion of Mary hostel. The Legion of Mary was a lay Catholic organisation founded in the 1920s by Frank Duff. It operated as a rescue organisation, and ran hostels in various cities for the reclamation of women in need of 'moral rescue' and as homes for unmarried pregnant women.[37] Despite the stated purposes of each institutional type, the cases herein have demonstrated their flexibility of function, including as sites of punishment for convicted women.

Paternalism, Catholicism, postcolonialism

The use of religious homes as places of punishment can be further understood under the broadly tripartite influences of paternalism, Catholicism and postcolonialism, often acting as overlapping forces. Paternalism has historically framed solutions to the problem of 'deviant' women around ideals of 'womanhood'. Female offenders have been considered more malleable to reform and more susceptible to informal control. In particular, under a 'welfarist' ethos, prison was considered a corrosive environment for women, leading to the establishment of female-specific institutions tasked with moral reform.[38] These developments occurred in a period of rising penal welfarism in which there was support for the establishment of a range of institutions catering to specific populations (of men and women), such as inebriates and the 'feeble-minded'.[39] While the embrace of women-only reform institutions in Britain and the United States occurred under penal welfarism, the penal welfare ideology did not achieve like dominance in Ireland.[40]

Nevertheless, the Irish preference for religious homes over imprisonment was laced with paternalism borne of a deeply patriarchal society.[41] As explored above, for women reprieved from a sentence of death, a 'merciful' outcome was often a double-edged sword, with notions of chivalry, and the protections afforded women *qua* women, entwining with paternalism to justify lengthy periods of religious confinement in a system with little oversight. The same ambiguities of leniency were clearly evident throughout the cases of women convicted of lesser offences, many of whom found themselves in religious detention. The paternalism which guided punishment ideologies in these years was underpinned by patriarchal gender relations under which women were viewed as a class apart. Paternalism imagined women as childlike, inferior in rationality and lacking the capacity for full citizenship. This was particularly so for younger unmarried women who became pregnant. As Earner-Byrne writes, the unmarried mother, who formed the majority of those sent to religious homes within the present research, demonstrated 'the conditional nature of female citizenship'.[42]

Ireland in these decades can be characterised as a traditional patriarchal society in which women retained an 'Othered' status bound up with their symbolic role as moral guardians of the new nation. Mahon, drawing on Walby's idea of private versus public patriarchy, characterised Ireland as a private patriarchy post-1922.[43] Under private patriarchy women are understood within the structures of domesticity and the marital family. This was reinforced by legislative initiative, pronounced through the 1920s and 1930s, which actively worked to suppress 'woman' as a public person and elevate moral purity to the status of national dogma.[44] Chief among these initiatives were tighter censorship laws, the banning of contraceptives, the prohibition of divorce, the exemption of women from juries and the introduction of marriage bars for women working in the civil service.[45] These were accompanied by other pieces of legislation which targeted morality, such as restrictions on dance halls and the Criminal Law (Amendment) Act 1935. The post-WWI retrenchment of gender roles was not unique to Ireland.[46] Nevertheless, the intensity of these moves was noteworthy in Ireland, and these legislative endeavours were nurtured under the twin influences of the Catholic Church and a post-colonial period of nation-formation.

This raft of legislative innovation cannot be understood without reference to the Catholic Church. The influential status of the Church on independence was a position that had emerged through the nineteenth century.[47] By mid-century, the Church was an 'independent power bloc', to which British administrators had ceded significant influence for the social control of the Irish people,[48] something which gifted the Church an extensive institutional network in areas such as health, education and welfare.[49] On independence and until the 1960s, the Church exercised influence 'without a rival institution'.[50] In 1937, this culminated in the highly symbolic provisions of the new Constitution, one article of which enshrined 'the special position' of the Catholic Church while another referenced women's place 'in the home'.

Critically too, religion was pivotal in the development of Irish criminal justice, such as its role in the institutional networks of 'coercive confinement',[51] in the 'legitimation process' of the new Gardaí,[52] within the prison system, identified in strands of pastoral penality characterised by Catholic conservatism[53] and in the development of probation services.[54] As McNally, and Healy and Kennefick, observed, professionalised probation services developed only slowly in Ireland, in part due to the extensive role of religious organisations.[55] It would seem hardly surprising that when it came to punishment and the female body, the Church would play a role.

The flourishing of such extensive Catholic control of various aspects of what would otherwise have been government policy can be linked to the Catholic principle of subsidiarity, which held that the state should promote voluntary organisations to fulfil various functions. Under this ethos, there were various areas of public policy that the Church monopolised, with the imprimatur of the state.[56] The policy arenas taken on by the Church were invariably those with 'moral' significance.[57] As infant murder was typically an offence of morality, involving the killing of illegitimate infants, it was a matter more properly situated under the jurisdiction of the Church rather than the state.

Crucially, as Chapters 4 and 5 demonstrate, this jurisdiction was possessed of a deeply coercive power. Despite notions of leniency, confinement in religious organisations revealed both the 'porous' and the 'sticky' institution. The aspirations for its coercive power were outlined in a 1941 letter from the Department of Justice to Archbishop McQuaid, the Catholic Archbishop of Dublin.[58] The Department outlined its wish that an institution be established for:

> girls against whom no specific offence could easily be proved but as regards whom the Court would be satisfied that they were leading a kind of life which if not actively and definitely immoral was bound to end up as such unless they were placed under restraint.

The letter proposed a gendered system of preventative detention for women not criminally convicted but considered 'immoral'. Within the present research there is evidence of such 'extra-legal' punishment. Annie Somerville, the daughter of Mary Somerville who had been convicted of the murder of Annie's illegitimate infant in 1944, was ultimately placed by a local Protestant clergyman in a home run by the Salvation Army in England.[59] Beyond those convicted women who spent time in religious homes, the profile of women and girls more generally who served time in these sites as inmates revealed that they did in fact become sites of detention for women who had committed no offence, beyond some perceived offence of morality.

This thread of immorality joins together the two cohorts of women confined in religious detention in these decades, creating a commonality between the convicted women and the women who were innocent of any crime. Early in the life of the new state, sexual immorality had been identified as a threat to the nation. This 'threat' was especially located within the bodies of young women of the working and labouring classes. Despite Catholicism's professed non-interference in the family, marginalised women and families experienced significant state and Church intervention, particularly in matters of morality and sex. While the sanctity of the family was respected, for lone women who posed a threat to this, there was no such protection. Hence, for women whose offences were deemed more 'sexual' than 'criminal', they were fitting subjects for religious rather than state control.

Crucially, one way of further understanding gender and punishment in Ireland, and the reliance on religious detention, is in their role as essential tools of post-colonial nation-formation.[60] As a very explicitly identified 'threat' to the new Catholic state, immorality became a behaviour that required extreme measures, reflected in the gendered system of detention which was tantamount to preventative detention. Ireland's positioning as an independent nation was explicitly predicated on its Catholicism and its purity.[61] Anything which jeopardised this required remedial action. As Fischer argued:

> Insofar as Ireland's national identity was premised on moral purity and virtue, women who constituted threats to this identity were constructed as bringing shame onto themselves, their families, and their nation, and were therefore deemed to be deserving of punishment and confinement.[62]

The network described by Luddy for the confinement of unmarried mothers also betrayed larger concerns about the need to hide evidence of deviant sexuality and to isolate contagion. Considering the profile of women sent there from the courts, the fact that these institutions were for the confinement of offending *and* non-offending women revealed their true purpose: not to punish crime, but to punish sin. While these women were not viewed as a danger to life and limb, they did represent a very real danger to the life of the nation.

In the post-colonial context, particularly when reinforced with religious justifications, many new nations have sought to curtail women's rights.[63] While many anti-colonial movements flirted with egalitarianism, bourgeois nationalist movements often settled into a form of ruling that remained patriarchal.[64] There is also an observed tendency for post-colonial nations to maintain authoritarian techniques for subjugating threatening populations.[65] In the Irish context, a nebulous moral threat, always located in the bodies of young women, represented a further motivating factor in the growth of religious detention and the use of religious homes as sites of punishment.

Conclusion

Gender instantly assumes greater salience in attempts to understand lethal violence when the perpetrator is a woman. This book offers a perspective which can contribute to the growing scholarship on women who kill, and gender and punishment. The penological literature has identified differential responses to male and female offending behaviour – noting the dominance of discourses such as pathology, 'double deviance', the idea of women as 'not dangerous' and the 'bad woman' – when seeking to explain responses to women's violence. Post-colonial Ireland offers a new background against which to examine these questions. The findings of the analysis herein suggest the ways in which the Irish example demonstrates both convergence and divergence with the existing literature, and presents novel ways of considering women's lethal violence.

Notes

1 Lizzie Seal, *Women, Murder and Femininity: Gender Representations of Women Who Kill* (Basingstoke: Palgrave Macmillan, 2010), p. 1.

2 Lindsey Earner-Byrne, *Mother and Child: Maternity and Child Welfare in Dublin, 1922–60* (Manchester: Manchester University Press, 2007), p. 222.

3 Anette Ballinger, *Dead Woman Walking: Executed Women in England and Wales, 1900–1955* (Dartmouth: Ashgate, 2000).

4 Ballinger, *Dead Woman Walking*.

5 Lynsey Black, '"On the other hand the accused is a woman …": women and the death penalty in post-independence Ireland', *Law and History Review*, 36:1 (2018) 139–72, p. 139.

6 Sarah Beth Kaufman, *American Roulette: The Social Logic of Death Penalty Sentencing Trials* (Oakland: University of California Press, 2020).

7 Gerard O'Brien, 'Capital punishment in Ireland, 1922–1964', in N. M. Dawson (ed.), *Reflections on Law and History* (Dublin: Four Courts Press, 2006).

8 Renée Heberle, 'Are women getting away with murder?', *Signs*, 24:4 (1999) 1103–12.

9 Siobhan Weare, '"The mad", "the bad", "the victim": gendered constructions of women who kill within the criminal justice system', *Laws*, 2:3 (2013) 337–61, p. 338.

10 Abigail Rowe, 'Tactics, agency and power in women's prisons', *British Journal of Criminology*, 56:2 (2016) 332–49.

11 Anette Ballinger, '"A crime of almost unspeakable cruelty and wickedness": gender, agency and murder in Scotland – the case of Jeannie Donald', *Social & Legal Studies*, 28:4 (2018) 429–49, p. 431.

12 Belinda Morrissey, *When Women Kill: Questions of Agency and Subjectivity* (New York: Routledge, 2003).

13 Karen M. Brennan, '"A fine mixture of pity and justice": the criminal justice response to infanticide in Ireland 1922–1949', *Law and History Review*, 31:4 (2013) 793–841.

14 Ballinger, 'A crime of almost unspeakable cruelty and wickedness'; Brennan, 'A fine mixture of pity and justice'.

15 Elizabeth Comack and Salena Brickey, 'Constituting the violence of criminalized women', *Canadian Journal of Criminology and Criminal Justice*, 49:1 (2007) 1–36, p. 25.

16 Frances Heidensohn, 'The future of feminist criminology', *Crime Media Culture*, 8:2 (2012) 123–34, p. 126.

17 Ballinger, 'A crime of almost unspeakable cruelty and wickedness'.

18 Lizzie Seal, 'Public reactions to the case of Mary Wilson, the last woman to be sentenced to death in England and Wales', *Papers from the British Criminology Conference*, 8 (2008) 65–84.

19 Ginger Frost, "'She is but a woman": Kitty Byron and the English Edwardian criminal justice system', *Gender and History*, 16:3 (2004) 538–60; Anette Ballinger, 'Masculinity in the dock: legal responses to male violence and female retaliation in England and Wales, 1900–1965', *Social & Legal Studies*, 16:4 (2007) 459–81; John Carter Wood, *The Most Remarkable Woman in England: Poison, Celebrity and the Trials of Beatrice Pace* (Manchester: Manchester University Press, 2012).

20 Marie Fox, 'Crime and punishment: representations of female killers in law and literature', in John Morison and Christine Bell (eds), *Tall Stories? Reading Law and Literature* (Dartmouth: Ashgate 1996), p. 145. See the typologies drawn from media reporting: Bronwyn Naylor, 'Media images of women who kill', *Legal Services Bulletin*, 15:1 (1990) 4–8.

21 Fox, 'Crime and punishment', p. 148.

22 Anthony Keating, 'Setting the agenda for the press: the 1929 case against the *Waterford Standard*', *New Hibernia Review*, 16:2 (2012) 17–32. For discussion of this in relation to specific examples, notably the reporting of sexual crimes and contraceptives, see: Anthony Keating, 'Sexual crime in the Irish Free State 1922–33: its nature, extent and reporting', *Irish Studies Review*, 20:2 (2012) 135–55; Mark O'Brien, 'Policing the press: censorship, family planning, and the press in Ireland, 1929–67', *Irish Studies Review*, 29:1 (2021) 15–30.

23 One per cent of the population was coercively confined in 1951. Eoin O'Sullivan and Ian O'Donnell, *Coercive Confinement in Ireland: Patients, Prisoners and Penitents* (Manchester: Manchester University Press, 2012).

24 Eoin O'Sullivan and Ian O'Donnell, 'Coercive confinement in the Republic of Ireland', *Punishment & Society*, 9:1 (2007) 27–48, p. 33.

25 Ian O'Donnell and Eoin O'Sullivan, '"Coercive confinement": An idea whose time has come?', *Incarceration*, 1:1 (2020) 1–20.

26 Frances Finnegan, *Do Penance or Perish: A Study of Magdalene Asylums in Ireland* (Oxford: Oxford University Press, 2004).

27 O'Sullivan and O'Donnell, *Coercive Confinement in Ireland*.

28 Ciaran McCullagh, 'A tie that blinds: family and ideology in Ireland', *Irish Economic and Social Review*, 22:3 (1991) 199–211.

29 James M. Smith, *Ireland's Magdalen Laundries and the Nation's Architecture of Containment* (Manchester: Manchester University Press, 2008).

30 Tom Inglis, *Moral Monopoly: The Rise and Fall of the Catholic Church in Modern Ireland*, 2nd edition (Dublin: University College Dublin

Press, 1998); Maria Luddy, *Prostitution and Irish Society, 1800–1940* (Cambridge: Cambridge University Press, 2007).

31 Luddy, *Prostitution and Irish Society*.
32 Una Crowley and Rob Kitchin, 'Producing "decent girls": governmentality and the moral geographies of sexual conduct in Ireland (1922–1937)', *Gender, Place & Culture*, 15:4 (2008) 355–72, p. 366.
33 Brennan, 'A fine mixture of pity and justice'; Clíona Rattigan, *'What Else Could I Do?': Single Mothers and Infanticide, Ireland 1900–1950* (Dublin: Irish Academic Press, 2012); Smith, *Ireland's Magdalen Laundries*.
34 Inter-departmental Committee to Establish the Facts of State Involvement with the Magdalen Laundries, 'McAleese Report' (Dublin: Department of Justice and Equality, 2013).
35 June Goulding, *The Light in the Window* (Dublin: Poolbeg Press, 1998); Mother and Baby Homes Commission of Investigation, 'Mother and Baby Homes Commission of Investigation Final Report' (Dublin: Department of Children, Equality, Disability, Integration and Youth, 30 October 2020).
36 Maria Luddy, 'Moral rescue and unmarried mothers in Ireland in the 1920s', *Women's Studies*, 30:6 (2001) 797–817.
37 Luddy, *Prostitution and Irish Society*.
38 Lucia Zedner, *Women, Crime and Custody in Victorian England* (Oxford: Clarendon, 1991); Nicole Hahn Rafter, 'Prisons for women, 1790–1980', *Crime and Justice*, 5 (1983) 129–81; Estelle B. Freedman, *Their Sisters' Keepers: Women's Prison Reform in America, 1830–1930* (Ann Arbour: University of Michigan Press, 1981).
39 Victor Bailey, *The Rise and Fall of the Rehabilitative Ideal, 1895–1970* (London: Routledge, 2019).
40 Louise Brangan, 'Pastoral penality in 1970s Ireland: addressing the pains of imprisonment', *Theoretical Criminology*, 25:1 (2021) 44–65.
41 Black, 'On the other hand the accused is a woman'.
42 Earner-Byrne, *Mother and Child*, p. 224.
43 Evelyn Mahon, 'Ireland: a private patriarchy?', *Environment and Planning A*, 26:8 (1994) 1277–96.
44 Crowley and Kitchin, 'Producing "decent girls"'.
45 Crowley and Kitchen, 'Producing "decent girls"'.
46 Adrian Bingham, '"An era of domesticity"? Histories of women and gender in interwar Britain', *Cultural and Social History*, 1:2 (2004) 225–33.
47 Daithí Ó Corráin, 'Catholicism in Ireland, 1880–2015: rise, ascendancy and retreat', in Thomas Bartlett (ed.), *The Cambridge History of Ireland*, Vol. 4 (Cambridge: Cambridge University Press, 2018), p. 726.

48 Inglis, *Moral Monopoly*, p. 102.

49 Colin Barr, 'The Re-energising of Catholicism, 1790–1880', in James Kelly (ed.), *The Cambridge History of Ireland*, Vol. 3 (Cambridge: Cambridge University Press, 2018).

50 Ó Corráin, 'Catholicism in Ireland', p. 726.

51 O'Sullivan and O'Donnell, 'Coercive confinement'.

52 Vicky Conway, *Policing Twentieth Century Ireland: A History of An Garda Síochána* (Manchester: Manchester University Press, 2013), p. 40.

53 Brangan, 'Pastoral penality'.

54 Deirdre Healy and Louise Kennefick, 'Hidden voices: practitioner perspectives on the early histories of probation in Ireland', *Criminology & Criminal Justice*, 19:3 (2019) 346–63; Gerry McNally, 'Probation in Ireland: a brief history of the early years', *Irish Probation Journal*, 4 (2007) 5–24.

55 Healy and Kennefick, 'Hidden voices'; McNally, 'Probation in Ireland'. In the 1928 case of Bridget O'Neill, the District Court judge noted the paucity of probation services, suggesting that such services were particularly needed for those before the courts on charges of infant murder. He explicitly understood probation services through religion, emphasising its voluntary and charitable nature: 'It is sad commentary on the religion we are supposed to profess … Fortunately, it is only a position which a charitable person would seek, and as such there is no remuneration attached to it.' 'Charge of Infanticide', *Kerry Reporter* (26 May 1928), p. 2.

56 As with other services provided by religious organisations, the use of religious institutions was strictly delineated by religion, which is hardly surprising in a climate of fevered fears of proselytising by Protestant churches. Of the institutions to which women were sent, the majority were Catholic Church organisations, while the Bethany Home opened in 1922 and had evolved from the Dublin Prison Gate Mission and Dublin Midnight Mission, and was affiliated with various Protestant churches. Mother and Baby Homes Commission of Investigation Final Report, ch. 22.

57 Earner-Byrne, *Mother and Child*.

58 Dublin Diocesan Archives, AB8/b/XXVIII/1160, letter from the Department of Justice to Archbishop McQuaid, 21 February 1942.

59 NAI, Department of Justice 18/3110B. Letter from Governor of Mountjoy Prison, 4 April 1939.

60 Smith, *Ireland's Magdalen Laundries*.

61 Inglis, *Moral Monopoly*.

62 Clara Fischer, 'Gender, nation and the politics of shame: Magdalen laundries and the institutionalization of feminine transgression in modern Ireland', *Signs*, 41:4 (2016) 821–43, p. 827.

63 Ania Loomba, *Colonialism/Postcolonialism*, 2nd edition (London: Routledge, 2014).

64 Robert J. C. Young, *Postcolonialism: An Historical Introduction* (Hoboken, NJ: Wiley Blackwell, 2016).

65 Mark Brown, 'Postcolonial penality: liberty and repression in the shadow of independence, India c. 1947', *Theoretical Criminology*, 21:2 (2017) 186–208.

Bibliography

Primary sources

State papers

Department of An Taoiseach files
Department of Justice files
Dublin Diocesan Archives
State Books at Central Criminal Court, 1922–64
State Files at Central Criminal Court, 1922–64

Official publications

Commission of Inquiry into the Reformatory and Industrial School System, 1934–1936, 'The Cussen Report' (Dublin: Stationery Office, 1936).

Commission on Itinerancy, 'Report of the Commission on Itinerancy' (Dublin: Stationery Office, 1963).

Howlin, Niamh, 'Report on the Trial of Myles Joyce, November 1882' (Dublin: Department of Justice, 2017).

Inter-departmental Committee to Establish the Facts of State Involvement with the Magdalen Laundries, 'The McAleese Report' (Dublin: Department of Justice and Equality, 2013).

McCormick, Leanne and Sean O'Connell, 'Mother and Baby Homes and Magdalene Laundries in Northern Ireland, 1922–1990' (Dublin: Inter-Departmental Working Group on Mother and Baby Homes, Magdalene Laundries and Historical Clerical Abuse, 2021).

Mother and Baby Homes Commission of Investigation, 'Mother and Baby Home Commission of Investigation Final Report' (Dublin: Department of Children, Equality, Disability, Integration and Youth, 2021).

Newspapers and archived publications

Anglo-Celt
Belfast Newsletter
Connacht Sentinel
Connacht Tribune
Connaught Telegraph
Cork Examiner
Donegal Democrat
Drogheda Independent
Evening Echo
Evening Herald
Fermanagh Herald
Garda Review
Irish Independent/Sunday Independent
Irish Press
Irish Times/Weekly Irish Times
Kerry News
Kerry Reporter
Leinster Express
Leitrim Observer
Liberator
Limerick Leader
Longford Leader
Meath Chronicle
Nationalist and Leinster Times
Nenagh Guardian
Offaly Independent
Strabane Chronicle
Waterford News and Star
Westmeath Independent

Secondary sources

Articles and book chapters

Allen, Hilary, 'Rendering them harmless: the professional portrayal of women charged with serious violent crimes', in Kathleen Daly and Lisa Maher (eds), *Criminology at the Crossroads: Feminist Readings in Crime and Criminology* (Oxford: Oxford University Press, 1987/1998).

Ballinger, Anette, 'Masculinity in the dock: legal responses to male violence and female retaliation in England and Wales, 1900–1965', *Social & Legal Studies*, 16:4 (2007) 459–81.

Ballinger, Anette, 'Feminist research, state power and executed women: the case of Louie Calvert', in Stephen Farrall, Mike Hough, Shadd Maruna and Richard Sparks (eds), *Escape Routes: Contemporary Perspectives on Life after Punishment* (London: Routledge/Cavendish, 2011).

Ballinger, Anette, '"A crime of almost unspeakable cruelty and wickedness": gender, agency and murder in Scotland – the case of Jeannie Donald', *Social & Legal Studies*, 28:4 (2018) 429–49.

Barclay, Katie, 'Performing emotion and reading the male body in the Irish court, c.1800–1845', *Journal of Social History*, 51:2 (2017) 293–312.

Barr, Colin, 'The Re-energising of Catholicism, 1790–1880', in James Kelly (ed.), *The Cambridge History of Ireland*, Vol. 3 (Cambridge: Cambridge University Press, 2018).

Beirne, Piers and Ian O'Donnell, 'Gallous stories of dirty deeds: representing parricide in J.M. Synge's "The Playboy of the Western World"', *Crime Media Culture*, 6:1 (2010) 27–48.

Bhreatnach, Aoife, 'Policing the community: homicide and violence in Traveller and settled society', *Irish Economic and Social History*, 34 (2007) 47–64.

Bingham, Adrian, '"An era of domesticity"? Histories of women and gender in interwar Britain', *Cultural and Social History*, 1:2 (2004) 225–33.

Black, Lynsey, '"On the other hand the accused is a woman ...": women and the death penalty in post-independence Ireland', *Law and History Review*, 36:1 (2018) 139–72.

Black, Lynsey, 'The pathologisation of women who kill: three cases from Ireland', *Social History of Medicine*, 33:2 (2020) 417–37.

Brangan, Louise, 'Pastoral penality in 1970s Ireland: Addressing the pains of imprisonment', *Theoretical Criminology*, 25:1 (2021) 44–65.

Breathnach, Ciara, 'Handywomen and birthing in rural Ireland, 1851–1955', *Gender & History*, 28:1 (2016) 34–56.

Brennan, Karen M., '"A fine mixture of pity and justice": the criminal justice response to infanticide in Ireland, 1922–1949', *Law and History Review*, 31:4 (2013) 793–841.

Brennan, Karen M., 'Punishing infanticide in the Irish Free State', *Irish Journal of Legal Studies*, 3:1 (2013) 1–35.

Brennan, Karen M., 'Traditions of English liberal thought: a history of the enactment of an infanticide law in Ireland', *Irish Jurist*, 50 (2013) 100–37.

Brennan, Karen M., 'Murder in the Irish family, 1930–1945', in Niamh Howlin and Kevin Costello (eds), *Law and the Family in Ireland, 1800–1950* (London: Palgrave, 2017).

Brennan, Karen M., 'Murderous mothers and gentle judges: paternalism, patriarchy, and infanticide', *Yale Journal of Law and Feminism*, 30:1 (2018) 139–95.

Brennan, Karen M., 'Social norms and the law in responding to infanticide', *Legal Studies*, 38:3 (2018) 480–99.

Brown, Mark, 'Postcolonial penality: liberty and repression in the shadow of independence, India c. 1947', *Theoretical Criminology*, 21:2 (2017) 186–208.

Buckley, Sarah-Anne, 'Family and power: incest in Ireland, 1800–1950', in Anthony McElligott, Liam Chambers, Ciara Breathnach and Catherine Lawless (eds), *Power in History: From Medieval Ireland to the post-Modern World*, Historical Studies XXVII (Dublin: Irish Academic Press, 2011).

Burney, Ian A., 'A poisoning of no substance: the trials of medico-legal proof in mid-Victorian England', *Journal of British Studies*, 38:1 (1999) 59–92.

Coen, Mark and Niamh Howlin, 'The jury speaks: jury riders in the nineteenth and twentieth centuries', *American Journal of Legal History*, 58:4 (2018) 505–34.

Comack, Elizabeth and Salena Brickey, 'Constituting the violence of criminalized women', *Canadian Journal of Criminology and Criminal Justice*, 49:1 (2007) 1–36.

Crowley, Una and Rob Kitchin, 'Producing "decent girls": governmentality and the moral geographies of sexual conduct in Ireland (1922–1937)', *Gender, Place & Culture*, 15:4 (2008) 355–72.

Daly, Mary E., 'Marriage, fertility and women's lives in twentieth-century Ireland (c.1900–c.1970)', *Women's History Review*, 15:4 (2006) 571–85.

Delay, Cara, '"Uncharitable tongues": women and abusive language in early twentieth-century Ireland', *Feminist Studies*, 39:3 (2013) 628–53.

Delay, Cara, 'Kitchens and kettles: domestic spaces, ordinary things, and female networks in Irish abortion history', *Journal of Women's History*, 30:4 (2018) 11–34.

Delay, Cara, 'Pills, potions and purgatives: women and abortion methods in Ireland, 1900–1950', *Women's History Review*, 28:3 (2019) 479–99.

Delay, Cara and Annika Liger, 'Bad mothers and dirty lousers: representing abortionists in postindependence Ireland', *Journal of Social History*, 54:1 (2020) 286–305.

Doyle, David M. and Ian O'Donnell, 'The death penalty in post-independent Ireland', *Journal of Legal History*, 33:1 (2012) 65–91.

Earner-Byrne, Lindsey, 'Reinforcing the family: the role of gender, morality and sexuality in Irish welfare policy, 1922–1944', *History of the Family*, 13:4 (2008) 360–9.

Earner-Byrne, Lindsey, 'The rape of Mary M.: a microhistory of sexual violence and moral redemption in 1920s Ireland', *Journal of the History of Sexuality*, 24:1 (2015) 75–98.

Earner-Byrne, Lindsey, 'The family in Ireland, 1880–2015', in Thomas Bartlett (ed.), *The Cambridge History of Ireland*, Vol. 4 (Cambridge: Cambridge University Press, 2018).

Farrell, Elaine, '"Infanticide of the ordinary character": an overview of the crime in Ireland, 1850–1900', *Irish Economic and Social History*, 39 (2012) 56–72.

Farrell, Elaine, '"Poor prison flowers": convict mothers and their children in Ireland, 1853–1900', *Social History*, 41:2 (2016) 171–91.

Farrell, Elaine, '"The salvation of them": emigration to North America from the nineteenth-century Irish women's convict prison', *Women's History Review*, 25:4 (2016) 619–37.

Finnane, Mark, 'The Carrigan Committee of 1930–31 and the "moral condition of the Saorstát"', *Irish Historical Studies*, 32:128 (2001) 519–36.

Fischer Clara, 'Gender, nation and the politics of shame: Magdalen laundries and the institutionalization of feminine transgression in modern Ireland', *Signs*, 41:4 (2016) 821–43.

Fitzpatrick, David, 'Divorce and separation in modern Irish history', *Past & Present*, 114 (1987) 172–96.

Fox, Marie, 'Crime and punishment: representations of female killers in law and literature', in John Morison and Christine Bell (eds), *Tall Stories? Reading Law and Literature* (Dartmouth: Ashgate 1996).

Freedman, Estelle B., *Their Sisters' Keepers: Women's Prison Reform in America, 1830–1930* (Ann Arbor: University of Michigan Press, 1981).

Frost, Ginger, '"She is but a woman": Kitty Byron and the English Edwardian criminal justice system', *Gender and History*, 16:3 (2004) 538–60.

Garrett, Paul Michael, 'The abnormal flight: the migration and repatriation of Irish unmarried mothers', *Social History*, 25:3 (2000) 330–43.

Garrett, Paul Michael, '"Unmarried mothers" in the Republic of Ireland', *Journal of Social Work*, 16:6 (2000) 708–25.

Gavigan, Shelley A. M., 'Petit treason in eighteenth century England: women's inequality before the law', *Canadian Journal of Women and the Law*, 3:2 (1989/1990) 335–74.

Gibbons, Pat, Niamh Mulryan and Art O'Connor, 'Guilty but insane: the insanity defence in Ireland, 1850–1995', *British Journal of Psychiatry*, 170:5 (1997) 467–72.

Godfrey, Barry S., Stephen Farrall and Susanne Karstedt, 'Explaining gendered sentencing patterns for violent men and women in the late-Victorian and Edwardian period', *British Journal of Criminology*, 45:5 (2005) 696–720.

Gurevich, Liena, 'Parental child murder and child abuse in Anglo-American legal system', *Trauma, Violence & Abuse*, 11:1 (2010) 18–26.

Hahn Rafter, Nicol, 'Prisons for women, 1790–1980', *Crime and Justice*, 5 (1983) 129–81.

Hannan, Damian F. and Patrick Commins, 'The significance of small-scale landholders in Ireland's socio-economic transformation', in J. H. Goldthorpe and C. T. Whelan (eds), *The Development of Industrial Society in Ireland* (Oxford: Oxford University Press for the British Academy, 1992).

Hay, Douglas, 'Property, authority and the criminal law', in D. Hay, P. Linebaugh, J. G. Rule, E. P. Thompson and C. Winslow (eds), *Albion's Fatal Tree: Crime and Society in Eighteenth-Century England* (London: Allen Lane, 1975).

Healy, Deirdre and Louise Kennefick, 'Hidden voices: practitioner perspectives on the early histories of probation in Ireland', *Criminology & Criminal Justice*, 19:3 (2019) 346–63.

Heberle, Renée, 'Are women getting away with murder?', *Signs*, 24:4 (1999) 1103–12.

Heidensohn, Frances, 'The future of feminist criminology', *Crime Media Culture*, 8:2 (2012) 123–34.

Howlin, Niamh, 'Controlling jury composition in nineteenth-century Ireland', *Journal of Legal History*, 30:3 (2009) 227–61.

Howlin, Niamh, 'Passive observers or active participants? Jurors in civil and criminal trials', *Journal of Legal History*, 35:2 (2014) 143–71.

Hynd, Stacy, 'Deadlier than the male? Women and the death penalty in colonial Kenya and Nyasaland, c.1920–57', *Stichproben – Vienna Journal of African Studies*, 7:12 (2007) 13–33.

Inglis, Tom, 'Origins and legacies of Irish prudery: sexuality and control in modern Ireland', *Éire-Ireland*, 40:3/4 (2015) 9–37.

Inglis, Tom and Carol MacKeogh, 'The double bind: women, honour and sexuality in contemporary Ireland', *Media, Culture and Society*, 34:1 (2012) 68–82.

Irish Human Rights Commission, 'Assessment of the Human Rights Issues Arising in Relation to the "Magdalen Laundries"' (Dublin: IHRC, 2010).

Jaffary Nora E., 'Maternity and morality in Puebla's nineteenth-century infanticide trials', *Law and History Review*, 1–21, online first, 26 January 2021, https://doi.org/10.1017/S0738248020000292.

JFM Research and Adoption Rights Alliance, 'Submission to the Working Group on Discrimination Against Women in Law and in Practice' (Dublin: JFMR/ARA, 2015).

Johnson, Nuala C., 'Building a nation: an examination of the Irish Gaeltacht Commission Report of 1926', *Journal of Historical Geography*, 19:2 (1993) 157–68.

Johnston, Helen, 'Imprisoned mothers in Victorian England, 1853–1900: motherhood, identity and the convict prison', *Criminology & Criminal Justice*, 19:2 (2019) 215–31.

Jones, Richard, 'Populist leniency, crime control and due process', *Theoretical Criminology*, 14:3 (2010) 331–47.

Keating, Anthony, 'Setting the agenda for the press: the 1929 case against the Waterford Standard', *New Hibernia Review*, 16:2 (2012) 17–32.

Keating, Anthony, 'Sexual crime in the Irish Free State 1922–33: its nature, extent and reporting', *Irish Studies Review*, 20:2 (2012) 135–55.

Kelly, Brendan D., 'The Mental Health Treatment Act 1945 in Ireland: an historical enquiry', *History of Psychiatry*, 19:1 (2008) 47–67.

Kelly, Laura, 'Sexual knowledge and family planning practices in Ireland, c.1950–80: an oral history', 17 September 2020, CHOMI, University College Dublin.

Linders, Annulla and Alana van Gundy-Yoder, 'Gall, gallantry and the gallows: capital punishment and the social construction of gender 1840–1920', *Gender and Society*, 22:3 (2008) 324–48.

Logan, Anne '"Building a new and better order?" Women and jury service in England and Wales, c.1920–70', *Women's History Review*, 22:5 (2013) 701–16.

Luddy, Maria, 'Moral rescue and unmarried mothers in Ireland in the 1920s', *Women's Studies*, 30:6 (2001) 797–817.

MacLaughlin, Jim, 'The political geography of anti-Traveller racism in Ireland: the politics of exclusion and the geography of closure', *Political Geography*, 17:4 (1998) 417–35.

McAuliffe, Mary, 'Irish histories: gender, women and sexualities', in Katherine O'Donnell and Mary McAuliffe (eds), *Palgrave Advances in Irish History* (Basingstoke: Palgrave Macmillan, 2009).

McAvoy, Sandra, 'The regulation of sexuality in the Irish Free State, 1929–1935', in Greta Jones and Elizabeth Malcolm (eds), *Medicine, Disease and the State in Ireland, 1650–1940* (Cork: Cork University Press, 1999).

McAvoy, Sandra, 'Before Cadden: abortion in mid-twentieth-century Ireland', in Dermot Keogh, Finbarr O'Shea and Carmel Quinlan (eds), *Ireland in the 1950s: The Lost Decade* (Cork: Mercier Press, 2004).

McCarthy, Áine, 'Hearths, bodies and minds: gender ideology and women's committal to Enniscorthy Lunatic Asylum, 1916–1925', in Diane Urquhart and Alan Hayes (eds), *Irish Women's History* (Dublin: Irish Academic Press, 2004).

McCormick, Leanne, '"No sense of wrongdoing": abortion in Belfast 1917–1967', *Journal of Social History*, 49:1 (2015) 125–48.

McCullagh, Ciaran, 'A tie that blinds: family and ideology in Ireland', *Economic and Social Review*, 22:3 (1991) 199–211.

McLoughlin, Dymphna, 'Women and sexuality in nineteenth-century Ireland', in Alan Hayes and Diane Urquhart (eds), *The Irish Women's History Reader* (London: Routledge, 2001).

McNally, Gerry, 'Probation in Ireland: a brief history of the early years', *Irish Probation Journal*, 4 (2007) 5–24.

Maguire, Moira J., 'The Carrigan Committee and child sexual abuse in twentieth-century Ireland', *New Hibernia Review*, 11:2 (2007) 79–100.

Mahon, Evelyn, 'Ireland: a private patriarchy?', *Environment and Planning A*, 26:8 (1994) 1277–96.

Malcolm, Elizabeth, '"Ireland's crowded madhouses": the institutional confinement of the insane in nineteenth- and twentieth-century Ireland', in Roy Porter and David Wright (eds), *The Confinement of the Insane: International Perspectives, 1800–1965* (Cambridge: Cambridge University Press, 2003).

Miller, April, 'Bloody blondes and bobbed-haired bandits: the execution of justice and the construction of the celebrity criminal in the 1920s popular press', in Su Holmes and Diane Negra (eds), *In the Limelight and under the Microscope: Forms and Functions of Female Celebrity* (London: Continuum, 2011).

Mohr, Thomas, 'The Rights of Women under the Constitution of the Irish Free State', *Irish Jurist*, 41 (2006) 20–59.

Moulds, Elizabeth F., 'Chivalry and paternalism: disparities of treatment in the criminal justice system', *Western Political Quarterly*, 31:3 (1978) 416–30.

Murray, Peter, 'A militant among the Magdalens? Mary Ellen Murphy's incarceration in High Park Convent during the 1913 Lockout', *Irish Labour History Society*, 20 (1995) 41–54.

Nagy, Victoria, 'Narratives in the courtroom: female poisoners in mid-nineteenth century England', *European Journal of Criminology*, 11:2 (2014) 213–27.

Naylor, Bronwyn, 'Media images of women who kill', *Legal Services Bulletin*, 15:1 (1990) 4–8.

Ó Corráin, Daithí, 'Catholicism in Ireland, 1880–2015: rise, ascendancy and retreat', in Thomas Bartlett (ed.), *The Cambridge History of Ireland*, Vol. 4 (Cambridge: Cambridge University Press, 2018).

O'Brien, Gerard, 'Capital punishment in Ireland, 1922–1964', in N. M. Dawson (ed.), *Reflections on Law and History* (Dublin: Four Courts Press, 2006).

O'Brien, Mark, 'Policing the press: censorship, family planning, and the press in Ireland, 1929–67', *Irish Studies Review*, 29:1 (2021) 15–30.

O'Brien, Patricia, 'Crime and punishment as historical problem', *Journal of Social History*, 11:4 (1978) 508–20.

O'Donnell, Ian, 'Lethal violence in Ireland, 1841 to 2003: famine, celibacy and parental pacification', *British Journal of Criminology*, 45:5 (2005) 671–95.

O'Donnell, Ian, 'Killing in Ireland at the turn of the centuries: contexts, consequences and civilising processes', *Irish Economic and Social History*, 37 (2010) 53–74.

O'Donnell, Ian, 'An interfering judge, a biddable executive, and an unbroken neck', *Irish Jurist*, 60 (2018) 112–22.

O'Donnell, Ian and Eoin O'Sullivan, '"Coercive confinement": an idea whose time has come?', *Incarceration*, 1:1 (2020) 1–20.

O'Donovan, Katherine, 'The medicalisation of infanticide', *Criminal Law Review*, May (1984) 259–64.

O'Hanlon, Roderick J., 'Not guilty because of insanity', *Irish Jurist*, 3 (1968) 61–77.

O'Sullivan, Eoin and Ian O'Donnell, 'Coercive confinement in the Republic of Ireland: the waning of a culture of control', *Punishment & Society*, 9:1 (2007) 27–48.

Prior, Pauline M., 'Prisoner or patient? The official debate on the criminal lunatic in nineteenth-century Ireland', *History of Psychiatry*, 15:2 (2004) 177–92.

Rattigan, Clíona, '"I thought from her appearance that she was in the family way": detecting infanticide cases in Ireland, 1900–21', *Family and Community History*, 11:2 (2008) 135–52.

Robb, George, 'Circe in crinoline: domestic poisonings in Victorian England', *Journal of Family History*, 22:2 (1997) 176–90.

Rowe, Abigail, 'Tactics, agency and power in women's prisons', *British Journal of Criminology*, 56:2 (2016) 332–49.

Ruggles, Steven, 'Fallen women: the inmates of the Magdalen asylum of Philadelphia, 1836–1908', *Journal of Social History*, 16:4 (1983) 65–82.

Ryan, Louise, 'The press, the police and prosecution perspectives on infanticide in the 1920s', in Diane Urquhart and Alan Hayes (eds), *Irish Women's History* (Dublin: Irish Academic Press, 2004).

Schoen, Johanna, 'Between choice and coercion: women and the politics of sterilization in North Carolina, 1929–1975', *Journal of Women's History*, 13:1 (2001) 132–56.

Seal, Lizzie, 'Public reactions to the case of Mary Wilson, the last woman to be sentenced to death in England and Wales', *Papers from the British Criminology Conference*, 8 (2008) 65–84.

Seal, Lizzie, 'Issues of gender and class in the Mirror Newspapers' campaign for the release of Edith Chubb', *Crime Media Culture*, 5:1 (2009) 57–78.

Seal, Lizzie, 'Ruth Ellis and the public contestation of the death penalty', *Howard Journal of Criminal Justice*, 50:5 (2011) 492–504.

Seal, Lizzie, 'Imagined communities and the death penalty in Britain, 1930–1965', *British Journal of Criminology*, 54:5 (2014) 908–27.

Seal, Lizzie, '"She killed not from hate, but from love": motherhood, melodrama and mercy killing in the case of May Brownhill', *Women's History Review*, 27:5 (2018) 669–87.

Shepard, Bonnie, 'The "double discourse" on sexual and reproductive rights in Latin America: the chasm between public policy and private actions', *Health and Human Rights*, 4:2 (2000) 110–43.

Stanko, Elizabeth A., 'Challenging the problem of men's individual violence', in Tim Newburn and Elizabeth A. Stanko (eds), *Just Boys Doing Business? Men, Masculinities and Crime* (London: Routledge, 1995).

Streib, Victor L., 'America's aversion to executing women', *Women's Law Journal*, 1 (1997) 1–8.

Sutton, Rian, 'A "matter for the consideration of the executive alone": the court of public opinion and narratives of mercy in the clemency cases of Elizabeth Gibbons and Chiara Cignarale', *Irish Jurist*, 60 (2018) 123–33.

Urquhart, Diane, 'Ireland and the Divorce and Matrimonial Causes Act of 1857', *Journal of Family History*, 38:3 (2013) 301–20.

Urquhart, Diane, 'Irish divorce and domestic violence, 1857–1922', *Women's History Review*, 22:5 (2013) 820–37.

Valiulis, Maryann Gialanella, 'Power, gender and identity in the Irish Free State', *Journal of Women's History*, 6:4/7:1 (1995) 117–36.

Walsh, Oonagh, '"A lightness of mind": gender and insanity', in Margaret Kelleher and James H. Murphy (eds), *Gender Perspectives in Nineteenth-Century Ireland: Public and Private Spheres* (Dublin: Irish Academic Press, 1997).

Weare, Siobhan, '"The mad", "the bad", "the victim": gendered constructions of women who kill within the criminal justice system', *Laws*, 2:3 (2013) 337–61.

Wood, John Carter, '"Those who have had trouble can sympathise with you": press writing, reader responses and a murder trial in interwar Britain', *Journal of Social History*, 43:2 (2009) 439–62.

Worrall, Anne, 'Discourse analysis', in Eugene McLaughlin and John Muncie (eds), *The Sage Handbook of Criminology* (Thousand Oaks, CA: Sage, 2005).

Books

Arensberg, Conrad M. and Solon T. Kimball, *Family and Community in Ireland*, 3rd edition (Ennis: CLASP Press, 2001).

Bailey, Victor, *The Rise and Fall of the Rehabilitative Ideal, 1895–1970* (London: Routledge, 2019).

Ballinger, Anette, *Dead Woman Walking: Executed Women in England and Wales, 1900–1955* (Dartmouth: Ashgate, 2000).

Brady, Conor, *Guardians of the Peace* (Dublin: Gill and Macmillan, 1974).

Brennan, Damien, *Irish Insanity, 1800–2000* (London: Routledge, 2013).

Brewer, John D., Bill Lockhart and Paula Rogers, *Crime in Ireland, 1945–95: 'Here Be Dragons'* (Oxford: Clarendon, 1997).

Carlen, Pat, *Magistrates' Justice* (London: Martin Robertson, 1976).

Conley, Carolyn A., *Melancholy Accidents: The Meaning of Violence in post-Famine Ireland* (Lanham, MD: Lexington Books, 1999).

Conley, Carolyn A., *Certain Other Countries: Homicide, Gender and National Identity in Late Nineteenth Century England, Ireland, Scotland and Wales* (Columbus: Ohio State University Press, 2007).

Conway, Vicky, *Policing Twentieth Century Ireland: A History of An Garda Síochána* (Manchester: Manchester University Press, 2013).

Cox, Catherine, *Negotiating Insanity in the Southeast of Ireland* (Manchester: Manchester University Press, 2012).

Daly, Mary E., *The Slow Failure: Population Decline and Independent Ireland, 1920–1973* (Madison: University of Wisconsin Press, 2005).

Deale, Kenneth E. L., *Beyond Any Reasonable Doubt? A Book of Murder Trials* (Dublin: Gill and Macmillan, 1971).

Dooley, Enda, *Homicide in Ireland: 1972–1991* (Dublin: Stationery Office, 1995).

Dooley, Enda, *Homicide in Ireland: 1992–1996* (Dublin: Stationery Office, 2001).

Dooley, Terence, *'The Land for the People': The Land Question in Independent Ireland* (Dublin: University College Dublin Press, 2004).

Doyle, David M. and Liam O'Callaghan, *Capital Punishment in Independent Ireland: A Social, Legal and Political and History* (Liverpool: Liverpool University Press, 2019).

Earner-Byrne, Lindsey, *Mother and Child: Maternity and Child Welfare in Dublin, 1922–60* (Manchester: Manchester University Press, 2007).

Fanning, Bryan, *Racism and Social Change in the Republic of Ireland* (Manchester: Manchester University Press, 2002).

Farrell, Elaine, *'A Most Diabolical Deed': Infanticide and Irish Society, 1850–1900* (Manchester: Manchester University Press, 2013).

Finnane, Mark, *Insanity and the Insane in post-Famine Ireland* (London: Croom Helm, 1981).

Finnegan, Frances, *Do Penance or Perish: A Study of Magdalene Asylums in Ireland* (Oxford: Oxford University Press, 2004).

Garland, David, *Peculiar Institution: America's Death Penalty in an Age of Abolition* (Oxford: Oxford University Press, 2010).

Goulding, June, *The Light in the Window* (Dublin: Poolbeg Press, 1998).

Green, David A., *When Children Kill Children: Penal Populism and Political Culture* (Oxford: Clarendon, 2008).

Griffin, Diarmuid, *Killing Time: Life Imprisonment and Parole in Ireland* (London: Palgrave Macmillan, 2019).

Heidensohn, Frances, *Women and Crime*, 2nd edition (Basingstoke: Palgrave Macmillan, 1996).

Hood, Lynley, *Minnie Dean: Her Life and Crimes* (London: Penguin, 1995).

Inglis, Tom, *Moral Monopoly: The Rise and Fall of the Catholic Church in Modern Ireland*, 2nd edition (Dublin: University College Dublin Press, 1998).

Jackson, Mark, *New-born Child Murder: Women, Illegitimacy and the Courts in Eighteenth-Century England* (Manchester: Manchester University Press, 1996).

Jaffary, Nora E., *Reproduction and Its Discontents in Mexico: Childbirth and Contraception from 1750 to 1905* (Chapel Hill: University of North Carolina Press, 2016).

Kaufman, Sarah Beth, *American Roulette: The Social Logic of Death Penalty Sentencing Trials* (Oakland: University of California Press, 2020).

Kelleher, Margaret, *The Maamtrasna Murders: Language, Life and Death in Nineteenth-Century Ireland* (Dublin: University College Dublin Press, 2018).

Kennedy, Finola, *Cottage to Crèche: Family Change in Ireland* (Dublin: IPA, 2001).

Kilday, Anne-Marie, *A History of Infanticide in Britain, c. 1600 to the Present* (Basingstoke: Palgrave Macmillan, 2013).

Lacey, Nicola, *Women, Crime and Character: From Moll Flanders to Tess of the D'Urbervilles* (Oxford: Oxford University Press, 2008).

Lloyd, Ann, *Doubly Deviant, Doubly Damned: Society's Treatment of Violent Women* (London: Penguin, 1995).

Loomba, Ania, *Colonialism/Postcolonialism*, 2nd edition (London: Routledge, 2014).

Luddy, Maria, *Women and Philanthropy in Nineteenth-Century Ireland* (Cambridge: Cambridge University Press, 1995).

Luddy, Maria, *Prostitution and Irish Society, 1800–1940* (Cambridge: Cambridge University Press, 2007).

McCorkel, Jill, *Breaking Women: Gender, Race and the New Politics of Imprisonment* (New York: New York University Press, 2013).

McCormick, Leanne, *Regulating Sexuality: Women in Twentieth-Century Northern Ireland* (Manchester: Manchester University Press, 2011).

McMahon, Richard, *Homicide in pre-Famine and Famine Ireland* (Liverpool: Liverpool University Press, 2013).

Milne, Emma, *Criminal Justice Responses to Maternal Filicide: Judging the Failed Mother* (Bingley: Emerald Publishing, 2021).

Morrissey, Belinda, *When Women Kill: Questions of Agency and Subjectivity* (New York: Routledge, 2003).

Naish, Camille, *Death Comes to the Maiden: Sex and Execution, 1431–1933* (London: Routledge, 1991).

O'Donnell, Ian, *Justice, Mercy, and Caprice: Clemency and the Death Penalty in Ireland* (Oxford: Oxford University Press, 2017).

O'Sullivan, Eoin and Ian O'Donnell, *Coercive Confinement in Ireland: Patients, Prisoners and Penitents* (Manchester: Manchester University Press, 2012).

Phelan, Mary, *Irish Speakers, Interpreters and the Courts, 1754–1921* (Dublin: Four Courts Press/Irish Legal History Society, 2019).

Prior, Pauline M., *Madness and Murder: Gender, Crime and Mental Disorder in Nineteenth-Century Ireland* (Dublin: Irish Academic Press, 2008).

Quinlan, Christina, *Inside: Ireland's Women's Prisons Past and Present* (Dublin: Irish Academic Press, 2011).

Raftery, Mary and Eoin O'Sullivan, *Suffer the Little Children: The Inside Story of Ireland's Industrial Schools* (Dublin: New Island, 1999).

Rattigan, Clíona, *'What Else Could I Do?': Single Mothers and Infanticide, Ireland 1900–1950* (Dublin: Irish Academic Press, 2012).

Reddy, Tom, *Murder Will Out: A Book of Irish Murder Cases* (Dublin: Gill and Macmillan, 1990).

Reddy, Tom, *The Murder File: An Irish Detective's Casebook* (Dublin: Gill and Macmillan, 1991).

Redmond, Jennifer, *Moving Histories: Irish Women's Emigration to Britain from Independence to Republic* (Liverpool: Liverpool University Press, 2018).

Rogan, Mary, *Prison Policy in Ireland: Politics, Penal Welfarism and Political Imprisonment* (London: Routledge, 2011).

Rose, Lionel, *Massacre of the Innocents: Infanticide in Great Britain 1800–1939* (London: Routledge & Kegan Paul, 1986).

Sarat, Austin, *When the State Kills: Capital Punishment and the American Condition* (Princeton, NJ: Princeton University Press, 2018).

Seal, Lizzie, *Murder and Femininity: Gender Representations of Women Who Kill* (Basingstoke: Palgrave Macmillan, 2010).

Seal, Lizzie, *Capital Punishment in Twentieth-Century Britain: Audience, Justice, Memory* (Abingdon: Routledge, 2014).

Smith, James M., *Ireland's Magdalen Laundries and the Nation's Architecture of Containment* (Manchester: Manchester University Press, 2008).

Tata, Cyrus, *Sentencing: A Social Process – Re-thinking Research and Policy* (London: Palgrave Macmillan, 2020).

Vaughan, W. E., *Murder Trials in Ireland, 1836–1914* (Dublin: Four Courts Press, 2009).

Walby, Sylvia, *Theorizing Patriarchy* (Oxford: Basil Blackwell, 1990).

Wiener, Martin, *Men of Blood: Violence, Manliness and Criminal Justice in Victorian England* (Cambridge: Cambridge University Press, 2004).

Wood, John Carter, *The Most Remarkable Woman in England: Poison, Celebrity and the Trials of Beatrice Pace* (Manchester: Manchester University Press, 2012).

Worrall, Anne, *Offending Women: Female Lawbreakers and the Criminal Justice System* (London: Routledge, 1990).

Young, Robert J. C., *Postcolonialism: An Historical Introduction* (Hoboken, NJ: Wiley Blackwell, 2016).

Zedner, Lucia, *Women, Crime and Custody in Victorian England* (Oxford: Clarendon, 1991).

Index

EU authorised representative for GPSR:
Easy Access System Europe, Mustamäe tee 50,
10621 Tallinn, Estonia
gpsr.requests@easproject.com

www.ingramcontent.com/pod-product-compliance
Lightning Source LLC
Chambersburg PA
CBHW051953270326
41929CB00015B/2633

9 781526 182340